NOT ONE OF THE BOYS

NOT ONE
OF THE BOYS

Living Life as a Feminist

BRENDA FEIGEN

ALFRED A. KNOPF   *New York*   *2000*

THIS IS A BORZOI BOOK
PUBLISHED BY ALFRED A. KNOPF

www.aaknopf.com

Knopf, Borzoi Books and the colophon are registered
trademarks of Random House, Inc.

ISBN 0-679-40842-8

Manufactured in the United States of America
First Edition

To my daughter, Alexis

and

To my partner, Joanne

Contents

Acknowledgments

This book took many years to write. Without the urging of my editor, Victoria Wilson, I may never have started on the journey. Without her terrific sense of humor, as well as her skills as the best editor New York has to offer, I wouldn't have been able to complete it. Vicky waited patiently while I tried to find my voice and, when I did, encouraged me on throughout the process. Toward the end, her compassion and devotion surpassed all her other contributions. She deserves the most thanks any author can give her publisher. I also am indebted to Jane Garrett, who watched over the process, and to photographer Michele Smith, for her patience, flexibility and skill.

All feminists everywhere are in my heart, having inspired the writing of the book as I observed and participated with them in the demand for justice, equality and power. A number of special feminists deserve to be singled out for having contributed—one way or another—to the making of this book. They helped me understand more than I had before, and they helped me clarify what I was trying to say in various sections of the book: Professors Nancy Baker, Deborah Tannen, Catherine Stimpson and Sandra Harding paved the way for my more educated position on women's-studies academics and their penchant for categories like postmodern feminism. Other more than helpful feminists, such as Lindsy Van Gelder, Kate Millett and the late, great Bella Abzug, lent insight into various aspects of the state of the current Women's Movement. Professor Chris Littleton helped clarify the issues surrounding feminist jurisprudence, while Professors Linda Nochlin, Mary

Garrard and Norma Broude have taught me about women artists and how their art relates to feminism today. Robin Morgan inspired me on many levels, not the least of which was to continue our ongoing dialogue about the differences between boys and girls.

Without the help of Professors Catharine MacKinnon and Diana Russell, as well as my friend Andrea Dworkin, I would not have had the clarity I needed for the chapter on pornography.

My new friend the Right Honorable Kim Campbell inspired me to ask why, if Canada can have a feminist like her as its prime minister, we in the United States can't seem to find even a single woman who would be considered qualified to run our country.

My old friend Justice Ruth Bader Ginsburg served as a brilliant light shining the way for every feminist lawyer I knew, myself certainly included. I watched in admiration as she wrote the most brilliant briefs I've ever read, and I now look to her as a role model for every girl and woman who aspires to be not only the best lawyer she can be but a judge as well. I hope I have done her justice as I attempt in this book to describe her contribution to feminist jurisprudence, as well as to the cause of equality for women. I express here my sincere hope that Ruth will become the first woman Chief Justice—a mantle she would wear with great panache, a position for which no one is better suited.

Marc Fasteau has participated in much of this story. I thank him for his patience, strength, support and mostly just for getting it.

Other friends and relatives who have lent support in important ways, sometimes just an arm or shoulder to lean on when I needed it most, especially toward the end of the writing of this book: Richard and Peggy, Philippa, Gerry and Kathy, Evelyn, Virginia and J.O., Pam, Erica, Christine, Christina, Regina, Patti and Sandy, Frances, Kirsten and Diana, Umberto, my colleagues on the board of California for the Arts, Pam and Steve, Mitch and Janice, and numerous others, for whose unintentional omission from this list I apologize.

I owe a special debt to the women with whom I worked at William Morris. Often we were afraid to speak freely there, but at the same time, in silent recognition of our collective plight, we supported each other.

I cannot omit mention of my own special SEAL team, which made *NAVY SEALS* possible. You know who you are. The only question is whether you're reading this book!

My closest friends, who have stood by me throughout the span of time from before the book's inception to my recent ordeal, must be mentioned individually. Gloria Steinem: Where would any feminist alive today be without you? You've been there for me since that day in May 1970 when we met, as I've tried to be there for you. If we've had any disagreements, they pale in comparison with the strength I've derived from your intelligence and compassion. I have never seen anyone work so hard to bring so many different women together. Gloria, your dislike of conflict has made you the peacemaker, the one person who has held this movement together when it could have splintered into a thousand pieces. You appear all over the book; I can only hope that you will find my rendition of times we spent together accurate. As the book neared its completion I was detoured, and when I needed you more than ever, you were of course there, ready not only with advice but with love. Jane Alexander, one of the most gifted actors I'll ever know, has been another source of inspiration, a perfectionist in the best sense of the word. You helped not only me but real artists all over the nation. You are a trusted friend whose wisdom has and always will guide me. Lily Tomlin: There is no one else like you anywhere. Not only do you make me—and the rest of the world—laugh on a rather constant basis, but you have been there for me, as has the brilliant Jane Wagner, whenever I've needed anything, including help with this book. There are no others more generous than the two of you, our favorite dinner companions. Harriette Kaley, you are one of a kind. You helped shed light where there were only shadows. Through thick, through thin, you've been there, obviously hoping that eventually I would find my way by myself. I hope I'm in the process.

I don't know what would have happened to me or the book without the wonderful doctors who have not only been a great source of strength in the darkest hours but have helped me find the path back into a healthy life: Marilou Terpenning, Karen Blanchard, Patricia Wolfson, Leslie Botnick, Wing Hsieh and Mitch Lewis. I also want to acknowledge my old friend Barbara and my new

friend Jody, who went through the whole deal with me—two wonderful women with whom I could and still do compare notes.

Of course I must thank my mother, Shirley Kadison, who looks
only on the bright side, urging me to go for the brass ring, encouraging me to believe I can accomplish anything I set my heart on. I
only wish that were true. And I want to thank my father, Arthur
Paul Feigen, who before his untimely death wisely instructed me
to be happy above all else. He was the first person from whom I
felt unconditional love. Thanks also to my brother, Richard Feigen,
for pushing me every which way for as long as I can remember.

Joanne Parrent means so very much to me in every way. She
spent hours talking with me about many issues that arose in the
writing of this book, helping me say what I really meant. She has
been a feminist as long as I have, and she gave me the inspiration
to plunge forward in writing some of the more difficult and controversial chapters. She pushed me time and time again to finish a
manuscript I found hard to bring to completion. She contributed
intellectually to this book and, at a much more mundane level,
when I needed help in taking care of all the details of writing the
manuscript, she was there for me. Her understanding and generos-
ity of spirit has made this labor so much easier. After she came into
my life, suddenly the work became more fun. Without her, during
this past year, I have no idea how I would have survived, much less
how I would have finished the book.

Finally, my daughter, Alexis Feigen Fasteau, must be acknowledged. Her energy and excitement, her eagerness and joy, have
given me the ride of my life. Many sections of this book were written with her directly in mind, and I thank her for giving me the
clarity to write them. She rose to the challenge of having a sick
mother during the summer and fall of 1999. It was hard on her, but
she never let me think I was a burden. I am so grateful that she
came into this world, first looking to me and her father for guidance, and now striking out on her own, inspiring me with her kind,
loving, generous spirit and her keen intellect. Alexis already does
feminism proud, and I know that she will continue to carry the
torch.

NOT ONE OF THE BOYS

Introduction

THE BEGINNING—
HARVARD LAW SCHOOL,
CLASS OF '69

In 1966, I graduated from Vassar College. By that time, women were beginning to aspire to careers previously off limits to them. Most of my college classmates were satisfied with graduating from one of the Seven Sisters after having found an eligible Ivy League husband, but some of us applied to graduate and professional schools.

Once admitted to Harvard Law School, I decided to go there, because it would provide a good base for almost any career I could think of, including law itself. One reason I didn't take Columbia up on its offer to enter its joint law/business program, with a full scholarship, from which I would have emerged with a J.D. and an M.B.A., was that I felt I should be in a different city from the guy I had been dating since I was in the ninth grade. Deep down, I didn't think that marriage was in store for us, so my instinct was to head to Cambridge and the most famous law school in the country.

When I got to Harvard, however, my eyes were opened wide. I didn't realize then that a survey to be conducted during that year would reveal that of 2,708 lawyers employed by forty top law firms in six major cities, only 186 were women.[1] Another more sweeping statistic, also then unknown to me, was that women constituted only 3 percent of the nation's lawyers.[2] Perhaps the anti-Semitism I'd grown up with on the near north side of Chicago, my hometown, had prepared me for what I was about to experience.

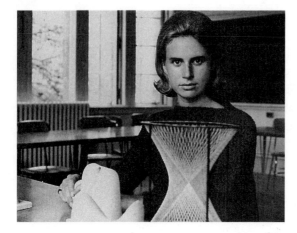

*My Vassar
graduation
photograph (I was
about to graduate
with honors in
math—June 1966).
The peculiar-
looking object in
front of me was used
to calculate spatial
relations in our
topography class.*

When I was ten, the Women's Athletic Club, which sponsored after-school swimming classes for the girls in my school, tried to exclude me because I was Jewish. And that was just the beginning. Throughout high school, there were annual New Year's Eve parties at a private club that wouldn't even allow Jews in as visitors. So every New Year's Eve, my fun would begin after midnight, when the boys were finally allowed to leave the party. I wasn't invited to the Fortnightly Club dances that all my friends, except the very few other Jews in my class, attended every other week. When I was sixteen, I was told that I couldn't visit my boyfriend's apartment after his eminent doctor father had a heart attack, because he hated Jews so much that seeing me there with his son might kill him.

It was common knowledge that former Harvard Law School Dean Erwin Griswold issued a traditional annual admonishment to women entering their first year: they were taking up valuable spots needed by men who, unlike their female counterparts, would have to support families. To the 32 women out of 565 students in my class, this was an ominous echo in our ears as we tried to live up to the expectations that our LSAT scores had predicted—on average, they had been higher than the men's.

Maybe we should have been grateful. When Ruth Bader Ginsburg entered Harvard Law School exactly ten years before I did, there were only nine women in a class about the same size as mine.[3]

Women were required to wear skirts in class; men, jackets and ties. Short skirts were the fashion in those days, and I'd occasionally note snickers from guys seated below me in the amphitheater-type classrooms who merely had to turn their heads to look up my skirt. Eventually, I decided that if they were distracted it was their problem, not mine.

After classes had been in session for a few weeks, I was startled to discover that A. James Casner, my property-law professor, who later was the role model for the professor in the movie *The Paper Chase*, held Ladies' Day—the one day of the year when he would call on women. The other days he'd spar, in Socratic fashion, only with men, whom he could try to intimidate without worrying that they'd burst into tears, the way he imagined women would. When one woman dared to raise her hand on a regular day, Casner curtly answered her question, then redirected his remarks to one of the male students. Harvard was noted for its case-study approach, and a big part of learning was to engage in verbal duels with the professor about arguments used or decisions rendered in various cases. We women were not getting the same education that the men were, and for some reason, probably because I didn't know her, I didn't approach the woman who had tried to engage Casner to express my sympathy for the way our professor had treated her.*

Ladies' Day in property-law class was spent on two issues: the dower rights to which a widow would be entitled in her deceased husband's property and who actually owns the engagement ring when an engagement is called off.

In my criminal-law class, the relatively young professor (unlike the avuncular Casner) announced that on his Ladies' Day, we would be discussing rape. And when that day rolled around, the

---

* In Professor W. Barton Leach's section of property law, women were similarly excluded from the process. One male classmate remembered no women speaking—except on Ladies' Day. He also recalled Leach's locker-room humor and the tales about his former wives that he told in class.

specific question for us women was, How much penetration constitutes rape?

Virtually all our professors would enter the room and issue the standard greeting: "Good morning, gentlemen." It was probably an unconscious wish for the days before women were first admitted to the Law School—in 1950. And so it became clear, really from our first day of classes, that women were unwelcome at the Law School, and that came as a continuing shock to me. Whereas at Vassar my comments had always been valued, here in Cambridge I began to feel as though I had no right to speak up. During all those years before college when I had attended a coed day school, asking questions had never been a problem. But in this elite of all elite white-male institutions, I was intimidated. At first, instead of taking action, I cried tears of rage, not knowing what to do.

When I wasn't in class, I was bombarded, as were, I assumed, the other women, by male classmates repeatedly asking the same stunningly boring question: "What's a nice girl like you doing in a place like this?" I didn't try to answer that question, because it was such a poorly disguised come-on. They really weren't interested in the reasons I had chosen to study at Harvard. I didn't know any of my female classmates yet, so I couldn't tell whether they shared my feelings about the way the Law School was treating women. That was before the time that women went up to other women they didn't know to compare notes on problems they were having as women.

During my first year at the Law School, I lived in a big old house with two former Vassar classmates both studying for their doctorates: one, Alice, in intellectual history; the other, Marcia, in English literature. They didn't seem to empathize with my plight, because, I thought, their departments were so unlike the Law School. But much later I heard a story about a woman who had started studying for her Ph.D. at Harvard in 1961. Naomi Weisstein's field was brain science. And at Harvard she did a dissertation on parallel processing, which led academics in more recent years to talk about how the brain is creative and active and shapes reality—Naomi's discoveries. But as her husband, Jesse

Lemisch, put it at a Veteran Feminists reunion in 1997, "the male supremacist zealots who ran Harvard, people like Jerome Bruner, wouldn't let her use the experimental equipment there—since she was a woman, Bruner felt, she would likely break it." Naomi decided to switch to Yale in 1963 (three years before I entered Harvard Law School). She used the equipment there, then got her degree from Harvard, first in her class, three years later.

It wasn't until October 1998, at a weekend event called "Vassar and Hollywood," that I heard Vassar president Frances Fergusson's story. I had mentioned over lunch that I'd become a feminist thanks to the way I was treated at Harvard Law School (not that sexism in society at large wouldn't have hit me eventually). President Fergusson's immediate response was that she had become a feminist in the mid-1960s when she was a graduate student at Harvard, enrolled in the Ph.D. program in fine arts. At the end of her first year, the names of her fellow students who had been awarded fellowships were read. All were male. When Frances approached the head of the department, challenging the obvious sexism in the grants that had been awarded, he defended the practice, saying that women didn't need the money as much as male students did (another reminder of the lie that only men support families and therefore need money).

My personal life in Cambridge involved going out on dates during my first semester, one with a graduate of the Law School who's now a major real estate and publishing mogul. His question to me, which no man would ever be asked, was "Brenda, what makes you tick?" No answer came to me. One guy I went out with, clearly not a potential mate, did come through, however. Sometime late in the semester, right before winter break, he introduced me to another classmate, Marc Fasteau, as I was sitting in the cafeteria, eating lunch and reading a casebook. Marc was handsome; I was interested, so I agreed to let them join me, and then was shocked by the first question Marc asked me: "So what do you think of the *Schmerber* case?" We'd just been talking about that in criminal-law class, and it had to do with the constitutionality of taking blood out of a suspected criminal's arm without his permission (he was too drunk to give it). It wasn't so much interest in that particular case that got to me. It was the fact that I had just been asked a serious question by a male student who seemed genuinely interested in what I *thought*!

When I got home that night, I pulled out the booklet Harvard had distributed, containing a picture and a brief bio of everyone in our class. There was Marc. All it said was that he had graduated from Harvard College in 1963. So I mused that he *had* been at Harvard that night when I, in my first year at college, was walking to my dorm at Vassar, staring up at the stars, and was struck by the vision that my future husband was right then and there at Harvard. Marc had gone on to get a master's degree in American history from Georgetown before starting law school.

Winter break came, and I went home to Chicago. My father was very sick, and I was scared. He'd been in and out of the hospital because of the colon cancer with which he'd been diagnosed a number of years earlier. He'd also had several strokes. Mostly because of its terrible weather, I didn't like visiting Chicago, and when I was there I was flooded with all the memories of the discrimination I had faced as a Jew growing up in a high-WASP neighborhood. This time I had also to deal with my father's illness and my mother's understandable preoccupation with it.

Shortly after winter break, I was studying in the Langdell Hall law library when Marc, whom I hadn't seen since our first meeting in the cafeteria two months earlier, sat down next to me. That a guy would sit next to me, usually to ask me to go out or make chitchat while he was on *his* break, was not surprising. But Marc was different. He started whispering (obeying the "no talking in the library" rule) about some case we'd just been studying. The conversation picked up, as I realized that again he seemed genuinely interested in me as a person. Eventually, he asked if I wanted to have dinner that night. I was sure he was talking about the Harkness cafeteria, because that's where I always ended up— alone, not having taken the time to make advance dinner plans. I said I'd meet him in Harkness and asked what time. He looked at me as though I were a bit weird and said he'd meant at his place. I was pleasantly surprised and wrote down directions to get there.

When I arrived at his house, I almost fell on the very slippery, unsalted ice leading to the front door, but as he opened the door, the scent of chicken simmering in a wonderful-smelling wine sauce wafted toward me. Now I was really impressed.

Two days later Marc appeared at my front door, holding my red plastic pencil-and-pen case in his hand. I couldn't believe that I had left it at his house. And despite how much I wanted to, I couldn't invite him in. My old boyfriend from Chicago, now attending NYU Law School, was visiting me in Cambridge for the weekend.

It wasn't long before Marc and I began dating. I was impressed by an article he had written for *The Bulletin of Atomic Scientists* in 1963, way ahead of its time, on reasons for the United States not to send troops to South Vietnam. (At the end of 1963 about 16,000 U.S. troops were already stationed there, supposedly serving as advisers to South Vietnam's President Diem.[4]) But I think the night that really did it for me was when he started talking in fluent French, which I could just barely understand, about his feelings. We were at a party, and he was looser and funnier with me than he'd been before.

It turned out that Marc was contemplating ending a relationship with a woman he'd been dating for quite a while. After graduating from Bryn Mawr, she was now an artist living in Philadelphia. She had been planning on moving in with Marc before the upcoming summer. One day, however, he told me that he'd called her and ended their relationship. That same night, realizing that I was falling seriously in love with Marc, I formally broke up with Billy.

So Marc and I spent all our time together, studying, eating and some sleeping. And in the process, I watched how someone male was treated, how differently from the way women were.

One day I was walking with Marc through the underground tunnel that connects the different parts of the Law School. As we approached our constitutional-law professor, Paul Freund,

Freund looked at Marc and said hello, but he ignored me entirely. This happened before either of us had displayed any legal talent or had had occasion to charm him in any other way. It was merely a matter of gender. I was furious, and Marc saw for the first time what it meant to be a woman at the Law School.

At Vassar, I had learned to play squash and had come to enjoy it in the winter months when tennis was impracticable. So when I learned that Harvard Law School's contribution to sports at the university were several squash courts, I decided one day to visit them. Immediately, I was shooed out of the building by a very old male caretaker. "No women allowed!" he shouted at me. I left angry. Later, when I told Marc about it, he and I hatched an idea: I'd pretend I was a man and go in with Marc to play. I wanted to do what Marc could and what I enjoyed.

After we'd hit the ball for a while, my long hair, which had been piled on top of my head under a hat, began to fall down, and not long after that the little old man opened the door to our court and shouted, "No women! You get out." I felt like a bad dog as we scurried away, so upset and angry that tears rolled down my cheeks. Finally, it hit me that I felt the same as I had when I was growing up in Chicago. I felt isolated and still didn't know any of the other women in our class well enough to ask if they too were unhappy. This was well before the days when women sought each other out in consciousness-raising (C-R) groups to talk about our feelings, feelings that men may not get. In fact, it wouldn't be until C-R groups sprang up in New York and I joined one, in 1970, that I myself would find it easier to express to other women painful emotions like the ones I was feeling at Harvard.

Eventually, Marc told me that he'd been invited to join Lincoln's Inn. I hadn't heard of it. He confessed that it was an all-male eating club. I was shocked and pressed further. All male students and all faculty—then also all male—were invited to join, but women weren't. How could he join, I asked, when he too thought it was wrong? Marc decided to take on Lincoln's Inn with me, telling them that he wouldn't join unless women were admitted, and he began to work on a plan to get women in. Soon both he and I began to spread the word to other classmates about the squash courts and Lincoln's Inn. It took a while before we mustered any real support for our positions. This was, after all, 1967. The public's focus was on the Vietnam War. By the end of 1967, we had more than 500,000 troops there and polls were showing that most Americans were tired of the war.[5] Men my age were especially preoccupied with the subject, fearful constantly that their draft numbers would be called.

One day, in a constitutional-law class taught by the highly respected Paul Freund, the one who had acknowledged only Marc in the underground hallway, we were discussing a 1947 case, *Goesaert v. Cleary*,[6] in which the U.S. Supreme Court upheld a Michigan statute making it a crime for a woman to work as a "barmaid" unless her father or brother was the proprietor of the bar and present while she was working. The country's most highly respected constitutional-law scholar, our teacher, apparently found the reasoning in the case sound and asked if anyone disagreed with the Court. I put my hand up, heart beating wildly, and said, in that classroom of virtually all men, that I thought the decision was outrageous, cutting off yet another source of income for women while placing them on some kind of phony pedestal. Professor Freund burst out laughing, as did the entire class. When I turned around to look at Marc, in his assigned seat several rows behind me, I didn't get the reaction I had expected. He was just sitting there, not laughing with the rest of them but definitely avoiding looking at me. If there were any other women in that classroom, I definitely didn't see them, nor did they offer any consolation later.

After class, Marc made some lame excuse for not publicly agreeing with me—something about it not being his issue. I said that anything that put women down was his issue, just as it was mine. I was really feeling fed up with the Law School and its treatment of women. Marc told me not to take it out on him. But because I considered him to be my best friend, I definitely expected him to be more supportive.

Slowly, however, on the heels of that incident, I began to meet a few women in my class. At that point, they were just casual acquaintances. I didn't talk with them about my feelings concerning the Law School, because I didn't know them well enough.

It's interesting, as I look back on it, that at Harvard I felt a sense of entitlement. My anger was justified. My parents had paid just as much tuition as had those of everyone else, yet I was getting less out of the experience than my male classmates were.

All this was taking a toll on me. I had never had an easy time sleeping, especially when I was anxious about something. Since anxiety (another word in these days for my anger) permeated my life at law school, my insomnia had become so bad that I'd sought help from the psychiatrist who was assigned to treat law students. He refused to prescribe sleeping pills, referring me instead to the Harvard health services. There I met with a kind man who had a doctorate in education. After several meetings, he said that he and his colleagues would like me to take a battery of psychological tests. I agreed, and the next thing I knew they were offering to see me for two therapy sessions a week at no cost to me. They were interested in my complaints about the treatment of women at the Law School and eager to study the consequences of that treatment.

At the end of my first year in law school, I learned minutes after my last exam was over that my father had died early that morning. I had just started to unwind with Marc when my brother, Richard, called with the news. I burst into tears, as though I hadn't considered the possibility that his serious illness could come to this. I was distraught but tried to keep our plans and go to a party with Marc that night. He took me home because I was too upset to stay, and then he returned to the party. At that point, I was too out of touch with my feelings to care very much, but in retrospect, I wished he had stayed with me that night. The next morning I flew to Chicago.

Marc and I spent as much time together as we could that summer of 1967. I was working for his close friend Peter Goldmark (until recently president of the Rockefeller Foundation), at City

Hall in New York. Marc was working in Boston at a city government agency.

By the time I returned to Cambridge for our second year, I had decided to share a house with a classmate, Kimba Wood (now a federal judge), with whom I'd become friends. One day, Kimba and I were walking through the lower level of the Law School library, where we'd been studying in little, depressingly stark carrels. I saw a sign on a frosted door: PROFESSORS ONLY. Moving closer we heard a toilet flush, and realized that it was a men's room. It didn't need to say "Male Professors Only" because that would be redundant—all Law School professors were male. As Justice Ginsburg pointed out years later: "Up till 1963, barely a dozen women had ever taught on any U.S. law faculty across the country."[7] In fact, Ruth Bader Ginsburg would become, in 1972, the first woman to hold a tenured position at Columbia Law School.[8] The meaning of that sign on the library bathroom was the first feminist revelation that I shared with another woman in the Law School.

In the middle of our second year, I decided to write a paper for something called *The Women Lawyers Journal*. They were sponsoring an essay contest on civil rights, and my article was called "Civil Rights: Discrimination in the Legal Profession." I recently located a letter from the Secretary of Harvard Law School, certifying that my essay was the entry that he had chosen to represent Harvard Law School in the contest. Even today, I read a sentence in the first paragraph of that essay with shock: "A 1967 survey of over 25 major law firms in New York, Boston and Washington discloses not a single woman partner." I had obtained that information by carefully reading through the lawyers' bible, *Martindale-Hubble Law Directory,* for the year 1967. In my essay I set forth more sorry statistics about women in the legal profession. It seems as though Title VII of the 1964 Civil Rights Act, which had passed after heated debate and which prohibited discrimination by private employers, hadn't made much of a dent in my chosen profession.

During the summer of 1968, between our second and third years in law school, we were all expected to clerk at law firms. With that in mind, firms from all over the country descended on the Law School, putting notices on bulletin boards about who they were and when they'd be in which classrooms to conduct interviews. I began to talk with the hiring partner of one firm whose notice had appealed to me, but he stared at me and then bluntly admitted that they simply weren't hiring women. This exact same experience was replicated on three other occasions. Some firms were more creative: Coudert Frères, the Paris branch of the New York firm Coudert Brothers, told me they could not hire a woman because their "senior partners" would object. Milbank Tweed, a big Manhattan firm, told me that they had already hired their one woman for the year. Another large firm said that women would only be hired to do probate, trusts and estates work, the traditional domain of "lady lawyers." I wasn't interested.

I didn't know then that Supreme Court Justice Sandra Day O'Connor had graduated from Stanford Law School in 1952, at the top of her class, along with Chief Justice William Rehnquist. Yet while Rehnquist was rewarded with a Supreme Court clerkship, a much-sought-after job for young lawyers, of course Sandra Day wasn't even considered for such a clerkship. Nor would a single private firm hire her to do a lawyer's work. "I interviewed with law firms in Los Angeles and San Francisco," Justice O'Connor later recalled, "but none had ever hired a woman before as a lawyer, and they were not prepared to do so."[9]

Matters had slightly improved by the time I got to law school, and finally, for the summer between our second and third years, I landed a position at Foley, Hoag and Elliott, a respectable Boston firm. Marc took a job at another prestigious firm nearby.

By the time our third year in law school started, maybe having become aware of all my raging battles, many of the other women in my class were expressing their own disgust with the way women were treated. Still complicating our situation—not to mention that of world peace—was the Vietnam War. Most of us were furious at the government for U.S. involvement in that war. We would soon learn that an American infantry unit had massacred about five hundred innocent men, women and children in the village of My Lai. Nonetheless, President Nixon continued to ask the "great silent majority" of Americans to support this still-undeclared war and to refuse to join the antiwar demonstrations occurring across the nation.[10]

I was studying labor law that spring with the internationally acclaimed professor Archibald Cox, and it came as no surprise to me and my classmates when he was summoned to Columbia University in April to deal with a huge student uprising. This time students were protesting university plans to build a gymnasium in a park next to the campus; the university was apparently using hardball tactics to wrench concessions from the community.

Because of my relationship with Marc, I often was torn between sitting with him and other male friends at lunch, only to hear repeated angry outbursts by the guys over the war, and sitting with my women friends. Although the women all opposed the war too, we finally were discussing other subjects—like what we were feeling as women at Harvard Law School and what we should do to make things better not only for ourselves but also for the women who would follow. In retrospect, our conversations resembled those of the C-R groups that would start to form in the outside world within a year.

One day, as interviews for jobs after graduation were picking up steam, I asked Dean Derek Bok if I could meet with him. I was upset that the Law School was letting firms that discriminated against women use the school's facilities to conduct interviews. It seemed like such an obviously moral request that I couldn't believe it when Dean Bok pleaded with me to understand that much of the school's financial support came from just those firms about which I was complaining. Harvard Law School, he stated quite simply, could not afford to alienate the big money givers by thorough investigations of their hiring practices. When I reported back to my women classmates what the dean's response had been, they were as angry as I was. But he must have heard me. By the next year, firms that took blatantly sexist positions couldn't interview on campus. That, of course, didn't rule out the possibility that they were still discriminating against women in more subtle ways.

What law firm hiring partners felt about the role of women as lawyers was not surprising. Ridiculous stereotypes were constantly reinforced by professors, who warned us that women didn't do criminal work or labor law. These fields were regarded as too dangerous and unseemly for us. It was inappropriate for women to visit male criminal clients in jail, just as it was unbecoming for a woman to sit around a bargaining table full of men until all hours of the night.

Soon I was like a time bomb ready to go off at any further insults. At a faculty reception for third-year students, I got into an argument with the esteemed professor Louis Loss, who argued that women lawyers shouldn't use "Esq." after their names, because the appellation "esquire" refers only to men. I blurted out, "That is bullshit. This is not England!"

By this time, Marc had been anointed to the Harvard Law Review. Becoming an editor was the most prestigious position any law student could attain; it was reserved for those who had the very highest grades in the class. No women were on the Review, even though our LSAT scores had been higher on average than those of our male counterparts. This fact is relevant, because LSAT scores had generally been found to correlate with one's grades in law school. At Harvard Law School, at that time, they didn't. The reason for this deviation was obvious. Women at Harvard Law School, unlike at some schools where they made up a much larger percentage of their classes, were under such pressure from both male professors and students that most of us couldn't concentrate the way the men could. If it were the same today, it might be called a "hostile learning environment."

Shortly after Marc was elected to the Law Review, he was asked to join something called the Choate Club. Neither of us had ever heard of it. Soon we learned that the club was male only; there had never been any women members. It helped to be on the Law Review, but that wasn't a prerequisite, and it was good if the man was an athlete or from blueblooded lineage. The Choate Club had just, in the past few years, started to admit Jews. It had one black member. Many professors who had been students in the fifties and before and who were Jewish had been in the dark about the existence of this club until we started to make a fuss. It seemed, though, that as much as these professors had themselves experienced anti-Semitism, they didn't have any understanding of what women were experiencing at Harvard Law School.

Marc decided that he wouldn't join the Choate Club unless it eliminated the no-women policy, just as it finally had the no-Jews policy. Soon the club took a vote and the male-only policy was dropped. I was invited to join, and Marc and I both became members. But right after women were admitted, I heard men who'd been members for a long time saying that now the club had lost its cachet. What had been *the* secret elite club at the Law School, counting among its members former U.S. presidents, senators, and governors and all kinds of other prestigious person-alities, folded several years after I was admitted.

One day in the fall of 1968, while I was reading the news-paper, I was intrigued by a report about a group of two hundred women who had staged a "guerrilla" action at the Miss America contest in Atlantic City. They were protesting the contest by throwing bras, girdles, and other oppressive feminine parapher-nalia into trash cans. Although not as colorful, at least a few of our protests at the Law School were successful. Both Lincoln's Inn and the squash courts were integrated the year after we grad-uated. But before that, Marc and I had embarked on a significant personal journey. In the middle of our third year, we got married.

The morning of the wedding, before it was time for my brother to escort me down the aisle, I decided to walk around the second floor of the Harvard Club of New York City to calm my nerves.* I wandered into the musty library in my wedding gown. The elderly men who had been snoozing behind their newspapers

---

* I hadn't yet made the leap that a woman's being walked down the aisle by a male rel-ative was a sexist custom.

*Right after the Big
Event, at our
Harvard Club
wedding reception*

began to stare at me, but not with the gracious good humor that
brides usually experience just before they are married. As I
exited, I noticed a small sign with the words NO LADIES ALLOWED.

Finally, it came time for the walk down the aisle, at the end of
which we exchanged rings. Upon our marriage, I added Marc's
last name to mine, making me Brenda Feigen Fasteau. About a
year later, Marc added Feigen and became Marc Feigen Fasteau,
so we had exchanged not only rings but also names as well.

Weeks after our wedding, I learned that women were not
allowed to be members of the Harvard Club of New York City.

*Marc and I honeymooning on
the Caribbean island of
Anguilla, December 1968*

The only rooms we were even permitted to enter were the very
ones that had been reserved for our wedding and the reception
afterward.

Clearly, I couldn't let that go. It took about five years—and our
admission to the Massachusetts and New York bars—for Marc
and me to sue the Harvard Club of New York for sex discrimination. There were crazy debates, including statements like one in
the *New York Times* that women, once admitted, would put "green
tablecloths on everything." Our case was a four-pronged class
action: I was representing myself and all other women who had
attended any part of Harvard University and were, because of
their gender, unable to become members. Marc was representing
the class of men who refused to join a sexist club. The two other
classes were comprised of men who would resign their memberships if women weren't admitted, and women with "signing privileges," meaning that they had previously agreed to confine
themselves to a few rooms on the second floor of the club. They
were so browbeaten that they didn't even object to using a side
door, insisted upon by male members who didn't want women to
be seen going in and out the front door. Taken together, the four
subclasses were certified by the federal district court as one large

class of plaintiffs for the class action we'd brought, with much fanfare in the press.

At the last of several pretrial conferences, the judge ordered the Harvard Club to take one final vote before we proceeded to trial the next day, making it very clear, since he was, for the moment, both judge and jury, that he was not sympathetic to their pleas for more time to bring the membership around. He himself had graduated from Princeton and wasn't in the least bit impressed by the club's nine-lawyer team as they trooped into his courtroom. The last wail of the lawyers for the Harvard Club reverberates to this day in my ears: "Your Honor, can't we please at least keep the bar male only?" The judge looked at me, and I shook my head. "It's all or nothing," I proclaimed, sure that justice was on my side. My instinct was good. The next day, pursuant to the judge's order, the club voted to admit women as full members, and I was one of the first to join. There were no areas, except the men's bathrooms and locker room, that were off limits to us.

Our battle against the Harvard Club would lead to a general change in attitudes about male-only clubs, to the point now where any man running for high office knows he's in trouble if he belongs to a club that doesn't admit women, let alone Jews, blacks or other minorities.

In general, stopping the sexism at Ivy League institutions— supposedly liberal bastions—wasn't easy. Ruth Bader Ginsburg described litigation that started in the late 1970s after a tea given by Columbia University for all senior women faculty. There were only eleven of those women, but they made good use of the occasion, by discussing the sex differential then part of the university's retirement plan. Under this plan, women received lower monthly retirement benefits, because, on average, women live longer than men. A lawsuit was subsequently filed with one hundred Columbia women—teachers and administrators—as named complainants. It finally reached the U.S. Supreme Court, which resolved the issue in favor of the women.[11] But the sexism wasn't reserved for women at the top. During Ginsburg's first month as a professor at Columbia, in September 1972, the university sent layoff notices to twenty-five "maids" (all women) and not a single janitor (all men). The work of maids and janitors was essentially identical. So Ginsburg entered the battle, which, as she puts it, "happily ended with no layoffs, and, as I recall, the union's first female shop steward."[12]

Our victory against the Harvard Club in 1973 made it all the more gratifying for me, one day a few years later, to receive a call from a group called Harvard Law Women. They were organizing an evening event for all the women graduates of the Law School who lived in the New York area to attend a performance of the play *First Monday in October*, starring Henry Fonda and Jane Alexander. The play was to be followed by a reception at the Harvard Club, which I was once again thanked for having integrated, and to which they would invite Jane Alexander. She was playing the fictitious first woman appointed to the U.S. Supreme Court. I thought the whole thing was a great idea and was delighted when they called me shortly thereafter to say that Ms. Alexander had accepted the invitation to join us after the play for the reception in her honor at the Harvard Club.

When the big night rolled around, I was very excited. I had never been at the club to celebrate women from the Law School. When I introduced myself to Jane Alexander, we instantly clicked. Eventually, someone politely asked me if I would share Jane with the others.

The search for jobs after graduation intensified when Marc and I returned for our last semester of law school from our honeymoon in the Caribbean. I should have anticipated trouble. Paul Weiss Rifkind Wharton & Garrison, a large, prestigious firm in New York, interviewed Marc and me together—at our request—for positions at their firm. When the hiring partner saw that Marc was on the Law Review, he turned to him and said he had a job if he wanted one. "As for Brenda," he said, looking not at me, although I was right there, but at Marc, "we don't hire spouses, so that settles that." He hadn't even glanced at my folder. Both Marc and I were enraged, because the idea of work-

ing in the same firm had appealed to us. The partner went on to
rationalize that the reason for this rule was that if the firm
wanted to fire one but not the other of us, the work of the one
who remained might suffer. Marc thanked them but declined the
offer. Years later, when I told a Paul Weiss partner that story, he
seemed shocked, denying that such a thing could have happened
at his firm. That denial, of course, was after Title VII of the Civil
Rights Act had begun to be enforced against companies that discriminated against women. Excuses like the one given us
wouldn't pass legal scrutiny under the new law.

Our job-interview process quickly changed course when Marc
was offered a clerkship with U.S. Supreme Court Justice Abe
Fortas. I was able to land a fairly interesting-sounding job at the
Department of Housing and Urban Development. Meanwhile,
my spirit remained intact. When Justice Fortas, in a private
meeting he'd asked me to attend with Marc in his chambers,
advised me that I wouldn't be seeing much of Marc for the entire
year of his clerkship, my response was a determined, uppity "Oh
yes I will." I don't even think I added "Your Honor"!

Several months later, Fortas quit the Court, and we decided to
stay in Cambridge an extra year before moving to New York. We
took and passed the Massachusetts bar exam, before we started
the second half of our honeymoon to quaint and beautiful
places—cheap enough, though, for us to afford—all over Europe.
One incident from that otherwise lovely trip stands out. When we
arrived in Israel, of course the Wailing Wall was one of the first
sights we visited. As we approached, I got a sinking feeling in my
stomach. The men and women were on different sides of the Wall,
because men aren't supposed to be distracted by women when
they're praying. I started to make a fuss, which Marc stopped just
as several Israeli police approached. I agreed that it wasn't worth
getting arrested for, although in recent years groups of Jewish
women have publicly protested at the Wall.

My own experiences at Harvard were borne out in a study on
all the women who had graduated in the years up to 1970 from
Harvard Law School, since 1953, when the first class of women

graduated.[13] The survey showed that almost all the graduating men but only 45 percent of the women had received two or more job offers. Twenty-three percent of the women, but only 15 percent of the men, had had twelve or more interviews with law firms in the process of seeking a job. Fifty-two percent of female Harvard Law School graduates started out in law firms, as compared with 72 percent of the men. Sixteen percent of the women and 11 percent of the men were employed by the federal government, and this statistic conforms to the common notion that most jobs with the federal government are easier to get and pay less than jobs in private firms. Nine percent of the women but only 1 percent of men worked in Legal Aid (free assistance to the poor, subsidized by tax dollars).

More statistics revealed that recent female graduates had considerably less client exposure than men did. Twelve percent of women but only 1 percent of men saw no clients in an average week. Thirty-seven percent of women but only 17 percent of men saw fewer than four clients a week. (These statistics reflect the fact that women were encouraged to go into estates-and-trusts work, a field in which the client whose interests you're representing is usually a family where women's much-vaunted people skills are needed or someone who is—or soon will be—dead.)

These statistics, coupled with what happened to me at Harvard Law School, and subsequently in the suit against the Harvard Club, pried my eyes wide open. I had planned to have a traditional—and stellar—career, even though I wasn't sure exactly what I'd be doing. By now, however, I realized that such a career would be mine only with constant confrontation, even though I had justice on my side. I would settle for nothing less than treatment equal to that of my male counterparts. Little did I know then that the years I spent at Harvard would inform my politics for the rest of my life. The fervor with which I had tried to make all those anti-Semites like me back in Chicago had turned to anger. I wasn't about to spend another second waiting for things to change on their own, as my mother kept imploring me. If I sensed discrimination or a generalized hostility to women, anywhere, anytime, I had to do something about it, whatever the cost to me or my career. No longer would I try to please the kind of men who seemed forever likely to have a deep fear—even hatred—of women. I was glad that the worst offenders at Harvard Law School, the ones who had Ladies' Days and, in general, had deplored our existence there, were dying off. Maybe the next generation of professors would be more enlightened. Maybe it would even include women.

If I hadn't consciously identified myself before as a feminist, my experience at Harvard Law School certainly made me aware that I was one. This book is one woman's story of living life as a feminist. With eyes wide open, as they now were, I couldn't help but notice the instances in which either I individually or women in general were put down or negated in one way or another.

I remain convinced that feminism indeed has the potential to be the most revolutionary social movement since the founding of our United States. Unlike those in the civil rights and gay rights movements, we have never really asked for only equality with, or the same treatment as that accorded, straight white men. This may be related to the fact that women are the majority, not a small, isolated minority. We have as much right to rule the world, let alone address issues of importance to women everywhere, as men. I have told the stories that follow—some of which have been hard to write—in the hopes that they will resonate with other women.

Chapter 1

MY DISCOVERY
OF THE WOMEN'S
MOVEMENT

While I was in law school, the second wave of the Women's Movement began. (I consider the first to have started with the Seneca Falls Women's Rights Convention, in 1848, which ushered in the fight for women's right to vote—not achieved on the national level until 1920.) The influence of the civil rights movement and protests against the Vietnam War created an environment in which women finally felt it was time to look out for themselves and not simply join other groups demanding their rights. The internationally acclaimed book by Simone de Beauvoir *The Second Sex*[1] had already provided the theoretical framework for women's demands.

The National Organization for Women (NOW) had been formed in 1966. Its president in those days was Betty Friedan, whose best-selling 1963 book *The Feminine Mystique* I had trouble relating to because it was aimed at housewives. But NOW had led the campaign to end sex-segregated want ads, and in August 1968, the Equal Employment Opportunities Commission (EEOC) issued guidelines prohibiting newspapers from carrying separate ads for women and men. It took over six months for these guidelines to go into effect, because the American Newspaper Publishers Association sued the EEOC to try to stop the new policy.

Unbeknownst to me at the time, the first three occupationally oriented feminist groups were formed in September 1969: the Women's Caucuses of the American Sociological Association, and counterparts in political science and psychology. The Association for Women in Psychology, formed during the annual meeting of the American Psychological Association (APA) in 1969, in fact, made a dramatic demand the following year: $1 million in reparations from the APA for damage done to women by psychologists who had, according to feminists, viewed women's psychological problems from the vantage point of sexist psychological theories.[2]

In the same year, however, the National Association of Women Lawyers declined to participate in a joint survey on the status of women in the legal profession and in law schools.[3] The good news was that the fall of 1969 ushered in the first accredited Women and the Law class, taught at NYU Law School, which had been in the forefront of admitting women students.

After seeing a flyer in Cambridge about a "Women's Liberation" conference, called the First Congress to Unite Women, I flew to New York at the end of November 1969, and was amazed that over five hundred women had shown up for the Congress, which was closed to the media—and to men. At the door, I was told to pick a straw out of a jar. It turned out that my straw entitled me to be on the podium for a discussion about the status of women. I went along with a decision made by chance rather than reason. It would not be the last time I would experience this every-woman-is-equal theme that permeated many aspects of the Women's Movement.*

The first night of the Congress, the lights went out, then on again, and suddenly twenty women were on the stage all wearing T-shirts with letters spelling out the words Lavender Menace, the name of a lesbian feminist group. The next day, more women, again on stage in front of the whole auditorium, cut off the long hair of one of their members, to make the point that they would no longer be defined by what men want, only by what they themselves wanted to look like. All now short-haired, they called

---

* A number of years later, I would engage in a "transatlantic dialogue," subsequently published and disseminated widely, with Juliet Mitchell, the leader of the British feminist movement, and a socialist who felt one couldn't be a feminist without being a socialist. Needless to say, I disagreed with her.

themselves political lesbians, and although I didn't agree that having long hair was about pleasing men, I did agree that women do outrageous things to their bodies in a desperate attempt to attract men. Fortunately, a universally needed platform came out of the Congress, advocating passage of the Equal Rights Amendment and the repeal of all laws that made abortion illegal.

Just being at the Congress was a heady experience. I was part of something much bigger than my skirmishes at Harvard Law School. I was now a member of a large angry group that was poised on the brink of a real revolution.

After the First Congress to Unite Women, I went back to Cambridge and decided to join NOW, which was about to undergo a change of leadership. I called Betty Friedan, who was still the president, and in response to my saying that I wanted to become a member, she asked what I did. I told her I had just passed the Massachusetts bar exam. Not long after that, I received a phone call from Lucy Komisar, NOW's national vice president for publicity: Would I please consider running for national legislative vice president? They needed a lawyer to fill the position. There was a six-month membership requirement if you were running for national office in NOW, but they would bend the rules. And shortly after that call, I was on a plane to Des Plaines, Illinois, headed to NOW's 1970 annual convention, where I was handily elected to the legislative position.

Several weeks after taking over the NOW vice presidency, I was watching the *David Susskind Show*. The subject was "Working Girls," and Sandra, my brother's wife, was on the panel. I was particularly taken with a strikingly attractive woman with an intelligent-sounding voice spouting statistics about how shabbily women were treated in different occupations. I had seen her once before at a big party my brother had thrown, crowded with the jet set and New York's literati. When I first noticed her, at this party, she was escorted by Rafer Johnson, a black Olympic gold medalist. I had later asked my brother who she was, and he had replied, "Gloria Steinem."

As I watched the Susskind show I was transfixed by Gloria's

knowledge of facts and figures without so much as a glance downward at her notes. I wanted to meet her, and I decided I'd figure out how when Marc and I moved to New York in May.

We had lucked into a dirt-cheap rent-stabilized triplex penthouse in Tudor City on East Fortieth Street. The previous tenant had been Charlton Heston. When we first saw the apartment, we had had to imagine away the terrible olive green paint on the walls. The view, the light and the location, overlooking the East River, were wonderful, and we signed the lease.

As national vice president of legislation for NOW, my responsibility was to ensure that the Equal Rights Amendment would be passed by Congress and sent to the states for ratification that year. It had been introduced every year since 1923 but had never made it out of Congress. And its wording had remained the same:

> Equality of rights under the law shall not be denied or abridged by the United States or any state on account of sex.

Many "radical feminists" didn't care at all about passage of the ERA. To them, NOW members like myself were just liberals who "bought into the patriarchy." "Radical feminists" wanted to restructure society. So did I, but I couldn't figure out how to do that from *outside* the system, and I still can't. Actually, I have always considered myself a radical feminist, because I want to change the society in which we live, not just participate equally in it. But I also have a healthy respect for our Constitution, which can, of course, be amended. It is certainly true that our political system has flaws, among the most grievous being that women are grossly underrepresented everywhere. But it is equally true that if we were represented at least in proportion to our numbers in the population, the system would be very different from the male-dominated one in which women now must exist. The "radical feminists" who thought the ERA didn't matter were confusing the structure of our governmental system with the substantive decisions made under the rules of that structure. This resulted in their minimizing the importance of changing unjust rules. The Fourteenth Amendment to the Constitution, guaranteeing equality based on race, had not created equality between women and men under the law. The ERA would be a first step in rectifying that injustice, making the questions of whether and how the Fourteenth Amendment applied to gender discrimination moot.

There were other groups of women coming together that would fit into the same category as NOW. In 1970 a small group of African-American women met in New York to discuss the problems facing them and the opportunities available to them in light of both the civil rights movement and the Women's Movement. Calling themselves the Coalition of 100 Black Women, they hoped to build the organization's membership from the original twenty-four to a more substantial hundred-woman group. They quickly surpassed that original goal, with their programs involving career advancement, political and economic empowerment and the crisis of the black family.

Betty Friedan, during her presidency of NOW had dismissed welfare, the War in Vietnam and lesbian rights as not being women's issues. Our new administration disagreed, and the newly elected president, Aileen Hernandez, a former commissioner of the EEOC, was black, so I hoped that lesbians would be welcomed and more women of color would join NOW. NOW's focus would continue to be mostly on working women's issues, such as twenty-four-hour child care and equal pay for equal work, as well as the ERA and abortion rights.

To me, twenty-four-hour child care would help working parents as well as women who would otherwise just be housewives. I've always wondered why women who stay home while their husbands work don't seem to understand that sharing the roles of caring for the children and the home, as well as supporting the family, with the men in their lives is good for the entire family.

Shortly after I assumed the position of national vice president of NOW, I received a phone call from U.S. senator Birch Bayh. Senator Bayh was a Democrat from Indiana for whom I'd interned during the summer between my junior and senior years at Vassar. Now he was asking me if I would be willing to coordinate the "pro testimony" for the Equal Rights Amendment. He was chair of the Subcommittee on Constitutional Amendments, which would be holding hearings on the proposed amendment in early May. I gladly accepted the responsibility, promising that I'd get important and prestigious people to testify for the ERA.

Politically, it was crucial to get union women on our side. We needed to persuade them that their giving up hard-won "privileges" like shorter hours and protection from workplaces possibly hazardous to pregnant women was necessary in order for union women to achieve equality with their male counterparts. Ultimately, the ERA got the ringing endorsement of labor women, most notably the Coalition of Labor Union Women (CLUW), as well as the women in the UAW and the AFL-CIO.

I decided to call Gloria Steinem, who by now was well known as an intelligent New York journalist with good political connections. I was delighted that I finally had a reason to call her, and in what would become a very familiar response, Gloria conditionally agreed to testify, even though, she protested, she wasn't a lawyer and she knew so little about the ERA, if I would agree to help with her testimony. I happily assented. Although I've always been one for advance planning, Gloria isn't, and we agreed that she would go to D.C. on the night of May 5—the day before she was scheduled to testify—and call me once she was settled in. Meanwhile, three officers of NOW were scheduled to testify during that first day of hearings, and I was one.

I reviewed the process by which the Constitution had been amended in the past, as well as transcripts from past years' ERA floor debates. I studied recent legal writings on the ERA, concluding that it would, in fact, go further than the Fourteenth Amendment's Equal Protection Clause and prohibit *any* different treatment under the law between men and women unless a superior constitutional claim intervened. It was universally accepted by constitutional scholars, for example, that men and women would still use different bathrooms and be separated from each other in prisons, guaranteed the right of privacy by already existing provisions in the Constitution.

At the beginning of May, Marc and I lugged all our worldly possessions out of our Cambridge apartment into a U-Haul truck, which he was going to drive to our new home in New York while I flew to D.C. I would meet him in New York after the ERA testimony several days later.

So on May 5, 1970, I was called to the podium in my capacity as national vice president of NOW. I spoke on behalf of all women about the reasons we deserved to be protected by the Constitution, just as all men were, and how the way to accomplish that was through the ERA. The Supreme Court, in various sex-discrimination cases that had come before it, starting with Myra Bradwell's suit against the state of Illinois because it wouldn't let women become lawyers,[4] had failed us miserably, never so far deeming such discrimination a violation of the Equal Protection Clause of the Fourteenth Amendment.

After my testimony, three members of something called Washington, D.C. Women's Liberation were called to give their testimony. My curiosity was piqued because they called themselves Emma Goldman, Sarah Grimké and Angelina Grimké,* and when "Miss Sarah Grimké" started to speak I was reassured because she said that they had "come here today to support our sisters who have been working since 1923 for the passage of this amendment." But then she went on: "[W]e know that the amendment cannot guarantee real equality. . . . We will not be appeased! Our demands can only be met by a total transformation of society which you cannot legislate, you cannot co-opt, you cannot control."

"Angelina Grimké" was even angrier. I was dismayed as she stood and faced away from the senators, toward the gallery, con-

---

* The Grimké sisters were the first American-born women to take to the public platform, where they advocated abolition and women's rights.

cluding her remarks with "Constitutional amendments will not make any difference. . . . Only revolutionary change can meet the demands that women are making today." And then in what would become a refrain in future women's liberation protests: "Free our sisters, free ourselves, all power to the people." On that note, the three of them marched out of the room. I thought they had done a special disservice to the memory of Sarah Grimké, who, in 1838, had made one of the most impassioned pleas I had ever read for women's equality: "I ask no favors for my sex. I surrender not our claim to equality. All I ask of our brethren is that they take their feet off our necks and permit us to stand upright on the ground which God has designed for us to occupy."[5]

But these three modern-day self-dubbed radical feminists, I realized, just didn't want any part of the patriarchal system. Why couldn't they see that the ERA will help women even if it's only a first step? While they fancied themselves able to function outside "the system," I couldn't even envision what that meant. I heard genuine passion in their rhetoric, but I still couldn't find within their arguments anything substantive *against* the ERA. In fact, that kind of feminist would come around years later in support of the ERA.

While the "Grimkés" were testifying, I had an insight that was to sustain me for the rest of the early years of the movement: they will seem so far out that I and Gloria and every other feminist I'd count as an ally now and in the future would sound downright reasonable compared with them. I'd studied about revolutions in political science classes and already knew that most had a "lunatic fringe," useful to the more mainstream revolutionaries.

I was staying at Marc's parents' house in Falls Church, Virginia. What I didn't realize then was that Gloria tends to work in the middle of the night—something that hasn't changed in the thirty years that I've known her. And so the phone rang about 2:00 a.m., waking both of Marc's parents. Gloria didn't seem very contrite about the time, and we spent several hours on the phone. First I explained what the ERA would do constitutionally, then I listened to what she had drafted and made a few suggestions. She asked if we could meet before she testified, and I told her to go to Senator Bayh's office, where I'd be waiting, right before the hearings were to begin.

The next morning, I headed through the Senate hallway eager to meet Gloria in person. I rounded the corner, Birch Bayh's office now in sight, and there, leaning over a desk, busily scribbling, was the back of the long-haired, thin, graceful person I had so carefully scrutinized on the Susskind show. "You must be Gloria," I called out. She turned and smiled, greeting me in her gravelly voice with "Hello, Brenda."

Gloria's testimony went over well. She was eloquent, strong and sure of herself despite the stage fright with which she insisted she was afflicted. I was again impressed with her ability to remember statistics. And she received a rousing round of applause as she concluded her remarks to the senators.

At the end of the pro-ERA testimony, excited but tired, I returned to New York City, my new home. I felt even guiltier than I had before that Marc had had to do all the work of moving as he described how he was stopped by cops as he tried to drive the U-Haul onto the East River Drive and then how it took him hours to maneuver the truck through Manhattan city streets lined with double-parked cars. But I was glad to be able to settle into our new apartment, in the city that seemed to be at the heart of the Women's Movement.

The world around us was hardly peaceful. Nixon's order to invade Cambodia led to the horrific point-blank shooting of student protesters by National Guardsmen at Kent State University during the same month that I testified for the ERA and Marc and I moved to Manhattan.

My first job in New York was as an associate at a big corporate law firm—Rosenman, Colin, Kaye, Petschek, Freund and Emil. I was assigned to the litigation department and given as my first assignment the menial task of "digesting testimony," so the trial lawyers could be spared reading through thousands of pages of actual transcript from days of depositions.

One day, a partner in the firm came into my office and told me to do some research for a corporate client that was being sued by a group of consumers who had gotten salmonella poisoning eating their product. As I quizzed the partners working on the defense, I learned that the corporate client's product was, despite their statements to the contrary, infected with the kind of salmonella from which the plaintiffs were suffering. The plaintiffs didn't know that, which meant that part of defending our client involved covering up the fact that the salmonella types matched. I began to hate what I was doing.

My "night job" involved staying on top of what was happening with the ERA in Congress. When the House started its debate on the ERA, Emanuel Celler, an elderly Democrat from New York, who had been chairman of the House Judiciary Committee for years, surprisingly risked his political future, not to mention his reputation as a liberal, by opposing the ERA and refusing even to hold hearings. But Celler was in the minority, and on August 10, 1970, the House of Representatives passed the Equal Rights Amendment by a vote of 352 to 15. (In 1972, Liz Holtzman successfully ran in the primary against Celler because of his anti-ERA stance and went on to become one of the few women in Congress at that time.)

Four important feminist books were published in 1970: Robin Morgan's *Sisterhood Is Powerful,* Kate Millett's *Sexual Politics,* Shulamith Firestone's *The Dialectic of Sex* and Germaine Greer's *The Female Eunuch.* I was fascinated by each of these books, even if I disagreed with some of the points made. For example, Robin Morgan, who had achieved notoriety at the 1968 Miss America Pageant, referred to NOW in her introduction to *Sisterhood* as "the NAACP of the Women's Movement." She criticized NOW for fighting *within* the system but complimented us for helping to win the airline stewardesses' fight against mandatory retirement when the stewardess married or reached the age of thirty-five (they weren't called flight attendants until later). Robin was upset that NOW allowed men as members, although

An afternoon party with Robin Morgan and her husband, Kenneth Pitchford, in Katonah, New York

in fact there were very few. Both she and I were married to men who called themselves feminists, and as a matter of principle, I thought men should help accomplish mutual goals, such as universal twenty-four-hour child care, the ERA and abortion rights, NOW's big issues.

Kate Millett's book impressed me. Begun as a doctoral dissertation, it became a best-seller that challenged relationships of inequality within the family, envisaging different ways people could live together and raise children. Reading *The Female Eunuch* was more fun (although I know this isn't a literary standard) than *The Dialectic of Sex,* which argued, in my opinion tediously, that there is a fundamental biological inequality between the sexes. Firestone also set forth a class analysis of Freud, Marx and Engels and even shared with her readers her views on the current state of aesthetic culture.

In April, Representative Patsy Mink, a Democrat from Hawaii, urged that women's rights be given high priority. This prompted Dr. Edgar Berman, a pal of Hubert Humphrey's, on the Democratic Party's Committee on National Priorities, to argue that women are incapable of holding important jobs because of their "raging" hormones. Patsy asked for my advice about how to respond; then Berman resigned from the committee.

One day in late May, Gloria called. She had been asked to deliver the commencement address at Vassar. Graduation was only a few weeks off, and she wondered if I would go with her, since I knew the school so well. What I hadn't absorbed yet was how totally terrified Gloria really was of public speaking. I knew she'd been scared before her testimony for the ERA, but I had assumed that was because it was about a constitutional amendment, and she was not a lawyer.

The day before her address, Gloria and I drove up to Poughkeepsie. Although I had been inside President Simpson's house for various teas, I had never been upstairs, nor had I known that he used the many bedrooms to accommodate visiting dignitaries. After we had been shown to our twin-bedded, very New England room, I was proud to show Gloria around the beautiful campus, pointing out each dorm I had lived in, the math building, where I'd climbed five flights of stairs early in the morning for my favorite calculus classes, the Shakespeare Gardens, the stained-glass-windowed library, and especially the misty stream surrounding the music building. As we wandered, though, I noticed how nervous Gloria was about her upcoming address, and we spent the rest of the evening refining her already very good speech.

Gloria and I arrived at the breakfast table the next morning to find everyone else already involved in a heated discussion. We were introduced to the other guests, one of whom was Kingman Brewster, the president of Yale, who had a daughter in the graduating class. By that time, Vassar and Yale were involved in serious discussions about a possible merger. When I was admitted to Vassar it was virtually equal in distinction to the Ivy League schools, which then only admitted men. While I was there the Vassar–Yale issue started to come to a head. Now a heated confrontation ensued between Kingman Brewster and me. He maintained that if Vassar and Yale merged, most of the existing Vassar faculty would lose their jobs, because the professors at Yale, then almost all male, were, he was convinced, far superior. I defended my former female professors. The discussion became even more animated when Brewster intimated that once Yale was coed, women would never constitute more than 25 percent of its first-year class.* Furious, I decided that if that was the attitude of Yale's president, then I was opposed to the merger. President Simpson didn't seem to mind (or involve himself in) the uproar, but eventually I noticed that Gloria was growing uncomfortable. Glancing at my watch, I realized that the commencement exercises were scheduled to begin soon and she still had to put on her robe, look over her notes, and pull her still terrified self together. We excused ourselves in the middle of my brawl with Brewster. (Several years later Vassar, in fact, started admitting men; single-sex education was becoming less popular with young women, eager to combine their social lives with their academic experience and to see guys as more than just weekend dates.)

Not long after breakfast, as we arrived at the procession lining up on the path in front of the library, I felt a wave of nostalgia for that time four years earlier when my classmates and I started our graduation processional. I bade Gloria good luck. She smiled weakly, and off I went to find a seat amidst proud families at the stunning site overlooking the lake, where every commencement in Vassar's history—except those occurring during torrential downpours—had taken place. As the procession wound its way in, I was delighted to see painted on every graduating senior's cap the ubiquitous peace symbol. In 1966, when I graduated, political consciousness was at a low ebb, isolated as we were on this beautiful campus. But these women graduating in 1970, at the peak of the Vietnam War protests, had had four years to become politicized.

Gloria was finally introduced. I could tell that she was nervous, but she had really pulled herself together. Cheers and clap-

---

* I was reminded recently that in February of that year, on Yale Alumni Day, forty women undergraduates had disrupted the luncheon to protest the "token number" of women students at Yale. Kingman Brewster had earlier rejected their more than reasonable request that the ratio of men to women in each class be 700 to 300 because "nostalgia" of the alumni required graduating 1,000 men each year.

ping punctuated her remarks, and as the young women showed their appreciation, Gloria seemed to become more calm and sure of herself. The essence of what she said was that these young women were destined to become all that they knew they could be—not just wives and mothers but women with a strong sense of who they were and what they could do to help other women. They would have careers that she hoped she would live to see the results of. They could conquer the world, and indeed, she reassured them, they would. Gloria was the best commencement speaker I had ever heard. Apparently, the assembled families, not to mention the graduating class, agreed, because she received a long standing ovation at the end. I was extremely proud to be her friend and to be there with her at this, her first major public address.

Along with the entire Vassar faculty, we had been invited to a reception back at President Alan Simpson's house after the ceremony. As Gloria and I made our way to the punch table, several people stopped to congratulate her, and I headed for one of my favorite Vassar professors, Linda Nochlin. After hugs of greeting, I asked for her help: "Please tell me what to say to my brother when he flatly denies that there have ever been any great women artists. If he's right, why?" Linda, who knew my art-dealer brother from a wild party she'd given at her house during my senior year at Vassar, celebrating five contemporary artists, looked thoughtful and told me she wanted to contemplate her answer to my provocative question.

I got my answer seven months later. I was walking by a newsstand in midtown Manhattan when I spied the January 1971 edition of *ARTnews* with a caption in big letters: "Why Have There Been No Great Women Artists?" by Linda Nochlin. In her article, Linda explained carefully how women throughout history had wanted to paint but were denied admission to the great academies in Europe. Female artists were even prohibited from painting nudes, which might explain their many landscapes, or in the case of Rosa Bonheur, cows. Linda's piece would, in years to come, have significant influence on women in art and academics, as well as on women artists. As Professors Mary D. Garrard and Norma Broude state in their book *The Power of Feminist Art:* "The feminist-art phenomenon in 1971 that exerted the most seismic impact (and still boasts aftershocks some twenty years hence) was the publication of distinguished art historian Linda Nochlin's essay, 'Why Have There Been No Great Women Artists?' "[6] My brother's sexist attitude had actually paid off!

The worst aspect of the summer of 1970 was that I had to take a bar review course every night so that I could pass the New York bar exam in July. By late fall I would learn that I had passed, and in February of 1971 I would be admitted to practice law in New York. Because of my studying, however, I was barely aware of the fact that in July 1970, New York had liberalized its abortion law, and the same month New York City had passed a bill prohibiting sex discrimination in public accommodations.

Soon I learned that a big march down Fifth Avenue was in the offing. August 26, 1970, would mark the fiftieth anniversary of the Nineteenth Amendment, which gave women the right to vote. The march was dubbed Women's Strike for Equality, and the marchers were asked to wear white with yellow and purple ribbons, just as the early suffragists had. Rallies like the one in New York were planned throughout the country.

Gloria and I got together at a little coffee shop near her apartment and decided that we would each carry posters with enlarged photos of the My Lai massacre. To us, the Vietnam War was very much a women's issue. Simply put, the male "policy makers" were out to prove how tough they were, how they would never back down from any confrontation, regardless of how many young lives were being lost and how senseless the cause.

Betty Friedan, who seemed particularly out of sorts because she no longer had NOW as a platform to lend her credibility, wildly objected to the Lavender Menace, a lesbian group, with its purple banner, marching with the rest of us. She stated flatly that they would give the Women's Movement a bad name. What she accomplished was a backlash, with straight feminists donning purple armbands in a show of support with the lesbian contingent, who had reluctantly agreed to bring up the rear. At least they were marching with us, and we had proved that no one could divide us as women from other women.

What was most wonderful about the march in New York was that at first we were told by police to confine ourselves to the sidewalks along Fifth Avenue. Then, as our numbers grew, they started to relent but still insisted we stick to one-half of the street so that some cars could get through. Finally, a few courageous women, completely unfazed by the cops with their sticks and guns, began marching on the other side of the street as well. Soon throngs of women followed, and as I looked across, I realized that we filled all of Fifth Avenue and that we stretched as far as I could see both uptown and down. Something big was happening. Women hadn't taken to the streets over our own issues since the suffragists had marched for the vote more than fifty years before. Our demands were passage of the ERA, equal opportunity in employment and education, free abortion on demand and twenty-four-hour child-care centers. Now I saw visually the tremendous groundswell of support for the issues I'd be working on as national vice president of NOW. When I watched the news that night with Marc, it was clear that this wasn't just a New York happening. Women all over the country had rallied in marches of their own—and in huge numbers.

At the next national NOW meeting, Betty Friedan demanded that the Executive Committee meet in a closed-door session. She had three problems: women on welfare, the Vietnam War, and most particularly, lesbians were not, to her, feminist issues. In fact, she continued to harp on her fear that making lesbian rights a priority would destroy any chance of success for the movement. Having little sense of her lack of support, she called for a vote, and lost.

Then she rushed out of the room and called a press conference. (In those days, everything that happened within the movement was of interest to the press.) Because Betty had insisted that secrecy shroud our meeting, the press were even more eager for a story, and it hit the news that night in a big way. In fact, the next NOW National Conference, in September 1971, passed a historic resolution on lesbianism "as a legitimate concern of feminism." There is no doubt that Betty Friedan's tantrum had caused the organization to take a public position on the subject, distancing itself as far as it could from Betty.

By this time, the ERA had been approved by the Subcommittee on Constitutional Amendments, but it still had to get through the Senate Judiciary Committee. Our nemesis was Senator Sam Ervin, who insisted that the ERA would never pass unless it was amended to exclude women from the draft. There was no way that we would accept this "compromise," which would continue to put women on a pedestal, a position from which we would never achieve equality.

As NOW's spokesperson on the ERA, I became a regular on national television shows like *Good Morning America.* One day I debated General William Westmoreland, who was worried about whether women and men would have to share bunkers. He complained that the esprit de corps among the male soldiers would be destroyed by the presence of women. (The same arguments against permitting gays and lesbians to serve openly were raised in the 1990s.) My answer to General Westmoreland was that there should be an objective test, related to skills needed to serve, given to both males and females. (I was opposed to the draft for both men and women, but if men were called, women should be too.)

During the summer and fall of 1970, when I arrived home at night, after Marc and I had eaten dinner—usually at a little restaurant in our neighborhood—I would begin making calls to NOW chapters around the country to make sure their members were lobbying their senators and representatives to get the ERA out of Congress. Reports back confirmed that things were looking good.

NOW's annual national convention, at which the status of the ERA efforts would be assessed, was scheduled to take place over a weekend in Chicago about six months after I'd become associated with Rosenman Colin Kaye Petschek Freund & Emil. My bags were packed and with me that Friday morning as I headed for the office and, ultimately, an evening flight. But late in the afternoon, I was summoned into the office of one of the junior partners. "You have to work on [a male client's] divorce case this weekend. I want to file the papers on Tuesday," he told me. I explained, "I am due to be out of town at a NOW convention this weekend but I'll be happy to get into it on Monday." The junior partner told me that I was staying over the weekend; I said I wasn't and reminded him that my being vice president of NOW constituted my *pro bono* work, which had been approved by the firm when I was hired. By that time, it was late, and I had to catch my flight. I told him I had to go. He just glared at me as I rushed through the hall, clutching my coat, bags and briefcase, to catch the elevator—and my plane.

I didn't realize then what that flight was really all about, but by Monday morning it had sunk in. By defying that junior partner, I had effectively quit. I asked to meet with the managing partner to try to explain what had happened. But as soon as I walked into his office, his face told me what I needed to know. I had no choice but to tell him that because I couldn't do my *pro bono* work and carry out my duties as a vice president of NOW, as they had assured me I could, I would have to leave the firm. He seemed relieved at being taken off the hook. Obviously, he had been about to fire me for insubordination.

I had also taken a step in a direction from which I could not retreat, one that turned out to be a real turning point in my life. After gathering my possessions from my office, I took a cab straight to Gloria's apartment in the East Seventies.

I told her that I had just quit/been fired from my job at the law firm and what I'd done to get myself into that predicament. She offered her total support and reassured me that I had made not just the right decision but the only decision I could have made. Feeling better, I began remembering out loud a long conversation I had had with Richard Goodwin, former special counsel to President Kennedy. Dick had been fascinated by the burgeoning Women's Movement as a political phenomenon. It seemed to him to fit right in to Robert Kennedy's philosophy of political organizing: to rally folks at the "grassroots" level.

NOW did have local chapters, even though it wasn't really structured to do more than address the big issues from the top down. That's when I decided that there needed to be a group that would encourage women to confront sexist issues in their own communities. Gloria thought it was a great idea—true to her nature, she didn't see a conflict between my idea and the top-down structure of NOW. We talked about how terrific it would be for groups of mothers (and fathers) to look for sexist references in the textbooks their children were studying that had been approved by local school boards. It would be key to women's gaining employment if there were twenty-four-hour child-care centers near their homes or places of employment. These were issues best left to women in their own communities, and we could help them mobilize around those kinds of issues. We could also connect groups in different parts of the country that were struggling with the same problems. This was a way to show women not yet committed to feminism the reason for our wanting and needing equal rights and the right to control our own bodies. Once involved with issues that touched them personally, they might relate better to broader issues, and we would stand more of a chance of getting them to lobby their representatives in Washington—as well as their state legislatures—about those big issues.

We needed a name for this new organization, and we wanted it to be tax-exempt so that we could accept donations from foundations and so that individual donors could get tax deductions. Marc volunteered to obtain our tax-exempt status, leaving Gloria and me to struggle over a name. She wanted something with the word "sisters" in it. I wanted the name to sound as though we were into taking action. We were eventually incorporated as Sisters: The Women's Action Alliance, but almost immediately thereafter we became known simply as the Alliance.

We needed prestigious names for our board of directors in order to make an impression on foundations. Gloria pulled out all the stops. People like John Kenneth Galbraith, a friend from her

Gloria Steinem in her study in late 1970, drafting a memo for the Women's Action Alliance, the "newsletter" of which would become Ms. *magazine*

India and JFK days, gladly lent his name. Dick Goodwin and a number of others gave us further credibility. And Franklin Thomas, whom Gloria was seeing, became incredibly valuable to us as well. A black lawyer who had been extremely active in what is now called inner-city work, he was then head of the Bedford-Stuyvesant Development Corporation. I was impressed with his intelligence, his wit and his keen ability to deal with all kinds of political issues. (Frank actively helped us until the day he was appointed to the presidency of the Ford Foundation and had to resign from boards of other organizations that could present a conflict of interest.)

Finally, the Alliance had enough credible names to begin raising money. Gloria and I did our dog-and-pony show, as Gloria was fond of calling it, all over the foundation world. We wore jeans and T-shirts to meetings with important men in dark suits and club ties, taking pride in defying "the establishment." We weren't about being sex symbols or proper ladies. The first money we raised was from the Stern Family Fund, which was small and run by the younger generation of a very rich and civic-minded family.

It seems amazing now that it was only in December of that year that the first all-women professional tennis tour was announced, when twenty-eight years later professional women tennis players

*Frank Thomas,
Gloria and Marc—a
weekend in the
country, 1971*

would each make more than a million dollars a year. To get away from work, Marc and I began to go out dancing with Gloria and Frank. They knew all the new steps. So one night, in an attempt to bring Marc and me up to speed, Gloria took my arm, Frank stood next to Marc, and separately they showed us our respective moves. It was amusing to see how determined Frank and Marc were to avoid touching each other at all costs, reinforcing the stereotype of straight men—terrified of looking like they might be homosexual. Gloria, merrily holding my hand or arm, taught me complicated dance routines easily.

One day, Gloria started musing about how the Alliance might need a newsletter to inform women of what others elsewhere were doing. She volunteered to take that on as her special project. I agreed that communication was essential, but I had a question: "Why not go for a slick magazine?" By this time, Gloria had become quite well known and I thought that we should capitalize on that and spread the word much more than a little newsprint publication would be able to. Gloria's response was sharp and quick: "Brenda," she said in that tone that always sounded a bit chastising because I was acting less smart than she knew I was, "we can only do a slick magazine if we take advertising, and with the kind of feminist content we want, we'll never get any ads." I disagreed and told her that I would check out my hunch with a leading woman in advertising, Jane Trahey, if Gloria would take her word for it. She agreed but added another condition: "And we have to make sure that women writers and journalists feel the need for a magazine like this." I knew that would be easy. Every woman writer I'd met complained that within the magazine world as it was then, she couldn't write the kind of stories she wanted to read. They were all sick of writing articles on fashion and makeup. They wanted to do serious reporting, especially about feminist issues, and no publishers (then all male) in respectable mainstream publishing would let them. There had even been a feminist sit-in at the *Ladies' Home Journal* in 1970, but its effects had been minimal at best. Author Susan Douglas observed that media men made the mistake of assuming that "feminists, like the pods in *Invasion of the Body Snatchers,* cannibalized perfectly happy women and turned them into inhuman aliens."[7]

The meeting to which Jane Trahey (who ran her own high-powered advertising agency) had graciously agreed convinced me that my hunch was right: a magazine aimed at women who were tired of the old stereotypes would attract advertising.

I immediately and excitedly reported on that meeting to Gloria. She listened intently but was still insistent on having meetings with women writers. We set about making lists of names, culled not only from our mental notes about writer friends but also from magazine mastheads. We had absolutely no idea how many women would show up.

On the appointed day, early in 1971, we cleared some space in Gloria's then small, cluttered apartment. Soon women began

pouring in from everywhere. By the time we were fifteen minutes into the meeting, there were women covering every inch of
the floor, the sofas and chairs, and the stairs leading up to the
loft where Gloria slept. Some—like Robin Morgan, Adrienne
Rich, Susan Brownmiller and Jill Johnston—I knew. After each
woman spoke about what she'd wanted to write but hadn't been
able to get approved by male editors and publishers, I thought we
had enough proof. Gloria, on the other hand, announced that we
should have another meeting—at my apartment—just in case
some women hadn't been able to make it that day.

So within days we were going over the lists again, seeing who
had not shown up. We even went out and bought different magazines to make sure that women employed by publications like
Sports Illustrated had been invited. At the second meeting the
response was the same: women poured into my apartment and
told us more stories of how they couldn't write what they wanted
for magazines like *Ladies' Home Journal, McCall's, Vogue* and
Sports Illustrated. They were all going through the same kinds of
rejections, but before now they had never compared notes,
remaining, as I had in my first two years at Harvard, isolated from
other women in the same situation.

The Alliance "newsletter" was now taking on a life of its own.
Sure, it would spread the word about what women all over the
country were doing, but it would also meet the demand by women
writers to write what they wanted. It would be a magazine!

One day, I was in our office, donated to the Alliance by a large
advertising firm whose CEO was a friend of Gloria's and now a
member of our board. There was a phone call from Elizabeth
Forsling Harris, who wanted to fly in from San Diego and meet
with Gloria and me. She said she had experience raising financing for magazines.

At our first meeting with Betty Harris, I had asked Marc to
join us. This was business, and his advice would be useful. After
the meeting, as Marc and I headed down and across town to our
Tudor City apartment, he made it clear that he didn't like Betty.
Gloria thought that Betty knew more than we did about financing

a magazine, which wasn't saying much. I, meanwhile, had noticed that Betty had had at least a few drinks of hard liquor—straight up—during our meeting.

Gloria left it to Marc and me to have several more meetings with Betty. At one of the meetings, Betty began to scream at both of us. It was something about how we didn't know what we were talking about, even though we thought we were so smart because we had gone to Harvard Law School. Marc finally decided he'd had enough, muttering something about how nuts Betty was as he guided me to the elevator. Although all Betty had to show for herself was a thick black notebook filled with generalities about magazine start-ups, with which she'd arrived in New York, a few days later she told Gloria and me that she thought it was time to divide up the ownership of the magazine. I protested, saying that it was impossible to come up with a formula until we saw what each of us would contribute. Gloria didn't say much during that conversation, leaving it to me to confront Betty. I left that meeting feeling that Betty was pushing too hard too soon.

About a week later, Gloria called me, sounding more anxious than I'd heard her before. In her most conciliatory tone, she told me there seemed to be a "personality difference" between Betty and me—and Marc, with whom Betty found it extremely difficult to work. I responded sharply to Gloria that if Betty had problems with Marc there was something wrong with Betty. Gloria hates confrontation, even if she's not around to witness it. So rather than responding directly, Gloria suggested that I spend my time on the Alliance and that she handle Betty herself. Part of her reasoning was, no doubt, that neither Marc nor I had had anything to do with magazine publishing before—we were lawyers, after all—whereas she and Betty Harris (presumably) had. The discussion about dividing up the pie had apparently been resolved. I would have nothing more to do with the magazine except to write an occasional article for it. Instead I would run the nonprofit Alliance, the board of which Gloria chaired, and Gloria's "day job" would be with the magazine. I realized that Betty had created a fight between herself and Marc and me so that she would have a greater piece of the equity she so desperately wanted.

From then on, Gloria and I saw each other mostly for political or social events. She did ask me what I thought of naming the magazine *Ms.*—I thought it was a perfect way to reinforce our belief that women shouldn't be categorized by marital status.

Ms. magazine published its "preview" issue, after a thirty-page shortened version of it appeared as an insert in the December 20, 1971, issue of *New York* magazine. Pat Carbine, whom Gloria had recruited from her post as editor-in-chief of *McCall's,* was to serve as publisher and Gloria as editor (she refused to accept the hierarchical title of "editor in chief").

Finally, after a lot of pain and suffering, Pat and Gloria came to their senses and told Betty Harris that her involvement wasn't working out. To get her to leave, they paid her a generous settlement, even though she had raised virtually no money and had become a constant source of irritation. They probably feared that the negative publicity that Betty would inevitably generate just as the magazine was getting started might be fatal to it. I'm also sure that Gloria's penchant for conflict avoidance contributed to Betty's pot. The settlement included her right to receive half of the revenues from the first complete issue of the magazine and $2,000 a month for fourteen months. She also had stock in the magazine, which at the time she sold it (when the magazine became a foundation) would eventually amount to still more unjustified money in her pocketbook. A business adviser had helped Gloria and Pat devise a plan to sell a noncontrolling amount of stock to raise the necessary financing. Meanwhile, a colleague of Gloria's had by now unearthed the reason for Betty's being so eager to leave California: as Mary Thom, one of the early *Ms.* staffers, delicately put it in her book *Inside "Ms.,"* Betty left "a number of unhappy creditors behind in California."[8]

Later, in 1975, when Warner Bros. got behind *Ms.* and there was an infusion of cash that enabled the magazine to get off the ground, Betty filed a completely unfounded lawsuit against the magazine, as well as Gloria and Pat, based on some kind of fraud theory. Her suit was thrown out of court.

Gloria still viewed it as her responsibility to raise money for the Alliance. And she thought it best that my title be coordinating director, instead of the more conventional executive director, because the former sounded less hierarchical. I disliked having to explain continually what my title meant, but I accepted the fact that we disagreed and deferred to her. Gloria had so much more power to generate funding than I did, and I wanted her to be able to explain the new organization in the way she felt most comfortable with.

One day, in November 1970, I received a call from the New York Civil Liberties Union asking if I was interested in handling a new case. Gary Ackerman and his wife, who had a full-time job, had just had a baby. Ackerman, a young schoolteacher working part-time, wanted to take a "parental leave of absence." His employer, the New York City Department of Education, had denied him that right; it was only available to mothers.

At the trial, we persuaded the federal district court that fathers should be as involved in their children's upbringing as mothers and that not allowing our client to take a parental leave of absence was a violation of his Fourteenth Amendment equal-protection rights.

The underlying problem raised by Gary Ackerman and his wife was that there is no child care provided by the government in our country. In contrast, Sweden pays the caregiver—mother or father—sixty-four weeks' salary so that person can stay home with the baby. The job temporarily abandoned in order to give such care is guaranteed for the sixty-four-week period. Taxes are significantly higher there than they are here to pay for this, among other government benefits. It is not irrelevant that recently the prime minister of Sweden has been a woman. *When Mothers Work: Loving Our Children Without Sacrificing Our Selves,* by Joan Peters, makes an additional point: "When 50–50 division of labor between mother and father is agreed on before the couple has children, even fathers who feel unprepared for active parenting will rise to the occasion."[9]

Meanwhile, excitement was swirling within the feminist world. Kate Millett, because of her book *Sexual Politics,* had been tagged a leader of the Women's Movement. At a conference, she was asked whether she was a lesbian, and she answered, in a very soft voice, that she was a member of Radicalesbians. She was also married to a Japanese artist, which led the curious to the conclusion that she was bisexual. When they heard that Kate had talked to the press, the other members of Radicalesbians got angry. They had a rule that you couldn't give out first or last names of members, including your own. In sisterly support, Gloria helped organize a press conference for December 18, 1970, at which Kate would explain herself in her own terms. From the audience I watched as Gloria reassuringly held Kate's hand. Gloria, who is as straight as any woman I've ever met, has had a standard answer when asked over the years if she is a lesbian: "Not yet." The uproar landed Kate on the cover of *Time* magazine.

Besides the Radicalesbians, other groups in the movement's early days had colorful names: W.I.T.C.H. (Women's International Terrorist Conspiracy from Hell), New York Radical Women, Redstockings, Lesbian Nation, The Feminists. Those groups helped make liberal feminists seem reasonable.

"Liberal" feminists thought it was okay to look good—at least for themselves. "Radical" feminists thought that women's concern about their appearance, including being thin, was a symptom of the sickness of the patriarchal society. Hence the haircutting episode at the First Congress to Unite Women and the rallying cry that "Fat is a feminist issue," which many years later inspired the late Princess Diana to seek therapy from the author of a book by that name.

Finally, in July, the National Women's Political Caucus (NWPC) was started at a conference attended by more than two thousand women. A priority of the new organization was that women infiltrate the two parties from top to bottom and get elected to office around the country, on both the federal and state levels. The NWPC was necessary because NOW, the agenda of which was solely issue-oriented, would not involve itself in electoral politics. The NWPC was explicitly bipartisan. But I'd always wondered how feminists could be members of a party that flatly rejects abortion as a choice for all women. (In general, it seems to me, identifying as either a Democrat or a Republican first, rather than as a feminist first, can lead to positions that are downright dangerous to women.)

It turned out that the women who had just been elected to the Policy Council of the NWPC were all "older." Gloria was the youngest, at thirty-six, but it was mostly women in their twenties who had worked so hard to start this organization, and they were angry. So in a small room off the large meeting hall, I took it upon myself to tell Gloria that the situation was politically unacceptable. Gloria, ever a genius at avoiding confrontation, went back to her newly elected cohorts and forged a compromise: everybody under age thirty-five would be deemed part of the "Youth Caucus," which would, in turn, have the opportunity to elect two of its number to sit on the Policy Council. Probably because I was so vocal, I was one of them.

Helen Dudar, a writer for the *New York Post,* called me a week later. She said that her paper wanted to do a story on me as their "Woman in the News," because they'd heard about the NWPC election. What appeared the next weekend was a full-page story telling about how the Youth Caucus had achieved representation on the newly elected NWPC Policy Council. The article went on to describe my work, my hobbies and, of course, my marriage.

As fall approached, I received an invitation to appear on the *David Susskind Show* and participate in a panel discussion on November 1, 1971. The panel would consist of theater critic John Simon, columnist Anatole Broyard, moderator David Susskind, authors (and feminists) Susan Brownmiller and Germaine Greer, and me.

It proved to be a difficult experience. Brownmiller brought a whole contingent of radical feminist pals who cheered every time she opened her mouth. Germaine Greer lifted her long skirt very high, so she could show us and the studio audience the scars left from a rape she said she'd suffered years earlier. John Simon couldn't stop talking about how ridiculous feminists were, and David Susskind kept interrupting everyone. Anatole Broyard and I, both usually loquacious, were rendered almost mute by all the cross talk and sat there arguing quietly with each other.

Liz Smith, the well-known syndicated gossip columnist, wrote me in December to congratulate me on appearing in the December issue of *Cosmopolitan* and, in her characteristic style, signed off with "Available for lunches and Bar Mitzvahs or whatever whenever you are."

Other breakthroughs for younger women occurred in 1971. In February, the New York City Board of Education decided that boys and girls could compete in noncontact sports at school. In April, the Explorer Scouts began to admit girls. In May, for the first time in the 150-year history of the U.S. Senate, girls were appointed as pages.

By late 1971, the Alliance, the existence of which had not yet been publicly announced, was receiving calls for help from all over the country, and Gloria and I decided that we needed to clarify what we were about. We scheduled a press conference for January 12, 1972, in Washington, D.C.

The announcement landed us on front pages of papers across the country. The headline in the *Washington Daily News* sang out, "Gloria Steinem Gets Organized," while the *Washington Post* declared that a "New Action Group for Women's Lib Lists Youth Goals." (I don't know how they decided our emphasis was on "youth," since it wasn't.) Next to both captions were big pictures of Gloria and me. Years later I learned that those headlines had caught the attention of the CIA, which apparently became convinced that we were organizing the overthrow of the United States government. In fact, a CIA file on me was started, with those banner-headline articles beginning a series of news clips they were keeping about me.*

Soon Gloria called to tell me that she had been invited to give the Harvard Law Review Banquet address, the first woman in the history of Harvard Law School to receive that honor. She wanted to know if I would help her with her speech, and she wanted Marc and me to go to the dinner. I was excited at the prospect of having an ally as powerful as Gloria take on the sexism of the Law School, which she was planning to do, but I also knew it would take some research to give her talk the necessary impact.

Gloria asked me to tell her the whole story of my life as a student at Harvard Law School, and as I did, she muttered compassionately, praised me for my courage and took copious notes in her distinctive handwriting. She then, predictably, decided to talk with the women who were students that semester. Some things might have changed since my graduation less than two years earlier, and like any good journalist, she wanted to make sure her facts were current.

Meanwhile, I had had a personal scare. One day while I was talking on the phone, I suddenly felt a lump in my breast. I went into a total panic, and I now remember nothing more of the conversation. My gynecologist ordered a mammogram, which confirmed the lump but didn't reveal whether it was malignant or benign. I proceeded to schedule appointments with every breast cancer surgeon in New York whose name I had ever heard. Marc wanted to go with me, so appointments made, we started our rounds.

The first was with a kindly older doctor who said the tumor bore none of the indicia of being malignant. If he removed the lump and the frozen section test revealed that it was malignant, he

---

* A number of years later, some well-known feminists asked me to find out if they had FBI files. So under the Freedom of Information ACT ("FOIA"), I decided to request mine then, too. To my shock, not only did I have an FBI file, but that's when I learned that the CIA had started one on me, too. I wrote the director of the CIA a letter thanking him for running a clipping service for me but pointing out that I thought the taxpayers' money would be better spent on more important issues. I never received a response.

In our Tudor City apartment, which overlooked the East River, circa 1972

would wait until he and I could talk—after the biopsy—about the next step. After a number of other appointments, Marc and I went to Jerry Urban, who, because he'd operated on Betty Ford, was then the country's most famous breast cancer surgeon. He was not at all reassuring. If the biopsy he would perform while I was on the table revealed any malignancy, he would immediately do a radical mastectomy and remove all the lymph nodes in the area, leaving me with a right arm that would have little strength or range of movement—and I am right-handed. He didn't believe in lumpectomies, in radiation alone or even in modified mastectomies. I didn't like him and decided to put my faith in the first doctor we'd seen.

Soon I entered New York University Hospital, scared to death. As I awoke from the general anesthesia, Marc was there, reassuring me that a frozen section of the lump had led to the diagnosis of a benign fibroadenoma. I was overwhelmed with relief.

Gloria and I had planned to go up to Cambridge the next weekend to talk with the female students at the Law School. Weak (because of the anesthesia and the stress), I still insisted on sticking to our plans. But when we arrived in Cambridge, I couldn't get my coat off without Gloria's help, because the stitches in my breast made me so stiff. Then, as Gloria grilled the students, all I had the energy to do was lie on the floor (there was no couch in our meeting room) and listen. The students were terrific. They not only backed up my complaints but added their own, naming the names of professors who still treated women badly and giving details about that treatment. By the time Gloria was finished taking notes that day, she had enough material. She proceeded to write the first draft, but I had a problem with it: She had left out the names of the offending professors. I thought we had agreed that she'd "name names and kick ass." She thought it would be obvious to the people in the audience, professors as well as past and present Law Review members. But I insisted that Harvard Law School is a big school and that I couldn't understand any reason for protecting the offending professors from embarrassment among their peers, if indeed her naming them would cause that.

Toni and Abe Chayes, the latter a former professor of mine at the Law School, had a party the evening before the banquet honoring Gloria. After a while, I noticed Professor Paul Bator enter the room. He had been my professor of administrative law, in which we had studied the FTC, the FCC, and all the other important federal administrative bodies. By now, I was encouraging women to file complaints with the Equal Employment Opportunity Commission (EEOC), as well as the Office of Federal Contract Compliance (OFCC) when they experienced sex discrimination at work. So, confidently, I approached Professor Bator and asked him why he had never taught us about either the EEOC or the OFCC. His response, by which he may have meant to sound clever, was that he had heard of neither. I couldn't believe that a professor at Harvard Law School would never have heard of these two regulatory bodies, especially when he was an expert in the subject of administrative law. Later that evening, after the party, I told Gloria that she had to add Bator's remark to her speech.

The black-tie banquet was the following night. Marc and I sat at Gloria's table, surrounded, mostly, by recent male graduates. After she was introduced, in a low-key but emphatic voice Gloria started to reveal to the audience what was really happening to women at Harvard Law School. Explaining the means by which she'd gathered her information, she proceeded to issue a blistering attack on various professors, as well as on the school itself for tolerating their behavior. She criticized the administration for allowing sexist firms to interview on campus. In short, she really gave it to them, and then she thanked the audience for its attention and sat down. What followed was a standing ovation, especially from all the students there. I was jubilant.

Then suddenly, after the ovation, a professor with a gray crew cut went up to the podium. He started to rebut her statements in a sputtering fury. But Gloria had the facts—the truth—on her side. He was hissed by the women students and graduates in the room—and even by many of the men, who had been so impressed by Gloria's address. Finally, mid-sputter, he stopped, red-faced. Even I was surprised by his attack. I had come to expect almost anything from Harvard Law School, but I had never seen such a display of rude and childlike behavior. Never before had an honored speaker at a Harvard Law Review Banquet been rebutted.

Chapter 2

FEMINISM
TAKES HOLD

Although the Harvard Law Review Banquet left me fired up and ready to do more battle for feminism, I decided not to run for a second term as national vice president for legislation of NOW, preferring to focus on the Alliance. The country was reeling from the Vietnam War and Nixon, a national presidential race was looming and the Democrats had a chance at the White House.

For the first issue of *Ms.*, which came out that spring, 1972, in time for the Democratic National Convention, I coauthored an article entitled "Rating the Candidates In or Out." My favorite candidate was Shirley Chisholm, a black member of the House of Representatives, from Brooklyn, but I knew how slim her chances were, so I was also a George McGovern supporter. My coauthor was rabidly for Eugene McCarthy.

The Democratic National Convention would be held that summer in Miami. There was an election for delegates coming up, and each candidate ran a slate in every district. Gloria and I managed to convince Marc and my brother that the four of us should run as Chisholm delegates in our Upper East Side district. We acknowledged publicly that past the first ballot Chisholm didn't have a chance, and that we would then throw our votes to McGovern. The voters didn't seem to appreciate the symbolism of what we were doing, and the real McGovern slate (filled with Democratic Party bigwigs) beat us in the election for delegates. So Gloria and I would be attending just as members of the NWPC, especially interested in making sure that the party platform supported women's issues. The top priorities were ratification of the ERA and abortion on demand. We also planned to lobby for lesbian and gay rights, an issue that we saw as inextricably linked to feminism.

In March, the Platform Committee for the Democratic Convention met in Washington, and the NWPC decided that a delegation needed to be there. Before the committee's first session that evening, a number of members of the NWPC Policy Council attended a private meeting with George McGovern at his nearby home. Actress Shirley MacLaine was there. McGovern's wife was nowhere in sight.

McGovern wanted us to believe that he cared about our issues. But his commitment was too vague, especially about both abortion rights and lesbian and gay issues. Gloria, who had known McGovern for years, demanded more reassurance from him than he seemed willing to give that afternoon. But he promised that he would call her at our hotel around midnight. If he wouldn't give the necessary reassurances, the NWPC might well withhold its support, thus signaling to other women's organizations that we had a problem with McGovern.

As evening rolled around, I was anxious to get onto the third floor, secured from the public, where the various subcommittees of the Platform Committee were meeting. Gloria wanted to go to our room so she'd be reachable at midnight by McGovern. But I thought that no matter how much McGovern respected Gloria, Shirley MacLaine's obvious jealousy of her, coupled with his reticence about supporting our demands, weighed against a phone call. When I asked Gloria if she'd seen the way Shirley had looked at her as we had left McGovern's house, she told me not to be silly. McGovern had said he would call.

Finally, the clock struck midnight. No call from McGovern. We waited another hour before I left Gloria in the room and made my way to the third floor. My friend from Cambridge, Toni Chayes, was a member of the Platform Committee, and I figured that by saying that I needed to speak to her I might get past the guards at the elevator. But when the elevator doors opened, there was Shirley MacLaine. As I stepped out, she started shouting at me right outside a small room with *Newsweek* and *New York Post* signs above the doorway. "If you people had your way," she virtually screamed, "you'd have George support everyone's right to fuck goats." The folks who were inside the press room suddenly appeared. I told Shirley that her behavior was embarrassing. She replied, "Good." Now I knew not only that George McGovern definitely was not going to call Gloria but that I wasn't going to get anywhere near the Platform Committee.

When I arrived back at our room, it was close to 2:00 a.m. and Gloria was still waiting for the call from McGovern. She was also deep in conversation with several young women who somehow had found her. I told her what had just happened and suggested we go to bed. She may have given up waiting for the call, but that didn't keep her from continuing her advice to the young women. One of the remarkable things about Gloria is that she is able to say the same things over and over again to new people who have never before heard the message. The young women ignored me, probably figuring that Gloria would kick them out when she'd had enough. What they didn't know was that Gloria never tells people she's had enough. Eventually, I put a pillow over my head and tried to sleep. I remember the sound of the door finally closing and Gloria, in characteristic fashion, turning on the television to watch a very late old movie.

The next morning brought the news that although the subcommittee with jurisdiction over social issues had voted to include a minority plank for gay and lesbian rights, someone had cut the paragraph supporting that plank off the bottom of the page. (Abortion rights, however, did emerge as part of the minority plank.) So the full committee would not even have the opportunity to vote on all the issues, because there wasn't a single copy that had been spared the wrath of (I suspected) Shirley MacLaine's scissors. Rumor has it that she and a Democratic National Committeewoman from Manhattan, furious at the vote of the subcommittee and determined that the issue of gay and lesbian rights never reach the light of day, had crept into the

room where the group had earlier met and in the middle of the
night literally cut out the offensive language.

As for the confrontation between MacLaine and me, two days
later, back in New York, I picked up a copy of the *New York Post*
and read that Shirley MacLaine had accused feminists of wanting a plank in the Democratic Platform giving people the right to
"make love to lampposts."

The ERA was approved by the Senate on March 22, 1972, and
sent to the states. I was now receiving calls from university and
women's groups around the country to discuss its significance,
and Marc and I were becoming known as *the* feminist couple, so
many of the invitations were to both of us. Marc was routinely
asked what it was like living with a feminist. Did he share the
household chores? Did he feel slighted by a wife who put so
much priority on being a feminist? How did he think the ERA
would affect men?

I often enjoyed our little trips, because they were like mini-
vacations. Once we were asked to keynote a weekend meeting of
a group celebrating a "Peak Experience" in Vancouver. Another
invitation came from a group of CPA/lawyers who were having
their annual meeting in Puerto Rico. When we arrived, we
learned that I was to address the wives over their lunch and Marc
was to address the CPA/lawyers, all male. And while the wives
were served salads, the CPA husbands dined on steaks.

The Democratic National Convention was scheduled for
Miami in July. The NWPC had reserved the Betsy Ross Hotel,
because its name honored a woman out of American history, and
again Gloria and I agreed to share a room. The NWPC's goal of
ensuring that women would constitute 40 percent of each state's
delegation had been achieved. The right to abortion was at the
top of our agenda, because it needed to be guaranteed at the
national level. (*Roe v. Wade* had not yet been decided.) The ERA
was out for ratification in the states. Lesbian and gay rights, as
important as they were to us, were unlikely to get more than a
nod from a few relatively powerless Democrats. And we were
becoming increasingly interested in supporting Sissy Farenthold,

a state legislator from Texas, if she decided to seek the vice presidential nomination.

The Policy Council of the NWPC chose Gloria to be its spokesperson at the Democratic Convention. Neither Gloria nor I had been present during the vote, and Gloria expressed no pleasure at having been awarded the honor.

By the time we flew to Miami, I had developed a self-help routine for protecting myself from Gloria's groupies on airplanes. Gloria, in the past, had usually sat by the window, but now I realized that by letting her do so, I was creating a situation in which people from all over the plane would approach us and lean over me to talk with her. And she seemed to encourage it, which meant armpits in my face for most of every plane ride. On the plane to Miami I sat by the window.

I did have Gloria to thank, though, for single-handedly ridding me of my fear of flying. As we were first getting to know each other, plane trips would be a solace for Gloria, who wasn't bothered so much then by strangers. She would promptly fall asleep, but I would sit there bug-eyed and white-knuckled as the plane bounced along. On several occasions, I'd elbow Gloria awake to announce that I was sure we were about to crash. She was kind enough, given that plane rides were among the rare times that she actually slept, to reassure me that we weren't going to crash, and she'd promptly fall back to sleep. After observing her, in astonishment, as the plane lurched hither and yon, I finally, over a period of several years, concluded that in fact we probably weren't going to crash, since she seemed so positive and so peaceful.

We were excited to check into the hotel we'd be occupying for a week, so the truly terrible quality of our accommodations in Miami didn't sink in until we arrived at our room. There was no shower curtain. The bathroom door didn't really close. The paint was peeling, and the lightbulbs had no shades. As Gloria poked around in the bedroom, she philosophically mused that we wouldn't be in the room very much.

Because we weren't delegates, we needed some form of "credentials" if we were ever to get to the floor of the convention to lobby delegates about feminist issues. Clearly Gloria had decided to use her considerable muscle when she asked me if I minded stopping at the headquarters of the Democratic National Committee before we headed to the Convention Hall.

When we arrived at the big fancy hotel that housed the DNC, Gloria was greeted by several apparently important men. We reached the top floor, where the receptionist seemed to be expecting Gloria, who motioned for me to wait as she was ushered into an office. In two minutes she was out, grinning and holding four press passes. I was impressed. Gloria, of course, had no intention of our hogging those passes. Her plan was for all of us from the NWPC to share them in fifteen-minute intervals.

My first time out on the floor was exciting. I took my cues from Bella Abzug, who was a delegate-at-large, and Gloria. They were introducing themselves to the women delegates from each of the states. I made my way to California's large delegation, several members of which I knew. They were a lively bunch, including a number of movie stars, not at all like the more professional political types from New York, who were taking themselves very seriously.

We still had to convince George McGovern to get behind the minority plank for abortion rights. As Gloria stayed up that first night drafting the statements of the three women who would introduce the plank, she made sure that the focus was on reproductive rights in general, including decrying involuntary sterilization of poor women and ensuring access to birth control by everyone. We, of course, ignored Shirley MacLaine, who was claiming that our insistence about abortion, however it was phrased, would cost McGovern the nomination.

On the issue of the vice presidential nomination, a number of members of the NWPC held an impromptu meeting in the ladies' room in the lobby of the Convention Hall—there were no other rooms available. We sat on the cold tile floor, blockading any poor soul who might need to enter. Our agenda was to be sure that Sissy Farenthold's name was put into nomination, despite McGovern's insistence that Eagleton be his running mate. By the meeting's end, it was determined that Gloria would nominate Sissy, and that Fannie Lou Hamer and a young Chicana would second her nomination so that all the caucuses—women, black, Spanish-speaking, and youth—would be represented. It worked, and Sissy became a candidate for vice president. Although she didn't win, she got a lot of votes.

The night of the vote on the proposed platform was the worst night of the convention for us. After some time had passed and the minority plank on abortion rights had still not been resolved, Gloria decided to confront Gary Hart, who was then managing McGovern's campaign. In the front of the middle section, Gloria got Hart's attention. Suddenly, he started shouting that all we wanted was to use the platform as a launching pad for our issues. Not only did he make no commitment to the abortion-rights plank, he made it fairly clear that McGovern and his supporters opposed it. At that, Gloria started shouting back at him. As she got angrier and angrier, she began to cry. The commotion was not lost on the press. Within seconds, all three networks—their logos blazing on the sides of their cameras—had started to descend on us. I took Gloria's hand and firmly said, "Let's get out of here, *now.*" She obediently followed as I headed for the shortest route to an exit. That was the first—and last—time I've ever seen Gloria cry. As she's been quoted, she cries when she's angry. My years at Harvard Law School more than demonstrated that I'm the same way. Neither of us had been encouraged or had felt free to show our emotions as children.

Gloria witnessed my crying when I got really angry at her one day at the magazine. I was getting increasingly upset that she always talked about race and sex discrimination as being equally bad but omitted mentioning anti-Semitism. When I asked her why, her response sounded like she thought it wasn't as bad. I blew up and left the magazine office in tears of rage. Gloria didn't try to stop me. And it wasn't until four days later that Marc, who had grown tired of my dejected state, called Gloria and asked her to please apologize to me. She did. And in recent years, I have noticed that Gloria occasionally mentions anti-Semitism in remarks she makes in public. After all, she is herself half Jewish.

After the convention, which left all of us exhausted, Marc and I planned an escape to St. Martin in the Caribbean. Then Gloria mentioned that she wanted to take her mother on a vacation somewhere, so after I checked with Marc, we decided that the four of us would go together. And soon off we flew to the beautiful half French, half Dutch island. On the beach one day Gloria tried to prove that she was indeed athletic by performing an in-the-air twirl she'd borrowed from tap dancing (her favorite "sport"). And there was a walk on the beach that she and I took at sunset one day, while Marc read and Ruth took a nap. We had been hearing a lot about lesbianism in C-R groups and in general from friends in the Women's Movement. We talked about what it must be like. To Gloria, women are her *sisters.* Sex with another woman seemed like incest.

Consciousness-raising groups had by now sprung up all over the country, but especially in New York. A few of my friends were attending one each week, and I decided to join it. From the start, I felt that I didn't quite fit in, having already fought my own battles in Cambridge against sexism. These women were just coming to terms with their anger at the ways they were treated by sexist male chauvinists. But my ears perked up when the discussion turned to sex, especially when it was related to the politics of feminism. At one meeting, I remember, I was harangued by a friend who, though not a lesbian herself, lit into me for enjoying the perks of white male society, because I was married to Marc. She went on to accuse me, and the other straight women present, of being sexist because we had ruled out sleeping with more than half the human race—namely, women. My C-R group was hardly in the vanguard on the subject. Many women were beginning to tell the truth about the problems they were having in their relationships, both sexual and otherwise, with their husbands. As Sheila Rowbotham put it in her highly regarded book *A Century of Women:* "Lesbianism began to be presented as the means of discovering one's real identity as a woman through a more fulfilling alternative sexuality."[1]

One day an editor at McGraw-Hill called Marc. She was interested in his writing a book. After all, he was one of the few well-known male feminists and there were an awful lot of men who needed enlightenment. The book should be about his perspective on the Women's Movement and what was in it for men. Women certainly would buy the book for the men in their lives.

Marc agreed to write the book, which would be called *The Male Machine,* and while one of the partners at his law firm was supportive of his decision, Mort Janklow, the firm's senior partner, was apparently spreading the word that I had "pussywhipped" Marc into leaving his firm to write the book. In fact my most active involvement had been to encourage Marc to ask Gloria if she would write the introduction. Soon Marc and his book had taken over what had been our dining room.

Jill Johnston, a well-known lesbian and a dance critic for the *Village Voice,* and I decided to begin a different kind of C-R group that would be a dialogue between straight women and lesbians. The disturbing chasm, started by Betty Friedan in 1970, seemed to be widening within the movement.

On one occasion, the meeting was in our apartment. Marc had absented himself, because there were no men in our C-R group. But when Jill got there she breathlessly announced that "John and Yoko" would arrive soon. Over murmurs of astonishment, as well as objections, she protested that they had invited her to a party on the *QE2* that night. She'd tried to get Yoko to join our group, but Yoko wouldn't go anywhere without John. When the doorbell rang, I found myself facing John Lennon and Yoko Ono. Jill jumped up, shrieked and led them into the living room. Then we had to decide whether to throw John out or just relax and make the best of what might turn into an interesting few hours. We all chose to let him stay, and John started talking about the women in his life, his mother and his aunts, who had raised him. His father hadn't been around, and he'd had no family male role models. He felt he understood and really liked women. Unlike Yoko, who seemed somewhat supercilious and austere, John was sympathetic. I realized later that I'd been unconsciously comparing John to Marc. Whereas John seemed to be very much in touch with his feelings, Marc often had problems knowing and expressing his. At times, when I had to prod Marc to tell me what he was feeling, I felt as though he was off in his head somewhere and I was alone, unable to confide my own innermost feelings to him.

At our next meeting to better foster the dialogue between straight women and lesbians that she so badly wanted, Jill volunteered her house in upstate New York. We drew up a list of names, and several weeks later a caravan including Gloria, Kate Millett, Susan Sontag (who brought her young son), Liz Smith, Pat Newcomb, Jill, a few members of my regular C-R group and I headed upstate. We gathered in Jill's cozy living room in the early afternoon and stayed there until sundown. Although the idea had seemed like a good one, nothing much came from that get-together, partly because Kate and her friends arrived late and somewhat inebriated.

One summer in the early 1970s, Marc and I rented a house in East Hampton with Leon Friedman and Gail Marks, his wife. Leon, another Harvard lawyer, was an old friend of Gloria's, and we had asked him to join us in our lawsuit against the Harvard Club of New York City. He not only was our co-counsel, he also represented the class of male graduates who were members but who would resign their memberships if women weren't admitted. During that period, Leon and Gail had become close friends.

One afternoon, Gail, naked from the waist up, was happily washing her car on our rented property, just outside the house, at the end of the long driveway from the street. I was inside reading but noticed that a patrol car had passed by the house twice. It was quite a distance away, hard to see through the trees and shrubs separating our property from the city street. Then, all of a sudden, it started up our driveway, heading right for Gail. The next thing I knew, two officers were shouting at her to get dressed and get inside their car. She must have had a shirt nearby, because she didn't come into the house. Dressed in shorts and a tank top, I jumped into our car and took off after her.

When I reached the station, I demanded that the desk officer let me see my friend who had just been taken there. He took one look at me and said, "No." I asked what she was charged with and he rattled off some obscure section of the New York State penal code. Seeing a copy of the penal code on a shelf, I started flipping through the pages until I found the section he'd cited. Just as I saw the words "bare breast" and "aureola," the officer literally slammed the book closed with my hand still inside. I looked squarely into his huge face and told him I was Ms. Marks's lawyer and that I was there to take her home. He stared back at me and said, "You're not a lawyer." I said I was. He said prove it. My only response was that I didn't have any cards on me. My shorts didn't even have pockets.

I called out to Gail that we'd be back and dashed home to find Leon or Marc—or my cards. As soon as he realized what had happened, Leon grabbed his cards, his wallet and the keys to the half-washed car and made a beeline for the station. Now in a rage over the general issue of how women ought to be able to go any-where we want—especially our own backyards—with no tops if men can, I stayed home with Marc. He knew better than to argue with me.

When Leon and a badly shaken-up Gail returned, Leon seemed happy that he'd been able to talk the police out of offi-cially arresting her. But Gail, who had never really proclaimed her feminist leanings before, was mad. Both of us wanted to go after the police for hauling her in like that, and I wanted her to sue the State of New York for having an unconstitutional statute, which treated women and men differently. Leon told me to forget it. Gail and Leon fought. But in the end, Leon won. Gail decided not to sue. I still think that statute and others like it all over the country are unconstitutional and occasionally think about chal-lenging them, especially when I'm uncomfortably clad in a soggy bikini top. For some reason, it's different on the Riviera, where beaches are filled with topless women.

By the spring of 1973, we had formed a *Ms.* softball team that would gather monthly in Central Park to play against women from other magazines. I was considered part of the team because of my founding efforts and was routinely drafted to play center field or left field because I could throw the farthest. Gloria, who didn't play, occasionally would come to the games to root for us. One day she brought along a woman named Herta Wittgenstein, with whom she had recently become friends.

Gloria introduced her as a doctor—and then, the bombshell— who had leukemia. Herta soon also became a frequent cheer- leader at our *Ms.* games. Unfortunately, Herta turned out to be a fraud and ultimately, a fugitive, a convict and an ex-convict. That incident, along with the Betty Harris mess, was another example of Gloria's inability to judge people critically enough.

After each game, the other *Ms.* players and I would go to a women's bar in the Village called Bonnie and Clyde's. There, in continuance of the celebration, the real party started. It was a birthday celebration for everyone who had been born during that particular month. The fact that the party was in a women's bar seemed perfectly appropriate, whether we were straight or not. Women danced with women and we all had a great time.

Although he was hard at work on his book, Marc and I contin- ued to do a lot of lecturing, still as the quintessential feminist cou- ple, but I occasionally felt lonely when we spent time together, and I was sometimes unhappy for reasons that I couldn't under- stand. Meanwhile, Marc seemed troubled as he worried about what he'd do when the book was finished. He reminded me of John Stuart Mill's description of the Rolls-Royce engine with no place to go. I, on the other hand, was more like a whirling dervish—dashing from my office to C-R meetings to softball games to lectures around the country. I was still spending a huge amount of time on the ERA, committed to ensuring that this con- stitutional amendment would be ratified by the necessary three- fourths of the states.

By 1977, all of us were focused on International Women's Year (IWY) and its celebration scheduled for November 18 to 21 in

Houston. Once again, there would be a conference, kicked off by a parade led by Gloria, Bella, Billie Jean King and numerous other well-known feminists. The mandate of that National Women's Conference was to adopt a National Plan of Action to be submitted to President Jimmy Carter and Congress. Some 20,000 women from all over the country attended. Among them were Coretta Scott King, widow of Martin Luther King, and the wives of three U.S. presidents—Rosalyn Carter, Betty Ford, and Lady Bird Johnson.

Little did I know that the success of that conference would rest on Gloria's virtually single-handed ability to draft a statement that would bring minority women—black women, Latinas and others—together. I watched as she, with Bella, talked to representatives of the various groups and tried to get them to draft something themselves. Finally, though, in the middle of the night, with only a few hours left before the statement was needed for the morning's plenary session, Gloria herself started to draft it. She continued to work, writing, rewriting and then checking her language with the spokeswomen for each group. I guess it was at that moment that I realized what a true leader Gloria was. What she so passionately cared about was that we all come together, united in our goals for women at home and around the world.

Out of the Houston conference came a Plan of Action approved by more than 80 percent of the delegates attending. A Roper Poll conducted a week before the conference revealed that only 19 percent of the general public felt that their views were represented by Phyllis Schlafly,[2] almost the same percentage as "anti-delegates" to the National Women's Conference, indicating that the Plan of Action passed by the delegates in Houston truly represented the will of the majority. In March 1978, *An Official Report to the President, the Congress and the People of the United States* would be published and transmitted by Bella Abzug, the presiding officer of the National Commission on the Observance of International Women's Year, in a letter to President Carter. It was called *The Spirit of Houston: The First National Women's Conference,* and it contained all twenty-five planks passed in Hous-

Bella Abzug, a perennial candidate for the House, the Senate or mayor of New York City, always enjoyed celebrity support— here, from actress Marsha Mason.

ton. They spoke to every major issue then of concern to women, from battered women and rape to child care, from business to education, from employment to the ERA, health, insurance, credit, the media, minority women, poverty and welfare and sexual preference.

As we were leaving Houston, Gloria gave each of her friends a beige T-shirt with the words in both Spanish and English, front and back, reading "Carry on the Spirit of Houston." I still cherish that by-now frayed and rather tight-fitting reminder of all that Gloria and the rest of us had been working on so hard that year. And for years after that, whenever I'd meet a feminist from another part of the country, she'd ask me if I was at Houston.

Although the National Women's Conference in Houston was a defining moment for the Movement, its accomplishments felt more ephemeral than specific victories like the decision in *Roe v. Wade*. After all, we'd come up with what we wanted, but it was up to male-dominated bodies like Congress to implement our goals. Nevertheless, we were full of hope as we boarded our planes for the trip home.

Chapter 3

THE ACLU, RUTH BADER GINSBURG— AND ME

At the biennial conference of the ACLU in June 1970, a strong policy resolution supporting women's rights was adopted, followed by a statement by the National Board of the American Civil Liberties Union declaring women's rights its top legal and legislative priority. The Women's Rights Project of the national ACLU was created late in 1971. Ruth Bader Ginsburg (then a professor of law at Rutgers) was asked to be the director. Years later, Ruth explained why she had agreed: "I wanted to be part of a general human rights agenda. Civil liberties are an essential part of the overall human rights concern—the equality of all people and the ability to be free."[1]

In late January of 1972, Mel Wulf, the legal director of the ACLU, called to ask me if I would be interested in directing the newly established Women's Rights Project with Professor Ruth Bader Ginsburg. Because she was a full-time professor of law, she wanted a partner. I was flattered, because I had practiced law for only about six months before I left to start the Alliance. But I was uneasy too, because we had *just* held the press conference—less than three weeks before—to announce the Alliance. I said that because of that I'd need a bit of time to decide.

I was confused and called Gloria. She had no doubts. Lots of women were qualified to run the Alliance but few, if any, feminist lawyers were around to do the job at the ACLU. Finally I let myself feel the thrill of the offer, no longer guilty at the thought of abandoning the Alliance.

So in February 1972, after sisterly hugs and tearful farewells, I moved to my new offices at the ACLU on Fifth Avenue and Twentieth Street and became director (with Ruth) of the Women's Rights Project. Late in the morning of my first day, Ruth appeared. She was a soft-spoken, thoughtful woman, with large, intelligent eyes.

Before I assumed my new position, I had made a point of reading the Supreme Court's opinion in *Reed v. Reed*.[2] This was the case Ruth had argued, and for the first time in history, in 1971, a majority of the Justices had agreed that women were a "protected" class, deserving recognition under the Equal Protection Clause of the Fourteenth Amendment. Articulating the standard of review, there had to be, they said, a rational relationship between a classification based on sex and a legitimate state interest. In *Reed*, the divorced mother of a deceased son was fighting for her right to be the administrator of her son's estate. The father was fighting back, citing the Idaho state law that gave him the automatic right to administer the estate because he was male. I felt that the decision in *Reed* was a partial vindication for the embarrassment I had suffered when Professor Freund had laughed at my outrage over the Supreme Court's opinion in the Michigan "barmaid" case.[3] Because of *Reed*, a new age was dawning for women, and I was excited by the thought that I might just be able to help in that revolutionary struggle.

During our first day in the office together, Ruth talked to me about several important cases on their way up to the Supreme Court. Meanwhile, we drafted a press release announcing the official formation of the Women's Rights Project. We wanted local ACLU affiliates to check with us about any questions that might arise concerning women's rights and sex discrimination. And we encouraged them to tell us about any lawsuits they were contemplating bringing on behalf of women. Ruth didn't want weak cases getting to the Supreme Court. At one point, I asked Ruth about a potential lawsuit challenging veterans' benefits, because women, not allowed in combat, couldn't qualify for them. Ruth agreed that such benefits might constitute discrimination against women, but she felt strongly that the spirit in the country, including that of the Supreme Court Justices, was to help veterans, and that it would therefore be unwise to challenge benefits directed at that particular group of men.

Ruth and I developed a pattern during that spring of 1972. I would arrive at the office at 9:30 a.m. At about 11:00 a.m. Ruth would call. My usual response when I heard her voice was "Hi, Ruth. How are you?" or "What's new?" My questions would be met with "Hi. Have you read the advance sheets yet?" or "Brenda, there's such an interesting case the Court just accepted!"

Ruth typically wasted few moments on chitchat. And she was a person just like me, late to bed—after her two children went to sleep, she worked at her desk until all hours—and late to rise. But she was able to stick to her own internal time clock. Law professors' schedules are irregular, and often they can pick the times when their classes meet. Her children were old enough, especially with the help of Ruth's supportive husband, Marty, to get themselves off to school early in the morning. And of course, they had someone to help with the kids, as most other working parents who could afford that necessary luxury did. Meanwhile, I was the one expected to conform to an office system with set hours by which people were expected to be at their desks. I didn't resent the different standards, though, because I had so much respect for Ruth's intellect and for the amount of work she put in on every brief we would come to write together.

Shortly after the Project started, we realized that we needed more space for law students and other support staff, many of whom were donating their time because of the excitement our existence was generating. The ACLU was about to move uptown and would be near our Tudor City apartment. When I visited the new offices, I picked a space for us separated from the rest of the ACLU by a hallway, and posted on our door a bright yellow sign: WOMEN WORKING. Ruth thought that was terrific.

Upcoming was the ACLU annual conference. The purpose was for lawyers from around the country to get to know others who were fighting similar battles and for national office attorneys to run seminars on topics of nationwide interest. The conference that year would take place in Boulder, Colorado.

After we gave the Women's Rights Project presentation, I suggested to Ruth that we go horseback riding. To my amazement, she agreed; she said she loved to ride. I doubted that Ruth would say she liked to do something she wasn't good at, so I found a place where we could rent horses and wasn't surprised when she proved herself to be a true horsewoman. Although each of us had ridden on English saddles, in Colorado we had to ride on Western saddles, which make much more sense in that terrain. We spent our time galloping in the beautiful desert outside Boulder. Ruth rode freely, almost wildly, but always in control. This is a woman who knows how to work—and play—hard, I realized.

By the spring of 1972, we'd joined the campaign for the passage of Title IX. It guaranteed that an equal amount of money be spent on girls and women as on boys and men in all publicly funded education and sports programs. No matter that the men's football team brought in station wagons full of fans and alumni; if that school wanted to retain federal funding, it would have to finance women's sports to the same extent. Needless to say, there was opposition. The National Collegiate Athletic Association, an organization of university presidents, mobilized against campaigns for a share in college budgets for women. They apparently had visions that their football teams would be completely destroyed. Amazingly, in retrospect, Title IX easily became law in June 1972.

One of the women with whom I'd become friendly during the Title IX campaign was Donna de Varona, who had won two Olympic gold medals for swimming in the 1964 games. She was president of the Women's Sports Foundation, a newly formed group. With her help, I worked out my own feelings about being forever "inferior" to men when it came to physical strength. (The high price they pay for all that testosterone is that they really do die younger.)

I realized recently that we're really only now beginning to feel the effects of Title IX, when I attended the opening game of the Women's National Basketball Association (WNBA). I saw young women in their twenties playing better basketball than most men. Tears streamed down my face as I read, the day after the league opener, about fathers and mothers bringing their little daughters, who happened already to love basketball, to see their role models. One dad said he thought it was just as important that his son see those women play, so he'd get the idea very visually that women can be strong, tough and athletic.

I wrote an article, which ended up being the cover story for the July 1973 issue of *Ms.*, featuring a large photo of Billie Jean King. In the article I explored all the issues that I could think of involving women in sports. I interviewed Billie Jean and asked her what would happen if she, who was then ranked number one in women's tennis, were to play against men. Her modest reply was that she'd come in "twenty-fifth or fiftieth." Nonetheless, when Billie Jean announced, in 1973, that she was challenging Bobby Riggs in a tennis match billed as The Battle of the Sexes, I was elated. Riggs had claimed that even an over-the-hill man could beat any championship-class woman player. At a party with all the *Ms.* folks I watched as Billie Jean soundly defeated him in straight sets in the five-set match (just the way men play but women still aren't allowed to). There they were in the Houston Astrodome, the match televised nationally. All I could think of was how proud I was of Billie Jean for taking up the challenge— and how dumb I was for not having bet a lot of money on her.

The ERA remained the real issue, and Ruth and I were in agreement that its ratification was of primary importance. Even though the principal work of the ACLU is litigation, lobbying for the ERA remained a priority for me. Sex-discrimination litigation would be forever changed once it was ratified. To Ruth in those days, too: "It [the ERA] is the bedrock issue. . . . [Without the ERA] the Supreme Court has no gun at its head."[4]

I appeared on numerous national television shows, such as *Good Morning America,* to debate the likes of Admiral Rickover

*Giving a pro–Equal
Rights Amendment
speech, 1972*

and General Westmoreland. They spoke about how terrible it
would be if women were drafted to serve their country alongside
men. My point, of course, was that if women were capable of
doing the job—judged by some objective test—they should have
the right to serve their country just as men did. Neither the admiral nor the general seemed to listen to what I was saying, let alone
care about equal rights for women in the military. They just
stared glassy-eyed into the camera while I was making my point
and then repeated theirs.

Debating ultra-right-winger Phyllis Schlafly of the Eagle
Forum, the organization she founded out of her hometown in rural
southern Illinois, became routine and almost always also involved
an argument about toilets and jails—and how she just knew that
both would become coed if the ERA were passed. So on the
Tomorrow Show, as well as in college auditoriums, I talked about
how the legislative history, developed during the ERA hearings,
would allow the government to have separate male and female

bathroom and prison facilities, because of another constitutional principle: privacy. One real problem debating Schlafly was that she lied. For example, at the beginning of our debates she said that all her children were grown. I did some research and learned that she had an eight-year-old son who was cared for by a nanny. When I confronted her with that on one show, she turned red-faced. On another occasion, she cited what she said was an Illinois case that deprived a woman of alimony because of the newfound spirit of women's independence. When I asked her for the cite, she muttered something that didn't sound as if it could be accurate. When I later checked for the case itself, there was none. But probably the worst aspect of debating Schlafly was that she didn't pause for a breath. The only way to get a word in was literally to speak over her, which on television doesn't work well and makes the one interrupting look uncivilized. Occasionally, though, I resorted to talking over her. It was my only choice if I wanted to get the feminist point of view across. For some reason, even talk-show hosts had trouble controlling her so that other guests would have an opportunity to talk.

Soon both Schlafly and Marabel Morgan, the author of *The Total Woman* (an early version of today's best-selling *The Rules*), started to harp on how the ERA would end marriage as we know it, cause divorce and harm "housewives," most of whom, although now happily married, would, once the ERA was in force, be abandoned by husbands and deprived by courts of alimony or maintenance of any kind. These were nothing more than ridiculous scare tactics, but I feared that Schlafly and her cohorts had a real constituency—insecure homemakers, as well as right-wing Christians.

By the late 1970s, even the so-called radical feminists of the early days who had not earlier concerned themselves with the ERA realized that its success would, in fact, help the women's liberation movement. But we finally realized that we were in trouble when Schlafly succeeded in scaring male legislators in some already ratified states to vote to rescind their ratification. In April

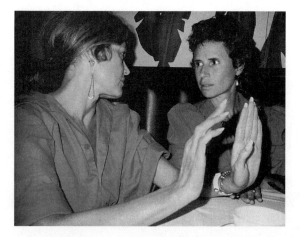

After the defeat of the ERA, Gloria and I talk feminist strategy and catch up with each other's lives over dinner.

1978, the first volume of the *Harvard Women's Law Journal* was published, and in it was an article by Marc and me entitled "Why a State May Not Rescind Its Prior Ratification of a Constitutional Amendment." Our thesis was that Article V of the Constitution gives the states power only to ratify a proposed amendment. Once that is accomplished, the duty imposed on a particular state legislature by Congress is discharged and that legislature has no more connection to the ratified amendment, no right to rescind it.

Unfortunately, even the issue of rescission became moot. It was beginning to seem that the ERA might not be ratified by the requisite three-fourths of the states. Thirty-seven states had ratified, but we were unable in the requisite seven-year period to secure a thirty-eighth state. After that, many feminists put their efforts into seeking an extension of the period during which states could ratify. I, however, had lost hope.

Ruth and I continued to put our emphasis on winning equal rights for women in the many cases that were coming to us. One day, while the ERA was still in the ratification process, Ruth told me about a sex-discrimination case that the Supreme Court had just agreed to review. The case was *Frontiero v. Richardson.*[5]

Sharron Frontiero was the plaintiff (and appellant), a married Air Force officer, living with her husband on a military base. She had requested that she be given the same housing and medical allowance for her husband as those her male cohorts in the Air Force received for their wives. The Air Force refused, because the federal statute providing such allowances for spouses of military personnel stated that while all wives were automatically entitled to such support, regardless of how dependent on their husbands they were, husbands had to prove that they were more than half dependent on their wives for support. Sharron Frontiero and her husband, who couldn't quite meet that standard, thought this was unfair.

The government, defending this preposterous statute, had won in the lower court. We didn't know Joe Levin, Sharron Frontiero's lawyer, but he worked out of the Southern Poverty Law Center, so his expertise was race discrimination, not sex discrimination. Ruth worried that bad law would be made if we didn't intervene, at least by filing an *amicus** *curiae* brief on behalf of the Women's Rights Project of the ACLU. And thus *Frontiero* became our priority.

Marc decided to help, so Ruth, Marc and I discussed our strategy. We wanted the Court to apply the highest level of scrutiny to sex-discrimination cases. That meant that in order for a distinction based on gender to be upheld, a court would have to rule that there was a "compelling state interest" in keeping that distinction on the books. Every race-discrimination case in recent years had been examined under this strict-scrutiny standard to see if there was a "compelling state interest" in maintaining whatever the particular racial classification was. But all that Ruth had been able to secure in *Reed* was that there had to be a "rational state interest" in maintaining a sex-based classification. That meant that the lowest standard of review could be applied, and that if there were any logical reason (it certainly didn't need to be compelling) for

---

* It has consistently struck me as antifeminist to use this Latin word for male friend, *amicus*, since we are female. I've pondered simply referring to it as an *amica* brief, but I don't know if I have any support within the feminist legal community for this, so I've decided that for this book, I'll use a word that all lawyers and many laypeople already know.

maintaining the distinction on the basis of gender, a court could uphold the provision containing that distinction. Of course, the issue in *Reed,* whether males were better suited than females to administer an estate, was easy. Requiring that men perform that function over similarly situated women does not have a rational relationship to any state interest. In *Frontiero,* however, it certainly would cost the government money to add benefits for husbands like those so far provided only to wives.

The government's argument was that the statutes allowing benefits for "dependents" of male service members presumed such dependent status of wives solely for "administrative convenience"; more wives were dependent. But although administrative convenience had been ruled an invalid test in *Reed* (it was not enough to satisfy even the lowest-level test that there was any rational relationship between preferring men and a state interest), we worried that the Court might deem avoiding a higher *cost* to the government not just administratively convenient but also a *rational* state interest. Therefore, we wanted the Court to apply the highest level of scrutiny (there would have to be a compelling state interest), not only because we cared about the outcome of the case on the merits but also because this was our chance to ensure that sex discrimination would become just as reprehensible as race discrimination. After all, the Equal Rights Amendment hadn't yet been ratified. To ensure that we covered all the bases, we asked the Court to rule that the classification in this particular case would also fail under the low-level rational-relationship test.

We started by outlining the arguments we wanted to make in the brief. Ruth's authority was clear. Marc and I would draft a section, spending hours finding relevant cases, and then hand it over to Ruth for editing. Meanwhile, she was busily creating the argument, stating in clear, almost poetic, language the reasons that women should be treated as first-class citizens. Eventually, after many long nights, a truly excellent brief emerged. I hadn't seen the part that Ruth herself had been working on until we were finished with the rest of it, but her summary of the history of discrimination against women through the years was stunning. Ruth didn't confine her observations to old cases and legal precedent. Instead, she took, from opinions going back centuries, those sections that revealed just how antiquated the government's position was, *and* she quoted authors of books and articles along with the cases. She described how men have traditionally viewed women and their role in society, quoting, among others, Thomas Jefferson, Alexis de Tocqueville, William Blackstone, Alfred Lord Tennyson, Henrik Ibsen, Gunnar Myrdal and Grover Cleveland. She even used the Court's own language in *Bradwell v. Illinois*[6] to show the ignorance of the Justices in the mid-1800s, when they agreed with the state that because she was a woman, Myra Bradwell had no right to practice law in Illinois. Much to my enormous pleasure, Ruth addressed the statute challenged in the ignominious "barmaid" case, *Goesaert v. Cleary,*[7] writing "like the classification challenged here, [it] was difficult to construe as a measure intended to assist women 'in the struggle for subsistence' or to safeguard women's competitive position."[8] She added that the ruling in *Goesaert v. Cleary* was "retrogressive in its day and is intolerable a generation later. . . . Goesaert was said by the appellant," wrote Ruth approvingly, "to be 'an unchivalrous desire of male bartenders to try to monopolize the calling.' "[9]

Ruth then proceeded through a history of the struggle for women's suffrage and cited passages from the Declaration of Women's Rights drafted at the 1848 Seneca Falls Women's Rights Convention. She quoted from Susan B. Anthony, Elizabeth Cady Stanton and Sojourner Truth, and continued to the 1963 statement from the President's Commission on the Status of Women, to language in recent legislation such as the 1964 Civil Rights Act, and to the legislative history of the Equal Rights Amendment.

I have never had an experience like the writing of our *Frontiero* brief, especially observing how Ruth used history to address the issues before the Court. I realized that, as with any other kind of writing, the point is to capture the attention of the read-

In the

Supreme Court of the United States

October Term, 1972

No. 71-1694

---◆---

Sharron A. Frontiero and Joseph Frontiero,

Appellants,

—v.—

Melvin R. Laird, as Secretary of Defense, his successors and assigns; Dr. Robert C. Seamans, Jr., as Secretary of the Air Force, his successors and assigns; and Col. Charles G. Weber, as Commanding Officer, Maxwell Air Force Base, Alabama, his successors and assigns,

Appellees.

On Appeal From The United States District Court For The Middle District Of Alabama, Northern Division

BRIEF OF AMERICAN CIVIL LIBERTIES UNION *AMICUS CURIAE*

Ruth Bader Ginsburg
Melvin L. Wulf
Brenda Feigen Fasteau
Marc Feigen Fasteau
    American Civil Liberties Union
    22 East 40th Street
    New York, New York 10016
    Attorneys for Amicus Curiae

The cover of the brief in the Frontiero *case, filed by the ACLU in the U.S. Supreme Court*

ers—in this situation, nine relatively old men—and persuade them, in eloquent language, that our position was the only tenable one.*

The government, in its brief on behalf of the Air Force, predictably argued that there were too few dependent husbands to warrant a change in policy, and furthermore that the policy was constitutional, applying the "rational-relationship" test set out in *Reed*.

Even Joe Levin, the lawyer for Sharron Frontiero, realized that his brief, the main brief for the Frontieros, was inferior to ours. He called to ask if we would be interested in writing a joint reply brief with him. Ruth jumped at the opportunity, and as it turned out, we wrote the entire reply brief. Levin just added his name.

Now came the moment to explore how determined Levin was to present the oral argument. And now was the time to try to negotiate with him to let Ruth present that argument, although any lawyer who has an opportunity to argue before the Supreme Court is unlikely to relinquish it. I placed the call to Joe Levin. He was glad to have had our "help" with the reply brief, and he was grateful for the *amicus* brief, as it enhanced his own, but he wanted to argue the case. The plaintiff had come to him, he had handled the case in the lower federal court, and as far as he was concerned, it was his to argue before the Supremes. I relayed the conversation to Ruth, and eventually a compromise was reached. Ruth would get ten of Levin's allotted thirty minutes to present our argument orally to the Court. This was exciting, because I knew that regardless of how few minutes Ruth was given, her appearance before the Justices would impress them.

Now Ruth began the very tough job of synthesizing the seventy-plus pages of material in the briefs into a very short presentation. I collected the various statutes and reporters to which we'd referred. I would be sitting at the counsel table with Ruth in

---

* Melvin Wulf's name was added to every brief that came out of the ACLU's national office, because he was the legal director. He did not participate in the writing of the *Frontiero amicus* brief.

the Supreme Court of the United States, and even though I wouldn't utter a word, I'd need to have each cite at my fingertips, ready for her use during the argument. The books I'd be lugging with me to Washington were big and heavy.

Ruth spent weeks preparing for the oral argument. I didn't go shopping for a proper suit or dress, and I later wished I had. Women were required to wear skirts when they appeared before the Court, and my wardrobe had not a single one that was the prim and proper length. (I ended up selecting a light-brown suede suit with a short skirt—fashionable in those days but not ideal for a woman lawyer sitting in front of the Justices.)

Early on the day of the oral argument, Ruth and I, accompanied by her husband, Marty, arrived at the Supreme Court. Ruth looked prim and appropriately dressed as always. She seemed a bit nervous. An eminent tax attorney, Marty had appeared before the Supreme Court and now took a seat in the section reserved for members of the Supreme Court bar.

Eventually, Ruth and I were escorted to the counsel table, where I stacked my pile of open books with yellow stickums in the order of the cases Ruth would cite as precedent. Joe Levin looked nervous as he joined us. The government lawyers were on the other side of the aisle that divided the room.

As the clerk finally called out the familiar "Oyez, oyez, all those . . ." and then "the Justices of the Supreme Court," my heart was pounding. Here I was, twenty-eight years old, overwhelmed and standing before the nine Justices of the Supreme Court as they filed in behind the bench in order of their seniority. The Court at that time consisted of Chief Justice Warren Burger and Justices Douglas, Brennan, Marshall, White, Blackmun, Powell, Stewart and, of course, Rehnquist.

The proceedings got under way, and Joe Levin went first, unimpressively. In a monotone, he emphasized the unfairness of female members of the military receiving fewer and more conditional benefits for their husbands than male members did for their wives. It was hard to tell what the Justices were thinking, because his remarks hadn't raised any particularly thought-provoking points, and everything he said was already in his brief. Mercifully, he did not take his full twenty minutes, leaving about twelve minutes (instead of ten) for Ruth.

Next it was time for Ruth, who stood and slowly and clearly declared, "May it please the Court." She proceeded to make our arguments brilliantly, pausing for effect, her voice changing to signal a different point or quote. And without any fanfare, she would give a cite, the name of the case, and the volume of the *Supreme Court Reporter* to which she was calling the Justices' attention. She even added the year, and I felt certain that if they had signaled that they wanted it, she'd have been able to give them the page reference as well. Although I felt a bit silly for having put so much time and energy into having the cases all there and the cites available, I was mesmerized by her performance. She was coming to the conclusion of her remarks. Not a single Justice had asked a question, but they all were listening very carefully. None seemed bored and none showed any sign of disagreement. But none had expressed his approval of what she was saying either. Should we be worried? Had she done something wrong? An oral argument without any interruption from at least one of the Justices is virtually without precedent. But as I looked at those nine male, mostly elderly faces, I saw the same fascination I was experiencing. They weren't bored; on the contrary, they seemed thrilled to see their craft performed so brilliantly. Ruth finished her argument and sat down. I leaned toward her and whispered, "Congratulations."

The government lawyers tried lamely to defend the federal statute we were challenging. Speaking on behalf of the Air Force, they argued that there were too few dependent husbands to warrant this change in policy and that there was a rational relationship—the only standard they felt the Court should apply—between the difference in the way male and female officers were treated and the rule that had been established to define dependency. The Justices grilled them, clearly trying to figure out if there was any way they could uphold the statute in question. I was feeling sure that we'd win on the merits. The tough question was what standard of review the Court would apply.

Then it was over and we were in the lobby of the Supreme Court. Marty came up to Ruth and seemed to be congratulating her, as he kissed her on the cheek, grinning from ear to ear. Then, as though he were talking to a twelve-year-old rather than one of our country's most distinguished constitutional scholars, he began to tell Ruth about how to take the shuttle back to New York. He had business in Washington and had to stay, while she and I were more than ready to return home. Finally, I told him that it was okay, I knew how to get to the shuttle. He looked relieved. And the truth is that as he had been explaining to Ruth how to get back to New York, I saw on her face a confused sort of look, as though comprehending that the task—at least at that moment—was a bit much. It was sort of touching. There had been nothing condescending about Marty's concern. Apparently, it was based on their many married years together, which by my count had, to that date, exceeded sixteen. (They had met when they were both at Harvard Law School. They married, and Marty, who graduated a year ahead of Ruth, accepted a position in a large New York law firm. Ruth then transferred to Columbia Law School to complete her third year and was immediately elected to the Law Review, as she had been at Harvard.)

As Ruth and I made our way back to New York, I told her that she'd probably given the best oral argument those Justices had ever heard. I couldn't see how they could disagree with a word we'd written or a sentence Ruth had said. It was then that I became convinced—and shortly thereafter told Ruth—that I was sure that she'd be the next Democratic appointee to the U.S. Supreme Court. Who knew that it would take twenty-one years for my prophecy to become fact?

After Ruth's argument before the Supreme Court, she and I anxiously awaited a decision in the *Frontiero* case. On May 14, 1973, it came.

Eight of the nine Justices agreed that the Air Force was wrongly discriminating against female officers by denying their husbands housing and medical benefits on the same terms as those offered to the dependent wives of male officers. Four of the Justices—a plurality led by Justice Brennan and joined by Justices Douglas, White and Marshall—agreed with our argument that sex should be a suspect classification. Justice Stewart, in an opinion concurring on the merits, simply stated that "the statutes before us work an invidious discrimination in violation of the Constitution." He concluded his elusive opinion by citing *Reed v. Reed*. Obviously, he thought the statutes had to be changed in our favor, but he wouldn't say that distinctions based on sex had to be scrutinized as closely as those based on race. I even looked up the word "invidious" in Webster's Second Unabridged and found the unhelpful definition "tending to cause animosity or imply a slight." What did that mean? Three of the Justices felt that the standard enunciated in *Reed* would require that the statutes questioned in *Frontiero* be held unconstitutional. And then there was Justice Rehnquist, who didn't see a problem with affording more benefits without conditions to military wives than to military husbands. The bottom line was that if a majority of the Court in *Frontiero* had held that there must be a compelling state interest in order to justify classifications based on gender, which should be, therefore, inherently suspect,* there would have been no need for the ERA.† Ruth was just as disappointed as I was that we hadn't gained the majority we needed to change the standard of review in all future sex-discrimination cases. But, and perhaps this is with the benefit of hindsight, she did seem more philo-

---

* Another adjective, such as "invidious," unfortunately isn't the necessary term of art to change the standard, so Justice Stewart's use of that word didn't help us.
† It was even argued at various times throughout the 1970s that a holding by the Court that all gender classifications were suspect and, therefore, subject to strict scrutiny would have been preferable to the ERA. Some experts felt the ERA would bring into question the constitutionality of affirmative action programs, which the Court otherwise might have been able to justify as meeting the compelling-state-interest test. The ERA would require an absolute ban on treating the sexes differently (except where overridden by other constitutional interests, such as privacy-related issues like same-sex toilet and prison facilities).

sophical about the situation, thinking, I believe, that inevitably the Court would eventually accept our point of view.

Starting immediately upon the announcement of the Women's Rights Project and continually throughout all the important litigation in which we were engaged, we constantly received huge numbers of calls from married women wanting to resume the use of their birth names. I advised them just to use those birth names consistently. There was no law preventing a woman from doing so unless she had some fraudulent intent. What was interesting about this was that no other single issue seemed to galvanize "regular" women as much when it came to their rights vis-à-vis men.

Sometime in June, Ruth and I received a call from the U.S. Commission on Civil Rights. Would we be interested in documenting all the federal statutes that distinguished on the basis of sex? By this time, Ruth was a full (and full-time) professor at Columbia Law School and had ceded her large corner office at the ACLU to me. She was interested, but she decided that the only way for us to complete that prodigious task properly was if she could involve her gender-discrimination (her new term for sex discrimination) class at Columbia Law School. First, however, the FBI had to conduct security checks on both of us. So we set a date in late July 1973 for our big meeting in Washington with the Civil Rights Commission.

After that meeting, our mandate was clear. We had been asked to review the entire federal code, and it took us a full school semester to complete our research and make suggestions for how the code should be changed.

Chapter 4

FASTEAU
AND FEIGEN

Once *Ms.* magazine was fully staffed, regular softball games and the ritual of monthly collective birthday celebrations began. No one seemed fazed that these parties were held at a lesbian bar in the Village. We were all feminists, some straight, some lesbian, some probably in between.

My birthday being on the seventh of the month, the *Ms.* birthday party in July 1973 had special significance for me. Soon after I arrived at Bonnie and Clyde's (the bar), I was greeted by a notorious lesbian I'll call Lila, who presented me with a wrist corsage perfectly laid out in a box. I didn't understand why me, except that she'd come to one of our softball games and claimed to be impressed by how far I'd thrown the ball. My response to this come-on was to drag a straight friend of mine onto the dance floor with me. I was flustered, maybe even flattered, by the attention Lila continued to shower on me, but I was determined to ignore her. Granted, I had felt some kind of attraction to a few women in college, but it was the sort of feeling that led to our putting our arms around each other when we walked through the hallways of our dorm. In fact, one spring vacation when a very good friend was scheduled to visit me in Chicago, I remember a vague sort of panic at our sleeping in the same room every night for two weeks and asked her to cancel her trip. I felt bad, but relieved. The attraction I felt toward those friends was physical in the sense that I wanted to be near them, even touch their hands or arms, but the idea of sex with them was nowhere near my consciousness.

Lila wasn't unattractive, but she was very butch, with short dark hair, and there was a swagger to her walk. She was shorter than I, and had a wiry build and a relatively flat chest. She grinned a lot and brimmed with a sexual self-confidence I hadn't witnessed before. I felt that I should stay away from her. I didn't feel attracted to her, but there was something in her aggressive approach that captured my attention. I also remembered seeing her at the First Congress to Unite Women, for which I had journeyed to New York while I was still living in Cambridge. And then, of course, I'd seen her at the softball game where we had exchanged a few words about the game. I didn't dance with her that evening at Bonnie and Clyde's, despite her many requests, but when I left the party I still felt flustered. The situation was unresolved.

Somehow I was able to separate that experience from my relationship with Marc. He was a man; men weren't invited to the after-game parties—and I'd done nothing wrong. I was happy to see him when I got home, but distracted. Then one weekend not long after the birthday party incident, I found myself sitting in the bay window of my brother's country house. I was alone. Marc had stayed in the city to work, and I'd driven to the country to get some fresh air, wishing that he'd take more time to relax with me. Meanwhile, I kept thinking about the incident at Bonnie and Clyde's, and I realized that the way I had behaved toward Lila reminded me of a decision I'd made years earlier that I wouldn't play on Vassar's varsity field hockey team because they practiced during dinner, spent all summer at field hockey training to ready themselves for the U.S. Olympic Team, and most telling, looked like—and probably were—a bunch of butchy lesbians. As I sat looking out at a beautiful view of the woods, I decided that apologies were in order. I phoned Lila. But as I did, I realized that I was frightened of what the call would bring. I didn't have an agenda, nor was I sure of exactly how I would explain the reason for the call, but when I heard her "hello," I told her that I was embarrassed at my behavior toward her at the bar. I also said that she had been awfully aggressive in a way that reminded me of a man who didn't care what I wanted, only what he wanted. Her response to my call was to invite me to stay at her home when I next visited D.C. so we could discuss the situation in person. It sounded like a reasonable request. I must have been in denial about the fact that I might be getting into something serious, something that would change my life.

Ruth and I were to meet in Washington with representatives from the Civil Rights Commission in just a few days. We still had to establish whether our review of the federal code would cover only sections that actually discriminated against one sex or whether it would have the broader scope of including any kind of distinction made between the sexes. Because the meeting was set for 10:00 a.m., I scheduled a flight for the evening before, having decided to stay at Lila's without really much thought at all. It was as though I were on automatic pilot. Something in me must have known what I was getting into, but I wasn't conscious of that knowledge. In fact, I had been curious about what sex with a woman would be like, especially after all my C-R group talk, and I probably wanted to experience it—sometime. None of this was real enough for me to feel concern about being unfaithful to Marc. That night, however, I simply rationalized that I needed a place to stay and that Lila's place was as good as any. Besides, I thought, we did need to talk about what had happened at Bonnie and Clyde's.

I arrived at Lila's big old house, which was not in a particularly safe part of town and had broken-down furniture. When she showed me to my room, which was the nicest in the house, I was relieved that it was far away from hers. I noticed—it wasn't hard because there was no spread—that the double bed had black satin sheets. After I hung my clothes in the closet for the meeting the next morning, I started for the hall door, but Lila, who was in the room too, stopped me with "Wait! Come sit down for a minute." There were no chairs in the room. She was sitting on the edge of the bed so I perched a few feet from her. She asked if she could kiss me, and in that moment I found her more appealing than I ever had before. I muttered something about how a kiss is never just a kiss. Then she leaned over and, in fact, kissed me in a sexy way that clearly wasn't just a friendly peck. It was the first real kiss I'd ever shared with a woman. I jumped up and said I was hungry, to which she responded with a report on the different restaurants in her neighborhood.

We chose one, left the house and eventually got around to discussing the ways we both had behaved at Bonnie and Clyde's. I had disliked her relentless pursuit of me. She hadn't seemed to care what, if anything, I felt about her, or, for that matter, that I was married. All I had wanted then, I told her, was to get away from her, whereas if she had behaved properly I might have been able to talk with her. (I didn't even think about whether I would have danced with her.) She apologized but blamed her behavior on being so attracted to me. I must have felt flattered, although I was unconscious (again) of that. I know I felt flustered. So flustered, in fact, that as she engaged in a conversation with an old friend of hers who had just entered the restaurant—probably trying to seem nonchalant about *me*—I went to the pay phone and called a former law school classmate. I told him that I was in town for the night and that I wasn't sure but I might need a place to stay. He reassured me that he and his wife would love to see me, asked about Marc (which made my heart sink) and told me that I could call back, because they stayed up late.

The dinner continued, and despite my anxiety, I decided to go back to Lila's. But I was terrified and felt like a teenage girl about to lose her virginity. I was married, but I rationalized that lots of people were having affairs. It was the 1970s and there were bestselling books on the subject of "open marriage." I couldn't think of a good reason not to experience sex once with a woman—something I had admittedly been curious about. It wasn't an easy night. A big part of me was resisting and I had a problem letting go. After all, I knew I didn't love Lila and I did love Marc. But still I wanted to experience lesbian sex! Eventually, I did, although at one point I found myself sobbing with exhaustion—and fear. In the end, though, the experience proved to be quite something. I arrived at the Civil Rights Commission the next morning bleary-eyed but secretly proud of myself. As I reflected on the night before, I realized that what had happened—my first experience with a woman—could only have occurred with someone as totally aggressive as Lila.

I went back to New York after the meeting. While I felt a certain degree of guilt about it, I never once thought that what I was doing with Lila was as bad as having an extramarital affair with a man. That would have qualified as real adultery, whereas in my warped mentality of the time, what I had done with Lila didn't. I grant that this rationalization is totally sexist! Something in me, however, obviously felt guilty about Marc, because I never told a soul in my C-R group about my affair with Lila, even though it was with them that I first got the idea to have sex with a woman.

Over the next few months, Lila and I occasionally got together in New York, where she had talked a gay man in the East Village into letting her occasionally use his depressing little apartment. For me, it was all about sexual experimentation. I continued to make love with Marc, who one night looked at me and said, "Something's changed." He thought I was much more fun in bed. Soon Marc guessed that I had had an affair with a woman. I didn't deny it. Maybe it upset him. I have to assume it did, but he didn't demand that I stop. I'm quite sure that I wished (unconsciously, of course) that he would ask me never to see Lila again—to prove that he really loved me. But absent a demand from Marc that it be over, the affair with Lila ran its course.

By Christmas of 1973, I'd had it with the first woman in my life. She had begun to pressure me to leave Marc on political grounds. It was "bad feminism" for me to be with a man, to enjoy male privileges through him. Meanwhile, what I wanted and missed most, I realized, was intimacy with Marc. I really felt like nesting now.

Marc and I had talked about having a baby, but at some indeterminate point in the future. Then my brother and his wife had their second child, a boy, in January 1974. Something in me awakened. Maybe it was my need to be tender, to nurture; in short, to be a mother. Before it had always been "someday." Now it was "Let's have one too." Not that minute, but soon. We would talk about it. The only concrete change was that because neither of us liked it, we used birth control only sparingly—during the middle ten days of my cycle.

In February we went skiing, after which we returned to our lives—I at the ACLU and Marc writing his book, which was tentatively called *The Male Machine.* We also continued on the lecture circuit as *the* feminist couple.

One night at a university in Ohio, about three weeks after our ski trip, I was talking about the effect Title IX was having on women in college athletics. But about halfway through my remarks, I got really dizzy and nauseated. I concluded quickly, and Marc, glancing at me with a puzzled look, gamely picked up where I'd left off. Finally, I heard Marc say "Thank you," which meant we were nearly free. As soon as we stood up to leave, he whispered, "What's wrong with you?" I told him that I needed to find a bathroom. As I unsteadily hurried off, I looked back to see the usual crowd surrounding him with their questions about what it meant to be a man and a feminist.

A little while later, when we were alone, waiting for our ride back to the hotel, I stated simply, "Either I'm very sick with an awful disease or I'm pregnant." The strange thing was that until that moment I hadn't had a clue that I might be pregnant.

In New York the next morning, I stopped at my gynecologist's office for a blood test, the results of which wouldn't be back for three days. I was scheduled to be on a plane when the results were due in, so we agreed that Marc would call my doctor. I'd get the news from Marc, who seemed to be in a state of shock, as soon as I landed. Maybe, he thought, it would be better if we waited six months, until we had more money. I, on the other hand, had been dealing with strange feelings all day, and by evening was downright excited to be pregnant.

The baby was due on November 28, 1974, Thanksgiving Day. As the weeks went by, I found that I loved being pregnant. I felt that I was doing something important every second of every day, without making any effort. By the summer, I was still feeling great. All went smoothly both at home and in the office until just before the July 4 weekend, which would be immediately followed by my thirtieth birthday.

The day before the long weekend started, Aryeh Neier, the executive director of the ACLU, asked me to come to his office. I was greeted with the announcement that they were letting me go. We hadn't seen eye-to-eye now for some time about how to run the Women's Rights Project. I was spending too much time lobbying for the ERA, which he granted I'd conducted with the full support of the organization. Aryeh maintained that the ACLU was best suited to litigation, and I hadn't been aggressive enough. That was one flaw I'd never been accused of before. "I thought we'd agreed," I said, "that until the ERA is ratified, we won't be sure that sex will be treated as a suspect classification." What mattered was laying the groundwork for sex-discrimination suits so they would be reviewed on our terms. While the ERA was still out for ratification, although I was certainly encouraging lawsuits—working hard, for example, on the Reproductive Freedom Project, spun off after *Roe* was decided—I was, I thought, spending an appropriate amount of time on the ERA.

Aryeh didn't seem to be listening. Despite his pompous attitude, it didn't occur to me that possibly the ACLU itself, the fighter of all fights to eliminate sex discrimination, was letting me go because I was five months pregnant and might not, in his antiquated opinion, return to work after the birth of the baby.

Needless to say, I was thunderstruck, devastated, barely able to get myself home to tell Marc. Here I was, a Harvard Law School graduate fired from a job I loved and for which I was more than suited. Marc was stung by the news. He himself had been casting about trying to decide what to do now that his book was almost finished. He had choices, among them to join a large law firm, but he was leaning toward going it alone. Would he, I asked, consider the possibility of our forming a law partnership? He didn't jump at the idea; instead, in his usual pensive way, he said that we should think about it. I remember the weekend after that meeting with Aryeh as about the most depressing of my life. Maybe it was my raging pregnant hormones, but I remained devastated, sleeping badly, waking up with knots in my stomach. Marc and I spent that weekend going over and over our options—and how upset I was that I felt I had so few.

But by the next week, we'd come up with a solution. We would start our own law firm, called Fasteau and Feigen. What that meant was hanging out a shingle on an upper floor of a midtown office building and hoping for the best. We wanted to be our own bosses and do what came our way and what we found interesting. We soon found a good two-office suite, conveniently located on the same street as our apartment, just farther west, on Madison Avenue.

We got ourselves a large glass door plaque with big black letters and subtle gold trim. We invested in malpractice insurance, very expensive but necessary. It was exciting—and terrifying. Marc's book was due out in October. The baby was due in November, and here we were in July starting a new law firm.

Sometime in August, the *New York Times Magazine* ran a story about Tay Sachs, a disease that fatally affects babies born to Jews from Eastern Europe if both parents have the defective gene. I immediately called the one hospital in the New York City area that tested for Tay Sachs, Albert Einstein in the Bronx. The person who answered asked if I was pregnant. When I said I was—six months—she said there was nothing they could do. If they tested me and Marc and we were both carriers, making it likely that the fetus would be afflicted with the horrible and fatal disease, they would have provided me with reason to get an abortion—legal, of course, but immoral to them and their Orthodox Jewish leanings. Completely unnerved and furious, I shouted into the phone that they had no right to impose their religious beliefs on us. After I hung up, Marc decided that he'd get tested to see if he was a carrier. If he was, we'd figure out later how to get me tested. If he wasn't, then the baby would be okay, because we both had to be carriers for our child to inherit the disease.

So Marc embarked on the long subway journey to the outer Bronx, and finally, three days later, we learned that the results were negative. Apparently, testing for Tay Sachs is now perfunctory. In our day, the lack of testing led to some very tragic consequences.

McGraw-Hill was planning the publication of Marc's book for the last week of October so that it would be in bookstores for the Christmas rush. The thought was that maybe some men would buy it, but certainly women would for husbands and boyfriends. Our baby was due in late November, and we figured that Marc would be through with his publicity tour, which was scheduled to last about two weeks.

By October, we had almost everything needed for the baby except a boy's name. We'd searched through innumerable baby-name books and had come up with Alexis for a girl. Now we really needed to figure out a good boy's name, and I needed to get the fact that this child could very well be male. I knew I'd love him, but I also felt lost at the thought of raising him. I would refuse to let him play football. I hated boy toys, like toy guns and swords, so he'd have to get along without them.

Amidst all the goings-on with Marc's book, clients, Lamaze classes and finding the perfect baby names, we received a call from *People* magazine. Would Marc and I consent to an interview about us, his book and our soon-to-be baby?

Shortly thereafter, a reporter from *People* magazine arrived at our Tudor City apartment, accompanied by her photographer. They took pictures of Marc and me in our living room and on our bed, in various Lamaze positions. After the interview, we all trooped to our office so they could get pictures of us at work. Finally, we went outside. It was rush hour, and without my noticing, they got a telling photograph—typical of us and our relationship—of me with my huge stomach waving frantically for a cab, while Marc looked on, more relaxed but somewhat bemused.

My mother had announced that her present to us was a baby nurse for three months. That was great news, because I knew they were expensive. We started calling around to various agencies to see who would have a really good nurse available by November 28. The first response was from someone named Happy Gannon. She came to visit, a short, stocky, elderly Irish nanny, full of energy, with a winning chortle and a self-assurance that made us feel we'd all be in good hands. She'd been doing this kind of work for thirty years. When I asked her what besides directly caring for the baby she'd be willing to do around the apartment, she looked at me quizzically. "Whatever needs to be done, ma'am," she replied. I had no idea what that meant, but it sounded good.

I had asked my brother if he'd have a book party for *The Male Machine*. He agreed. Marc and I got out the lists and with some help from Richard put together a great group, all sympathetic to the cause that men should get in touch with their feelings, be involved with their children and lose the machismo they had been brainwashed into afflicting on the world. And so, late in October, as I walked into the party, all eyes and many hands seemed to reach out to touch my huge stomach. The guests celebrated with us both Marc's book and our pending new arrival. Then began Marc's two-week book tour. The schedule called for Marc to start on the West Coast and work his way back East.

By the end of the first week in November, Marc was back. On the morning of Friday, November 8, right after I awakened and started to get out of bed, water began pouring out of me. I shrieked in surprise, and Marc, who was in the bathroom shaving, came running out. The day proceeded with slow contractions. The next day, November 9, began with pain, terror, chaos and finally an emergency C-section—with no anesthetic, because it might hurt the baby—at 2:49 a.m. Before I was put out of my agony, I heard the doctor say, "It's a healthy baby girl with a full head of black hair."

The next thing I heard was Marc's voice, saying, "She's fine. She weighs six pounds, thirteen ounces, and she's twenty-one and a half inches long. *You're* going to be fine." He'd seen the baby and seemed thrilled. "When can I hold her, have her, see her?" I kept asking, with the little strength I had, the various nurses milling

In our new Madison
Avenue law office—
Fasteau and Feigen—
October 1974

about. They ignored me, until finally one came over to me on my gurney and asked if I was ready to see my baby. I couldn't withhold my excitement, despite the absolutely extraordinary pain from the fresh incision and the pressure pack on top of it.

They wheeled me out of the recovery room and down a long hall, through two sets of swinging doors, to the newborn baby ward. I stared at the rows of bassinets, some with pink tags, others with blue. My feminist antennae were aroused, of course, but at that point, I had little energy for a fight with the maternity administrators. Then a nurse appeared behind the glass wall, picked out a pink-tagged bassinet from the second row and gently pushed it to the first row, right in front of us. I lay there staring, amazed, in love and awe. They had already told us that because she was a cesarean, we couldn't hold her until she was twelve hours old—standard practice in those days.

Marc was exhausted. He'd been up for almost twenty-four hours. As he left for home and a few hours of sleep, he told me to call him when they brought the baby in. Meanwhile, I lay in my room in a state of amazement, and pain too intense for sleep. They didn't want to give me any painkillers yet.

Around 1:00 p.m., the nurse came to tell me that they'd be bringing my baby into the room soon. I was deliriously excited. Reaching for the phone to call Marc took every ounce of my strength. He arrived just as she did, and together we fussed over her. Finally it became apparent that her diaper needed changing. The bassinet they'd brought her in had supplies galore, so Marc took our not yet officially named baby and changed her.

Later that day, the husband of the woman in the room next to mine could be heard bragging on the phone to relatives that his wife had virtually dropped the kid, the birth had been so easy. "What a woman she was," he crowed. I felt tears rolling down my face, convinced that I wasn't a real woman because I had to be cut open to deliver my own baby into the world. Marc spent a lot of time during those early days reassuring me that indeed I was a real woman. Recently I have seen notices of various self-help groups of mothers who've had cesareans springing up on bulletin boards and in women's magazines. Ever since my own childbirth experience, I've had terribly negative feelings about home births, even the use of midwives. Everything had gone so well for me until virtually the last minutes before Alexis was born. But if I hadn't had top-notch medical care, my daughter could easily have been born with severe brain damage from the "fetal distress" into which she had so suddenly descended.

On the Monday after Alexis (now officially named) was lifted out of me, I was roused by a huge, stern-looking nurse. What was I doing lying around in bed? I was a mother now. She unhooked the catheter, apparently on my doctor's orders took the liquids-only sign off my door and told me to get out of bed. She had a German accent and was a little scary, so, very slowly, I followed her commands and soon was sitting in the vinyl armchair in a corner of the room. Then our pediatrician came in and Alexis was summoned.

Sidney Cohlan was the head of pediatrics at University Hospital. I could see why, after a few minutes. I had a million questions, most of which he patiently answered, but then he said, "I want to show you something." Holding a naked Alexis by his two thumbs (which she was fiercely gripping) so that her tiny feet were just barely touching the bed, he made me watch my newborn infant taking what looked like real steps. See, he said, they're programmed; they're going to grow up and do these things despite you. When I proceeded to ask him about the kinds of foods she should be eating and by when, he responded that newborn babies in Portugal start their lives on Portuguese fish soup. Did I really think it mattered? I was impressed into relative silence. I got his message and it stayed with me. Over the years, as I would hear mothers, especially, fussing over various issues like disposable versus cloth diapers (before the days of environmental concern), I would realize that it was all silly. Our children would flourish if we focused on what really mattered as we gradually raised them into adulthood.

I was scheduled to stay in the hospital for eight days. Although weak, I was delighted that by the time Gloria and Frank came to visit, I was able to shuffle, bent-over, down the hall to show off Alexis to them. I still thought my idea of their having a baby too, so the children could keep each other company as they grew up, was a good one, but Gloria just laughed at me. She and Frank did, however, agree to be Alexis's spiritual "god" parents. (Years later I learned that Gloria had agreed to play that role for many of her friends' children.)

Soon we settled back into the apartment, our dining room—and Marc's book-writing room—now converted into a room Alexis would share with Happy Gannon, the baby-nurse. Marc continued on his interrupted book tour; I lay on the couch in the living room, under strict doctor's orders not to return to work—or climb stairs—for at least six weeks. That meant that Happy was my nurse too, because I couldn't get to the kitchen, which was upstairs. It was a wonderful luxury.

The arrangement with Happy was that she'd live with us five nights a week and then have her weekends to herself. The end of

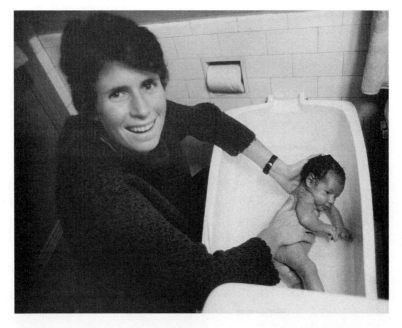

Alexis, ten days old, getting a bath, November 1974

that first Friday came, and Happy cheerfully waved goodbye as she exited our apartment. There we were, the three of us, all alone together for the first time. It was scary.

A big believer in cloth diapers, Happy had made arrangements with a diaper service, but Marc wanted everything as simple as possible. He immediately bought boxes of Pampers. Then he took to walking around with Alexis cradled in one arm as though she were a football. Alexis became all-consuming emotionally. And this state—of a mother totally loving her baby while feeling that she's on the front lines of the revolution, not to mention working full-time—has been a state in which I've lived for a long time.

The week after we left the hospital, we had an appointment with the pediatrician. This time, it was just me and Alexis. Shirley Stone, the pediatrician partner and wife of the head pediatrician, Sidney Cohlan, had—to my delight, because she was a woman with a sense of humor—taken over the primary responsibility for Alexis. Everything about the exam was going well until I noticed a small lump in Alexis's lower abdomen. I asked the doctor what it was. She took one look and excused herself. Drs. Cohlan and Stone returned to us together; he put his hand on the lump, feeling it carefully. Finally, he spoke: "I'm pretty sure that this is a hernia." I told him I'd never heard of girls having hernias, and he responded that Alexis's ovary was poking through her abdominal wall. It was, no doubt, something she had been born with. He suggested that we wait until she was about a year old and then have it operated on.

When I told Marc the news, we decided to get a second opinion from a pediatric surgeon. Within days, the three of us were heading to New York Hospital and the office of a little round stern-faced doctor with no sense of humor. He examined Alexis for about two minutes, then announced that she had two hernias, one on either side. He said that he'd like to operate when she was four months old—he definitely didn't want to wait a year. We were impressed that he'd found the other hernia, but in the meantime, the doctor asked Marc if he could talk to him alone. I stayed there with Alexis, dressing her as she wiggled. When we left, Marc relayed that the doctor had said it's very, very unusual for girls to have double hernias and that they wanted to do a Barr cell test. It dawned on me that the doctor was saying that he thought Alexis might be a boy.

I felt as though all my feminist battles had finally caught up with me. I didn't believe in god's wrath, but it seemed as though somehow I, a feminist, was being punished with the news that my totally female-seeming daughter might be a son. "So," I managed to squeak out, "what do they want to do about it?" They wanted, Marc replied, to take a throat culture, let it grow and see what the cells looked like in three weeks. My panic must have been evident, because Marc started reassuring me that the only reason all this was happening was that New York Hospital is Cornell's teaching hospital, so they want their interns and residents to do all sorts of tests, even unnecessary ones, including something as ridiculous as this. When I asked why the doctor hadn't wanted to give me the news too, Marc, probably trying to be diplomatic, responded that the doctor knew it might upset me and he didn't want to cause unnecessary alarm. It sounded patronizing to me.

We agreed to take Alexis back there again so they could do the test. During that three-week period, I tried to ignore my feelings of panic whenever I looked at her naked, so clearly a girl. Finally, Marc got a call from the doctor. He was terribly embarrassed, but one of their students had let the cells dry out. They couldn't get a reading. Would we mind bringing her in again?

In we trudged and another three-week period began. By now, I was trying to make a joke out of the whole thing—about my being punished for being a feminist—but I still wasn't laughing. Another few weeks passed; another call. This time, Marc reported, having trouble hiding his own amusement, they'd dropped the culture. Would we mind going through the whole thing again? I wasn't amused. The weather was terrible, and I was positive that my daughter was a girl. But in we went—again. At the end of that third three-week period, the more-than-welcome news was delivered: Alexis was a girl.

By this time, she was almost old enough for the surgery. The date was set without my realizing that a big feminist conference at which I was scheduled to speak and run workshops was being held on the third day after Alexis's operation. By the time I found out, I couldn't reschedule either one, but I figured it would all work out.

We got to the hospital early in the morning, and they came and took Alexis away on a little gurney with sides so she couldn't roll off. Marc and I sat waiting, near her bed in the baby ward. About an hour later, they wheeled a smiling baby Alexis toward us. She couldn't have been in much pain, I figured. Although she was fine, they wanted her to stay for four days. That was okay with us, because we, too, wanted to be sure everything would be all right.

The hardest part was what was going on around us. Mothers— and it was all mothers—were sitting next to the beds of their children, many of whom were hooked up to monitors. Some had had brain surgery; others heart operations. Nothing as ridiculous as hernias. We felt so sympathetic, in fact, that we tried not to bother the nurse, but she later admonished us that they were there for us too. The nurse asked me if I'd want to spend the nights at the hospital with Alexis. I responded affirmatively, but then I remembered that I would have to be out of town on the third night because of the conference. Marc, we explained, would stay that night. The nurse looked at me as though I were crazy. "No he won't," she said. "Only mothers are allowed to stay." I think both of us said the same thing in response, something like "You've got to be kidding." When we heard the words "hospital policy," that was enough for us to kick into high gear. We virtually attacked the hospital administrator's office. Once they realized what they were up against, they agreed that Marc could sleep in the nurses' lounge. That way, he wouldn't be around all the mothers, who they assumed would be in various states of undress. We knew this was ridiculous. Those women were completely involved with their own children. No one was taking off clothes, putting on nightgowns, or doing anything else that required privacy. Neither of us thought it fair to mother, child, or absent fathers that only mothers could stay with their children. So, of course, we were making the broader point as well, and hoped it got across.

Unbeknownst to me, at the same time, in the mid-1970s, Ruth Ginsburg was waging a similar battle. She was teaching at Columbia Law School, and she would receive monthly calls from the head of her young son's school. Would she please come in to meet and discuss her child's most recent escapade? "One afternoon," she has noted, "when I felt particularly weary, I responded, 'This child has two parents. Please alternate calls for conferences.' After that," she continued, "although I observed no quick change in my son's behavior, the telephone calls came barely once a semester. There was more reluctance to take a father away from his work, much more reluctance." And writing about this in 1997, she added, "There still is."[1]

Ruth then quoted a representative of the Women's Legal Defense Fund: "A woman who does less than everything for her child is seen as a terrible mother; a man who does more than nothing is praised as a wonderful father."[2] This resonates with me, because I always felt that if I didn't do everything for Alexis that could possibly be done, I wasn't a good mother. On the other hand, Marc, although he certainly did his share, rarely has felt guilt over not doing as much as possible. He's been able to be much more philosophical, and that's probably because society's expectations of him are much less.

One day before my six-week imposed convalescence was up, I returned to the office. By this time, I was feeling fine, and Alexis and Happy had their routine down. Happy made sure that Alexis's nap was quite late in the afternoon, so she'd be awake when Marc and I got home every evening from the office. We soon recognized how profoundly good that was for all of us, because we could play together every night, and Alexis wouldn't conk out until about 9:00 p.m. I had had no guilt about returning to work after Alexis was born, only an enormous desire to run home—literally—every day at about 5:30. I could finish whatever I was working on in our apartment after Alexis went to sleep.

By the time Alexis was two and a half months old, Happy had her sleeping through the nights. So as far as she was concerned, her days of living in were over. That meant that when Marc and I got home, Happy would have dinner for the three of us ready. Then she would leave and return by 7:00 a.m. the next day. The fact that Happy was still with us was due to the fact that Marc and I were earning enough to pay her salary. We were very lucky to be able to, unlike the millions of families who need the income of both parents and can't afford to pay for babysitters. That was the reason the Women's Movement was lobbying so intensively for universal twenty-four-hour child care.

Headlines in the *New York Times* screamed out one day in early spring that a substance called dioxin had been found in furniture recently imported from Italy. Apparently there had been an explosion in a plant somewhere in Southern Italy, which had caused the emission of this deadly chemical. In the middle of the night after that article appeared, Marc shot out of bed and ran from our room to Alexis's. I found him with a flashlight, underneath the desk we'd purchased recently so that we could bring work home, now that Happy's bed was no longer in Alexis's room. Soon he appeared in our room, looking like hell. What had been bothering him all day and had awakened him that night was his hunch that the desk we'd just purchased might be from the same region of Italy in which the explosion had occurred. The desk, now in our baby's room, could transmit through the air a horrible cancer. All we could do was suffer a sleepless night until we could research the next day whether the desk had been made and shipped out of Italy before or after the explosion. If before, there was nothing to worry about; if after, there was a lot.

To our enormous relief, after a few phone calls and searches through inventory records of the furniture store where the desk had been purchased, Marc learned that although the desk was indeed from the same region of Italy as the explosion, it had been shipped out of that country before the problem occurred.

That incident impressed me for one very good reason. Usually, we hear about maternal instinct and protectiveness being so fierce that women will do anything to save their children (like single-handedly lifting cars trapping a child underneath that they would never otherwise be able to budge). It's supposed to be instinctual, a gift only mothers have. Well, in fact, Marc's *paternal* instinct was at work overtime that day; he'd been right to worry about the dioxin issue, something I had ignored.

We continued to accept invitations to speak around the country. Now we had more to talk about than the ERA or even our feminist marriage: we had our baby. We could speak from experience about how important it was for both parents to be completely and equally involved. It was fun listening to Marc talk about what was going on for him, since we tended to take our daily lives for granted and didn't spend much time talking to each other about our feelings. While we were away on these short lecture trips, Happy, of course, would stay with Alexis.

In September 1976, at the age of twenty-two months, Alexis

entered nursery school—five days a week, half day. Happy wasn't at all excited about it, but Marc and I were. Unfortunately, we lost Happy not long after, because she was, *Happy Gannon, making sure that Alexis is ready for her second-birthday party*

after all, a baby nurse and this baby was now in school. That marked the beginning of an endless stream of nannies, house-keepers and au pairs. None came close to Happy, but Alexis was a very friendly, cheerful child, and to each, in succession, she became attached—from the Israeli dancer to the rural South-erner, from the Colombian to the Ecuadoran and the black male ballet dancer. The worst was Mary, from one of the Caribbean Islands.

One day, Donna de Varona, the former Olympic gold medal swimmer, was visiting. She'd had a long day and asked for a vodka with orange juice. We had some hard liquor left over from a recent party, so I opened our liquor cabinet, took out the vodka bottle and stared. It was completely empty. This went on as I took out bottle after bottle of all kinds of liquor I never would have checked out until the next party. Every single bottle was empty. Thus I discovered our first alcoholic nanny. Chicken that I was, although I knew she had to be fired on the spot I called Marc, who was still at the office, and asked him to come home. Donna, who had settled for just the orange juice, waited with me for Marc to arrive. He did, and after Donna left, I cowered in Alexis's room, pretending to be cheerfully playing with her. I hated to fire people. Mary wailed about being let go, promising never to drink another drop, but she'd been lying to us every morning about the reason for the headaches that had rendered her nearly useless in getting Alexis ready for school. It was scary to think about what could have happened to Alexis when she was in the care of someone without most of her faculties.

Even when our various caretakers had their wits about them, there was some question about the quality of those wits. I arrived home from the office early one day to find a four-year-old Alexis peering, as she leaned forward, through the legs of a window washer and out the window of our seventh-floor apartment. When I found that nanny, she was asleep in her room at the other end of the apartment. That was it for her.

Of course, all these caretakers had come with high references from agencies that are supposed to check their credentials. If anything, our experience highlights again the need for responsible loving child care for children of working parents. We ourselves needed what we'd been lobbying for since 1970.

During the summer between Alexis's nursery school and kindergarten years, we rented a house in Bridgehampton. One day Marc and I were relaxing on the beach, having left Alexis at a friend's house nearby. A man with a ball was trying to round up enough people for a volleyball game. Marc decided to play, and after he got up, I followed. I wanted to play and told the man with the ball to count me in too. He looked at me as though I were crazy and said, "No women." I was furious (hard to believe there was any more of that emotion left in me). It was a showdown. More people arrived. Some of the women sat down to watch their men. One or two others decided they wanted to play too. When

At the house we rented in
Bridgehampton, 1977

the man with the ball realized that he was
outnumbered, he took his ball, turned his
back and left. Unfortunately, many men don't want us to play in
their games or on their courts (unless that court is a bed).

It soon came time to take Alexis's schooling seriously. Nursery
school days were over, kindergarten was upon us, and we had a
multitude of schools near us on the Upper East Side, where we'd
recently moved. That a school had sports and other activities to
keep the kids occupied until at least 4:00 p.m. was one priority,
because the more time Alexis spent with her peers, the less
would be spent with housekeepers. Having somewhat narrowed
the search for the perfect school, we now faced a big decision.
Most of these schools were single-sex.

I had attended the Girls' Latin School in Chicago until I was in
the fourth grade. Then it merged with the Boys' Latin School and

Alexis wanted to be part of the conversation between Gloria and me (1978).

classes were all coed, until I entered Vassar. The only reason I went to an all-female college was that the Seven Sisters were supposed to be the best schools for women—as good as any in the male-only Ivy League. I remembered back to my first few months at Harvard Law School and wondered whether they would have been easier if I had been accustomed in college to classes in which men tried to dominate. Both Marc and I wanted Alexis to have boys as friends, not just as untouchable romantic heroes whom she would encounter on weekends. To make sure our instincts were right, we interviewed some of the admissions officers at the girls' schools. One was particularly notable. "What," I asked the head of admissions at Brearley, the most intellectually elite of the girls' schools, "would I tell Alexis when she asked me why there were no boys in her school?" The cold response was "Tell her that's just the way it is."

We knew then that Alexis would go to a coed school. I couldn't justify her being separated from boys based on an argument that she'd do better with them not around. It seemed too patronizing: the arguments that girls can't be themselves around boys or show that they have brains and do well in math, that they need to be protected from being humiliated, from having their bras snapped, from having trouble with numbers.

I loved math and science. I had never been intimidated by the boys. In fact, I remembered the day I got my report card in eighth grade. It was five A+'s and one A. A gang of boys, all of whom were near the top of our class, cornered me, clearly jealous but still trying to tease me. I was proud and not in the least bit flustered. When it came time for year-end awards, I received the "leadership cup," given to only one person in the seventh and eighth grades. I certainly didn't worry about whether the boys would be upset that a girl had won. This was the attitude I wanted to foster in my then four-year-old daughter. That meant we had one choice among the schools located anywhere near us. Dalton. And so, in the fall of 1979, Alexis entered kindergarten, unaware of all the fuss that had surrounded our decision about the school she would attend.

Chapter 5

CLOSING DOORS

By 1977, I was intellectually restless. The many matrimonial cases that came the way of our law firm were depressing. I decided to enroll in Columbia's Ph.D. program in political theory. I wanted to study revolutionary theory, comparing revolutions of the past with the Women's Movement, which seemed to me the most profound, and write a thesis about feminist political theory. Taking classes part-time, I also spent significant hours in the office so I could keep on earning a living. At the end of the semester, I was anointed an Honorary President's Fellow, which meant that I could take any class in all of Columbia University—for free.

Not long thereafter, I received a call from the head of the network news department at ABC. They were holding auditions for the position of network legal anchor and asked me to prepare two ninety-second segments on issues currently in the news. For one of the segments, I chose the *Rideout* case, in which a man had raped his wife and the state of Idaho had refused to consider his act real rape because the wife was considered to have "consented" to the rape simply by being married to her rapist. ABC didn't call me back, but preparing for the audition had taught me how much you can squeeze into ninety seconds.

My law practice, by now, consisted largely of matrimonial cases. A lot of the calls were from fathers who wanted custody—or at least joint custody—of their children. That was a direct result of the chapter "Family and Fatherhood" in Marc's book. It was, I think, the first time that the notion was advanced that men should have an equal right to (and responsibility for) child custody and care.[1]

One distraught father asked if I could get a court to overturn a part of his divorce decree that had granted his wife full custody of their son. The court had refused to take seriously his request for joint custody. And now he had evidence that his wife was verbally abusing their six-year-old and that she was so enmeshed in her personal love affairs that she spent little time with the child. I took the case.

The first day of the trial came, and I laid out the reasons that my client was the better parent. When it was the wife's turn, her lawyer took another tack, describing in detail some of my client's sexual liaisons. At the end of the first day, I told the judge that I would need more time for redirect the next day. I'd have to put on more about the wife's personal life than I'd originally thought necessary.

At about 9:00 that night, the phone rang. It was the attorney for the wife. She told me that if I put into evidence what she thought I was going to, she wondered how my bid for Congress, which she'd incorrectly heard I was planning, would go given rumors she'd heard about the sexual liaison I'd had with a woman some years back. This was the first time in my life I'd ever been threatened with blackmail. I may have acted nonchalant on the phone, but when I got off I nervously described the incident to Marc. His reaction was that I should notify the state bar. She could be disbarred, certainly censured, for what she'd done.

The next morning, as I walked to my side of the counsel table, I made a point of passing directly behind the wife's lawyer. "What you did last night could get you in a lot of trouble with the state bar. I'm ignoring your threats." She looked thunderstruck. In the end, despite everything, my client lost the case (the judge didn't think the mother was bad enough), but shortly thereafter he got a call from his former wife. She was sick of the responsibility and wanted him to have custody!

Another case I had involved a twenty-eight-year-old woman lawyer. She'd been diagnosed with pelvic inflammatory disease, and she thought the IUD she was using was causing scar tissue in her fallopian tubes. She had had a boyfriend; they'd had lots of unprotected sex and she'd never conceived. I warned my new client that she should be prepared for some rough questions about her sex life when the IUD manufacturer took her deposition. I also told her to have a laparoscopy so that we could prove that scar tissue had indeed formed. When I sensed her reluctance, I did some research and told her what I'd discovered: doctors could remove the scar tissue and possibly successfully suture the fallopian tubes together so that eggs could travel down them as they should. But my client refused to have the procedure. Finally, I realized that she actually didn't want to know what might be the awful truth—that she might never be able to have children. That case ended up getting settled, not for a lot of money.

In late 1977, Karen Burstein, still one of only two female members of the New York State Senate, called and made a strong case for my running for the State Senate. Neither she nor Carol Bellamy was running for reelection, but they wanted at least one woman to run for the Senate as they left it. I had come to know and respect Carol and Karen when I'd served as their counsel during the hearings on the New York State Equal Rights Amendment a few years earlier, so I considered their request. I would have to win the Democratic primary in September 1978. The Senate seat in my district, which covered the East Side of Manhattan, had been held for years by a rich Republican, Roy Goodman, who the summer before, when he was a candidate for mayor, had received less than 5 percent of the vote, a sure sign of his lack of popularity citywide.

Marc and I talked it over, and soon rumors in the press about my running began to appear. After I announced my candidacy, volunteers appeared, including Carly Simon, whose daughter, Sally, had been Alexis's best friend in nursery school. The *New York Post* erred when they wrote that Carly would sing at one of my fund-raisers, so I called and asked them to print a correction. They did, but then they got the date of the fund-raiser wrong, so I called again for another correction. Those three columns were the kind of valuable publicity that I never could have afforded. But then I hadn't really thought through very carefully how my campaign was going to be financed. And soon what had been a field of six Democratic candidates had narrowed down to me and William Woodward III. His was a multimillion-dollar, blue-blooded lineage, and he didn't hesitate to dip into his own very deep pockets. Midway through the campaign, I learned from a rich potential contributor to my campaign that Woodward had called and asked her merely not to give money to either of us. In this way, many potential contributors who knew both Woodward and me were neutralized, leaving me with very little in the way of a campaign fund while he had plenty of his own money to use any way he wanted.

One day, as I was approaching a subway station for a rush-hour stint of handing out my campaign leaflets, I glanced around at the four corners of the intersection at Seventy-seventh and Lexington Avenue. On each there was a youngish blond man, with a blue suit and a mustache. Woodward had hired look-alikes to hand out his literature! The voters would all think they'd met the actual candidate. Even if I'd had the money I'd never find one, let alone more, look-alikes, nor would I engage in what I considered Woodward's kind of immoral campaign high jinks.

Starting in March, I went into full swing, leaving the law firm in Marc's capable hands. Each day, I'd load myself down with campaign literature and start walking from Ninety-sixth Street and the East River to Fourteenth and Fifth. This would last until September! I continually exhausted myself; my feet hurt and my back was in spasms, but I wanted to meet the voters. Then in the evenings I went to the Democratic club meetings. By the end of the club endorsement process, I had received endorsements from five of the nine Democratic clubs in the district; Woodward got the other four. Although Woodward and I—both liberal Democrats—agreed on most issues, there was one that separated us. While I adamantly opposed federal funding of parochial schools, Woodward embraced it.

Soon it was time to register as a candidate with the City Board

*Getting ready to pose for my
first campaign photo. Alexis
is about three and a half.*

*Campaigning with two
Democratic Party leaders
on the East Side of
Manhattan*

of Elections. I wrote out my name, Brenda Feigen Fasteau, and shortly thereafter received a letter from the Board of Elections informing me that there were too many letters in my name to fit on the ballot. I could call myself Brenda F. Fasteau or B. Feigen Fasteau or even B. Feigen F. Of course, none of these was acceptable for me. I wanted to be known by my real name, and Marc decided to take the case to federal district court. Soon the ruling came down—in my favor.

The court ordered the Board of Elections to fit my full name on the ballot just like Helen Gahagan Douglas's and Franklin Delano Roosevelt's! In fact, the Board of Elections figured it out as soon as the court made its ruling. They put the letters of my name in a slightly smaller font, a suggestion Marc had made in his brief. This case was precedent-setting, because the same thing would happen to almost any woman who used both her own and her husband's last names. Before the *New York Times* went on strike for the duration of the campaign, its very last editorial was all about my name and how my name on the ballot should be the same as whatever names I was known by.

The name issue wouldn't go away. Alexis had been named Alexis Feigen Fasteau on her birth certificate. But by the time she was in kindergarten, she was growing upset that the teachers were referring to her as Alexis Fasteau. She complained about it to me, wanting them not to leave out Feigen, and that began a six-month-long experiment of writing her name with a hyphen between the Feigen and the Fasteau. (I insisted that she fully understand what she was doing.) She happily kept using her hyphenated last name. Eventually, convinced that she knew what she was getting into, Marc and I agreed that Alexis's last name would be Feigen-Fasteau, although the name on her birth certificate couldn't be changed until she was eighteen and able legally to give her consent.

Election Day for the primary came finally after a very long summer. We had invited to our apartment that evening all the volunteers in my campaign. I was so exhausted that Marc and I stayed in the bedroom alone, occasionally joined by a few really close friends, to watch the returns. By 11:00 p.m., the results were obvious: Woodward was maintaining a 52 to 48 percent lead over me in every part of the district from Fourteenth Street to Ninety-sixth Street. I went into our large, rambling living room and told my friends that I was conceding.

Then, at 2:10 a.m. the phone rang. It was UPI and they wanted to know, for the national editions of a number of papers across the country, what it felt like to have run along with four millionaires—not only Woodward but the man who would now be his opponent in the general election, the Republican Roy Goodman, as well as the Congressional candidates, Democrat Carter Burden and Republican Bill Green, both scions of zillionaire American dynasties. My answer was hardly polite: "How do you think it feels?" I blurted out. "Lousy!" And I hung up the phone. The East Side of Manhattan, dubbed the Silk Stocking District, had lived up to its name.

As I began to regain some "leisure" time to contemplate what I had just been through, I couldn't understand what I had been thinking. What would I have done if I had won? Would I have abandoned Marc and Alexis for five days each week to venture up to Albany, one of my least favorite cities in the country? Did I harbor the illusion that they would have moved up there? I had acted like an automaton. I wished Marc had asked me not to do it, but I wasn't sure that he'd focused on the realities of my winning either. Then I wondered what that said about our relationship.

In the spring of 1979, Marc, Alexis and I went skiing in Aspen. On the skis I'd had for years was embossed the name Brenda Feigen. So I decided that for that two-week period, I'd try just being Brenda Feigen. I liked it. I was sick of being confused for a French Catholic, even though Marc is Jewish. By the time we returned from Colorado, I had decided to go back to my birth name. Similarly, Marc, who'd adopted my name as his middle name about a year after we'd married, would now just be Marc Fasteau. Alexis continued using her hyphenated last name.

Frank Thomas, Gloria's friend, had been given a grant by the Rockefeller Foundation to conduct a study on U.S. policy toward

South Africa. Then, just as that grant came through, Frank was appointed president of the Ford Foundation. He asked Marc to direct the study on South Africa. Marc's background before law school was in foreign policy, so he was eager to accept the offer. That left me alone at our firm. Marc was really busy with his new responsibilities, so when I wasn't in the office I spent time with a friend I'd met during my campaign working on a screenplay. Eventually, I showed my draft to Gloria's former fiancé and my friend, movie director and writer Robert Benton. He told me that I had talent and that I should keep writing, whether or not this particular screenplay sold. But the more I thought about it, the more I didn't like the idea of a career that consisted mostly of being alone in a room, interacting with only (in those days) a typewriter.

One summer day in 1980, it came to me. I should become an entertainment lawyer. The following Monday, I drew up a list of lawyers in the field and began making calls. I reached Lee Steiner at Hess, Segall, Guterman, Pelz & Steiner, and a few days later I was ushered into his cigar-smoke-filled office in the Helmsley Building, high above Park Avenue. He grilled me about whether I was sure I wanted to go from being a partner in my own firm to being an associate in his. After all, I was thirty-six years old. I told him that I'd do whatever it would take to change fields,

Gloria and I chatting at my brother's pool, Katonah, New York, 1980

and so, having talked my way into a new job at a very low salary, I began closing down Fasteau and Feigen.

My immediate "boss" was a junior partner who worked for the clients Lee brought in. He had a sour face and no sense of humor. Because Hess, Segall prided itself on representing production companies, not "talent," all I really learned from him was how to draft definitions of "net profits" so that no actor, director or writer would ever see a penny in profits.

In the fall of 1981, full of excitement, as usual, about all her classes and activities, Alexis started second grade. One day she came home upset. The girls were required to take dance that fall, while the boys got to do sports. She didn't like dance, and she thought the whole thing very unfair. She wanted to know what I would do, but I held my tongue, sensing that this could be a defining moment in her young life. I wasn't sure, I said, demurring, but I'd definitely help her if she needed me. That night, she thought about her predicament and then, after calling a friend, came into our room with her decision. She was going to write a petition and get the other girls to sign it. Abbie, the friend on the phone, had already agreed. I told her that I thought it was a terrific idea and asked if she needed me for anything. "No," she said assuredly, "I'll write it myself. You can look at it after." A while later, she presented me with a draft of her petition. I suggested that she take it to school in the morning.

Alexis's petition was a success. She announced to me several weeks later that girls could play volleyball instead of dance, but that until winter—and only until winter—they'd have to use the smaller gym in which their dance class had been scheduled.

Jane Alexander and I had remained fast friends after our meeting at the Harvard Club reception in honor of her performance in *First Monday in October*—about the first woman on the Supreme Court. And now Jane and Gena Rowlands were starring in *A Circle of Love* for ABC. The story was based on a Texas case. Two women, both divorced mothers with children, had fallen in love with each other and moved their families in together. The husbands each brought a lawsuit seeking custody of the children on the grounds that lesbians are unfit mothers. And the court in Texas agreed with the fathers, stipulating that unless the mothers separated and never saw each other again, custody should be awarded to the fathers. It was an outrageous ruling, and the movie version was a heartrending account of the story. It was accurate except that ABC allowed Jane and Gena to touch each other only three times in the movie and only in non-sexual ways.

Everything seemed to be okay between Marc and me until the Wednesday before Thanksgiving of that year. Something Marc said caused me to reply, "You wouldn't have said that unless you're having an affair." To that, the cruelest words I had ever heard him utter came out of his mouth: "I am, and I want out."

I was stunned and crushed; then panic set in. My marriage might be ending and Marc, Alexis and I were due to fly to Falls Church, Virginia, the next morning to celebrate Thanksgiving with his parents, as well as my mother and my stepfather, Joe. Would we still go? Was he serious enough for us to tell them it was all over? What about Alexis? Would we tell her? I asked him who the other woman was, but he wouldn't tell me. I got the feeling that he'd been thinking about this for a while. I pleaded for him to reconsider, for us to go into counseling. Maybe it was just a midlife crisis. To everything I said he was either silent or negative. He refused to see a therapist with me. He had decided that our marriage was over.

It seemed like more than mere coincidence that Marc had made this decision just as he was turning forty. When we finally had a conversation, we agreed this would be a trial separation—I certainly wanted it to be only that—and that we wouldn't at that point discuss with Alexis the problems we were having.

Before I had any inkling that Marc was leaving, I had asked him to get names of analysts for me from his own doctor. The therapist in Cambridge had been helpful, but he told me that I had more work to do and that eventually analysis would be a good idea if I ever wanted to delve more deeply into my own psyche. So on the Monday after the worst Thanksgiving weekend of my life, I called Dr. Harriette Kaley.* All I knew about her was that she had a child and had been referred by someone with impeccable credentials. Because Alexis was so important to me, I wanted a doctor who would understand the parent-child relationship. Dr. Kaley must have detected how upset I was, because she asked if I would like to make an appointment for the next day. I said yes. And although usually I ponder important decisions, this time I went with my gut. I knew when I met her that she could help.

Although we were supposed to be separated and Marc had rented an apartment nearby, he never moved into it. Nor did we have a separation agreement. On Valentine's Day of 1982, from a pay phone in the restaurant where he and I were having dinner, Marc broke up with the woman he'd been seeing. Late in the spring of 1982, Marc and I were invited to the world premiere of the movie 9 to 5. Afterward, there was a huge party, and everyone was there, from the stars—Lily Tomlin, Dolly Parton and Jane Fonda—to the entire staff of Ms. magazine. The two most striking things about that evening were Dolly Parton's platform-like breasts, covered but sticking out so far that she really did look like a freak of nature, and how tightly I clung to Marc's arm, as though I were trying physically to keep him from leaving me. At that moment, I really wanted him back but felt an inexorable tug pulling him away from me.

By summer, Marc made up his mind that he was moving out. After Alexis left for camp, he took a small apartment in the East Fifties, not too far from where we'd been living on Park Avenue and Eighty-first Street since Alexis was thirteen months old. It was a long summer for me, every weekend alone in the Sag Harbor house we had rented together. We decided that when Alexis returned from camp, Marc would tell her that we were separated.

* I get angry when I read various feminist tracts trashing psychoanalysis. It isn't about penis envy or the other sexist mistakes Freud made. It is about being aware of one's unconscious self. I was out of touch with mine before I met Dr. Kaley, who continually urged me to articulate what I was really feeling. Feminists ought to come down harder on cigarettes, Prozac and other drugs that help disguise unpleasant emotions and think more clearly about their real issues with psychoanalysis, like how painful experiencing certain feelings can be, and, therefore, how easy it is to put down that which "causes" pain.

Nancy Baker, my oldest friend—from when I was four—joins my birthday festivities.

We agreed on joint custody, and by that summer Fasteau and Feigen, the marriage, came to an end.

The intertwining of Marc's and my lives had been so sweeping and intense that it was difficult for me to tell where the boundaries between us were. Marc was the only man on whom I had been able to count and the only one who truly knew me. I still loved him deeply. But I also realized that a certain intimacy had been missing in our relationship.

By 1984, I was about to embark on a new phase of my life, a phase that had not been part of my consciousness until the end

Gloria with Stan Pottinger, her new beau

of my marriage. Prior to that, I had held on to heterosexuality and to life on the fast, straight, upwardly mobile path that I had started on so many years earlier. Women like myself, who think of themselves as straight or mostly straight and who seem straight to the outside world, not to mention those who are, in fact, heterosexual during their early adult years, may take longer than others to make the decision to live life with another woman.

As Germaine Greer says in her recent book *The Whole Woman,* of renowned poet and feminist Adrienne Rich, who fell in love with a woman at age forty-seven after having lived as a wife and mother of three children, I do not believe that my marriage was a fraud or that the part of my life that I lived with my husband was wasted or lived wrong.[2] To me, too, it seems more profitable to consider the possibility "that there was a change. That new feelings and attitudes had developed out of changing conditions and consciousness."[3] I, too, feel that trying to find some biological component in sexual preference probably is futile. Instead it seems that there is a continuum of sexual orientation and that each of us is on that continuum somewhere, although the exact location may vary from time to time in our lives. As a feminist, I was not about to reject a lifestyle that seemed right for me now. True to Greer's observation about Adrienne Rich, I accepted the possibility that I might have finally rejected heterosexuality as unsatisfying. I was now open to a different kind of love—to having a serious relationship with a woman.

For the summer of 1984, I rented a house in Sag Harbor, on the North Shore of Long Island, a beach house next door to where several women I had heard about lived. And just as I was turning forty, I started the first serious relationship with a woman I ever had, with one of the women who lived next door. Vicky had a terrific sense of humor, and we had a lot of fun together. For the first time I experienced a mutual need for tenderness as part of sex. We saw each other almost every day during that summer, and I prepared to tell Alexis about my new relationship when she came home from camp.

When I first told nine-year-old Alexis about Vicky, her initial reaction was "Yuck!" But as time passed, Vicky and Alexis grew fond of each other. Nonetheless, Alexis complained. She was worried that her friends would find out, worried that if they came over to visit they'd see either Vicky or a picture of the two of us on the living room mantel. (I didn't realize that Alexis had been worried about her young friends' seeing that photograph until many years later when, in her early twenties, she told me.)

Meanwhile, I was learning a lot in my relationship with Vicky, especially about trusting the instincts I had never really known I had and about how important it is for two people in love to be emotionally "present" for each other. As our relationship continued, I experienced an increasing intimacy that hadn't seemed possible in my life before.

I wanted us to move in together. Vicky argued—and sometimes it sounded persuasive—that it wouldn't be good for Alexis. But I, the mother, wanted as solid a relationship as I'd had with Marc. We got into the same arguments over and over about who'd stay at whose place on the upcoming weekend, what to do with Vicky's various pets, and inevitable changes of plans often caused by fluctuations in Alexis's life. For me, being in a serious, committed relationship meant living together, but that wasn't happening.

About seven years after that relationship started, I began to give up on it. One signal—to myself—was my willingness, if not eagerness, to move to Los Angeles on a half-time basis as the first movie I was to produce went into pre-production. Alexis herself had decided that it was best for her to alternate living with Marc and me, three weeks at a time. Meanwhile, the uncertainty about whether I really wanted to *be* a lesbian was growing in me. Was I sure that I wanted to give up the perks of straight life? A man would certainly be easier in a lot of ways. So, as soon as I got to Los Angeles, I joined Great Expectations, a straight singles club. I did a video; the guys did theirs. We wrote up our profiles saying who we were and what we wanted in life—and what we wanted in the opposite sex. It didn't work. I wasn't sexually attracted to a single one of the men with whom I went out.

Then—out of the blue, it seemed—Alexis decided that she wanted to go to boarding school for her junior and senior years. Luckily for me, she picked Thacher, which I'd recently heard about and which was located in Ojai, California. It was a great school, and Marc knew this was right for her too, although he said somewhat sadly and, as it turned out, prophetically that he would lose his daughter to the West Coast.

I spent as many weekends with Alexis as I could justify—either in Ojai or in Santa Monica, where I was living. But my personal life had to improve. I missed New York, where I had constantly socialized with friends at book parties, cocktail parties or various feminist dos.

My life took a turn for the best, when, on a business trip in New York, I happened upon Robin Morgan in her office at *Ms.* As I greeted her, I surprised myself by blurting out that I was lonely in Los Angeles. Robin's response was that she had a close friend who lived there and who, when visiting Robin several months earlier, had said something about not meeting any smart feminists. Robin gave me her friend's address and phone number.

I returned to Los Angeles the next morning and called Joanne Parrent. Five days later we had dinner, and sometime during that evening, I realized that I just might have met the love of my life. That was May 20, 1992. In August, she moved in with me. In January, she gave up her own apartment. Soul/sole companions and life partners, she and I have found each other. A younger Alexis, who had been embarrassed by the whole subject and by Vicky's existence in my life, now by age nineteen was telling all her friends about us, and one weekend, when she was an undergraduate at Berkeley, decided to bring four of them down for a visit. They cared neither that Joanne and I were sleeping together in our bedroom nor that they had to make do with one sofa bed, one sofa and the floor.

One spring weekend almost a year after we'd met, Joanne and I visited my mother and her husband, Joe, in Palm Springs. My mother hadn't asked questions during the visit that I had made years earlier with my first real girlfriend, Vicky. But Joanne and I had been living together for months, and I knew it was a forever kind of relationship. From Chicago my mother had continually bugged me on the phone about how worried she was that I was "all alone." I had told her I wasn't—that I had lots of friends, one of whom was Joanne, with whom I was sharing a house and whom she'd meet. But apparently that wasn't enough to convey the information, and during dinner the first evening of our weekend in the desert, my mother finally forced the issue. By then, I'd even told her that Joanne and I were not only living together but also spent virtually all of our time together. In denial, she obviously was rationalizing that we were just roommates, because right in the middle of dinner, she started talking about how she wanted me to "find a nice young man"—I was forty-eight at the time—who would take me to "balls." I think she even said Joanne was so nice-looking that she could find herself a young man too. I told her that I wasn't looking for a man, that I didn't want a man, that I'd never be with a man again. I told her I was with the person I wanted to be with—and she was right there at the table with us. My mother, apparently taken aback by my bluntness, was quiet for the rest of the meal.

The next day, it was as though nothing had happened. We were sitting around the pool, and then Joanne got up and went to the other side to get out of the sun, which she hates. My mother immediately turned to me: "Brenny, just how important is she to you?" I was stunned by the directness of the question, but I stayed calm and replied, "Very." I hoped that my single-word response would allow her to hear the truth and accept it.

One night, at his invitation, Joanne and I were staying in my brother Richard's New York apartment. I didn't think I needed to tell him about the exact nature of our relationship. I thought he knew from the fact that I had been a total "tomboy" growing up, combined with his not having seen me with a man since I'd broken up with Marc—only with Vicky. When we arrived, he was

Joanne Parrent and I during our first summer together, on a drive down the Coast, near Big Sur

Joanne on a boat on the Seine during our trip to Paris in 1996

already out for the evening. My nephew, little Richard, had his own place downtown, and before we went to bed, I shut the hall door to his old room, as well as the door to ours, which was adjacent.

When we got up the next morning, little Richard was downstairs, where he'd apparently slept all night on the living room couch, having arrived very late from an uptown party and not wanting to journey to his apartment in the Village. He'd seen that his bedroom door was shut and, knowing that Joanne and I were staying, apparently figured—not unreasonably—that one of us was sleeping in his room. I felt terrible, but before I could get a cup of coffee, the phone rang. It was my brother on his way to the airport, shouting, "Do you realize that you made Richard sleep in the living room? I demand to know exactly what rooms you and Joanne were in. I never gave you permission to use Richard's room. *What room did you sleep in last night?*" He was furious. I started to say that I wished he'd told me that Richard had needed his room, there would have been no problem. But he was insistent, so I told him in plain English, "Joanne and I were both sleeping in Philippa's room." I felt relief that despite his roaring and shouting, I now knew he was completely aware of the truth.

These days most of my married Hollywood friends end phone conversations or tennis dates with "Give my love to Joanne." Several of them, who now have second homes near each other in Montecito, throw a traditional Thanksgiving dinner. They have invited Joanne and me, as well as Alexis, to many of their recent Thanksgivings, as well as to parties in the city.

Sadly, this isn't the way it's always been. One of my closest friends, a big-deal Hollywood wife, told me that it was fine with her that I was involved with women, but that I shouldn't "rub other people's noses in it." She sounded like the father of my friend who'd invited me to spend a spring vacation on Nantucket with them when I was sixteen. "You don't mind," he said, "if I mispronounce your name for these two weeks, do you, and call you Fagin?" Even though I was a fairly literate kid and had read Dickens, this man had flown below my anti-Semite-detecting radar and caught me off guard. I was confused, and my answer was meekly to say it was okay.

Sometimes I wonder about the straight feminists I know. A married friend of mine, a successful lawyer in New York, with whom I'd worked on many feminist causes before her marriage, tried with her husband, unsuccessfully, for years, to get pregnant. Finally, they adopted a baby boy, and when I next saw her, what she seemed most proud of was the size of her new baby's penis. Another, an actress for many years married to a director, was worrying aloud to me about her career, because of the lack of roles for women over forty. I told her that I thought she'd make a great director. She agreed, but added, "That's off-limits though, because [her husband] wouldn't want the competition." She actually believed that "competing" with him that way might spell the end of their marriage. Both of these women consider themselves feminists.

The most striking contrast between straight women and lesbians is revealed in their relationships with their partners. Many straight women will put up with all sorts of nonsense from men—because boys will be boys—and they don't want to lose their men to younger, prettier women.

It's a well-known fact that most lesbians prefer pants to skirts—they're more comfortable. I see far more straight friends in uncomfortable clothes—shoes, especially—than I do lesbians. Again the reason is that straight women try to be attractive to men who don't know or care how uncomfortable women's clothes can be—from underwear to shoes to short skirts and panty hose. Actually, the point about pants was made eloquently by Ellen DeGeneres in one of her *Ellen* coming-out episodes on which she said unequivocally that she doesn't wear skirts. My ninety-four-year-old mother spent years complaining whenever she saw me in pants. Her displeasure intensified after I told her that I was involved with a woman. Somewhat resignedly, after she saw a picture I sent of myself in a new Armani pants suit, she remarked on how good I looked.

A while ago, I was interviewed by Carolyn Heilbrun for her

biography of Gloria Steinem. She kept hammering at me for my opinion about the reasons Gloria still wore those very short skirts and heels. I did my best to defend my friend, saying that she wears pants frequently, but a very real part of me doesn't understand the appeal short skirts have had for her. Granted, she has great legs, but it seems crazy for anyone, let alone Gloria, to walk around in tiny skirts and nonfunctional heels. Not only are these shoes bad for your back, but if someone is stalking you, how can you run away if you can barely walk? So it's not just the hooker image that's a problem, it's also that you lessen your own self-defense ability if you can't move freely. The politically correct feminist position is that each of us should decide how she wants to dress, for her own pleasure, but that should include safety, as well as comfort.

Then, at the opposite extreme, there are male-identified butch lesbians, who mimic men in the often swaggering way they carry and comport themselves. They don't seem happy being *women,* and being a woman is, as far as I'm concerned, more a state of mind than a particular look. For the most part, this kind of lesbian will raise money for AIDS but not breast cancer. They are often caught up in role playing, so that their relationships with more "femme" women (often helpless victim types) mimic the worst of extreme heterosexual behavior. I have trouble understanding the desire to be with a woman who tries—whatever her method of doing so may be—to look and act like a man. If I wanted someone manly in my life, I would be with the real thing.

In any case, fortunately, role-playing lesbians seem increasingly to be in the minority. All women have the capacity for being both soft and tough, depending on the situation and the mood. Most lesbians I know are feminists who dress and act like normal/androgynous–looking women. In fact, many of the leaders and everyday run-of-the-mill members of the Women's Movement have been lesbians. In the old days, when Betty Friedan and others like her were trying to exclude them, they often were in the closet. But now they're mostly out, proud to be who they are and, most important, dedicated to the struggle for women's rights, including those of lesbians.

Annoyed by male transvestites who parade around in campy skin-tight dresses on stiletto heels, I have never been willing to refer to them as women. What they do is reinforce sex stereotypes about women, because they beg, in their ridiculous getups, to be called women (more likely, "girls") and to be treated the way they think men should treat women. Their intense focus on the differences between what men and women wear, especially their thing about wearing women's underwear, and their weird, campy behavior make clear the fact that they are no friends of feminists, who have a serious mission on this planet—not just play-acting and dress-up. I thoroughly agree with an essay I read only recently on transvestites written by Robin Morgan in April 1973, entitled "Lesbianism and Feminism."[4] She says:

> No, I will not call a male [transvestite] "she"; thirty-two years of suffering in this androcentric society, and of surviving have earned me the title of "woman"; one walk down the street by a male transvestite, five minutes of his being hassled (which *he* may enjoy), and then he dares, he *dares* to think he understands our pain? No, in our mothers' names* and in our own, we must not call him sister. *We know what's at work when whites wear blackface; the same thing is at work when men wear drag.*[6]

Transsexuals are the extreme. But on college campuses today, the only way for a lesbian and gay group to be politically correct is to include bisexual *and* "transgendered" people. I objected strongly, for example, to Renée Richards' being allowed onto the women's professional tennis circuit. The male hormones he once had provided him with muscles few women could lift enough

---

* In an earlier comment about transvestites, Morgan asked, "Maybe it seems that we, in our combat boots and jeans, aren't being mocked. No? Then is it merely our mothers and *their* mothers, who had no other choice, who wore hobbling dresses and torture/stiletto heels to survive, to keep jobs, or to keep husbands because *they* themselves could *get* no jobs?"[5]

weights to achieve. And, perplexingly enough, there are a number of transsexuals who, born male, had the operation to become "women" and ended up in relationships with women. They call themselves lesbians. So it was with great delight that I read a piece by Gloria in *Ms.* expressing almost identical views as mine on the subject of transsexuals—Gloria who is usually so tolerant of anyone who feels oppressed.

There continues to be blatant discrimination based on sexual orientation. The military chiefs don't know, even today, how many dedicated soldiers of both sexes they've lost because of their bigotry.

When President Clinton came up with his ridiculous "don't ask, don't tell" policy, all he did was thoroughly antagonize the lesbian and gay community. Our present policy toward gays and lesbians in the military—which prevents them from stating their sexual preference, as well as acting on it—is both immoral and, in my opinion, unconstitutional. Granted, military personnel lose many rights when they join up, but should they lose their right to free speech, their right to "Life, Liberty and the pursuit of Happiness," especially when it's about the very essence of their being?

During Ruth Bader Ginsburg's confirmation hearings, when the senators on the committee were engaging her in a discussion regarding President Clinton's "don't ask, don't tell" policy, she stated that sexual orientation should not be grounds for keeping anyone out of the military. And Clinton's support of the Defense of Marriage Act (DOMA) was appalling, a clear ploy to get conservatives on his side at the expense of one of his most loyal constituencies. DOMA is a federal statute that allows states not to recognize marriages legally performed and recognized in other states if such a marriage is between two people of the same sex. Not only does this run afoul of the full-faith-and-credit clause of the Constitution, it also blatantly singles out a particular group of people—lesbians and gay men—for discriminatory treatment. I don't see how either of the above-mentioned policies will ever pass constitutional muster, especially with Ruth on the Court.*

I am angry that Joanne and I can't get married. There are not only the emotional benefits one receives when one's relationship is confirmed by society, there are also practical considerations. She is a member of the Writers Guild of America, which has excellent health benefits. If she were married, her spouse would get the same health benefits at no extra cost. I suppose I'm fortunate that I'm considered her domestic partner for their purposes. We had to show that we were living together, sharing expenses and a bank account, and so forth. And then I was allowed to pay about $2,000 a year into the WGA's health fund to qualify for health insurance as her domestic partner. That $2,000 was in reality a tax payment for the WGA, a union, to pass along to the IRS, because the latter considered my health insurance additional taxable income attributable to Joanne. As far as we're concerned, if the WGA and other unions can't persuade the IRS that this is warped thinking, the WGA should pick up the additional cost, not pass it on to us individually. Since many employers don't recognize domestic partners at all, we're supposed to be grateful that I have a chance to obtain the same insurance that a spouse would get free—even if I do have to pay for it. I'm not grateful, firmly believing that the Writers Guild—and every other union or employer that treats same-sex couples differently from married ones—is liable for sex discrimination as well as sexual-orientation discrimination.

I think back to the perks I had because I was married to Marc, from travel savings to the automatic right to be by his side in a hospital should he have been sick, to social security and the right to file joint federal and state tax returns. Why should I have had those with him and not with Joanne? Back in the 1970s, practi-

---

* Commenting on *Marvin v. Marvin* about five months before she took her seat on the U.S. Supreme Court, Ruth mentioned the significance of "[the California Supreme Court's decision] recognizing for the first time that unmarried couples can sue each other. . . . [It] illustrates the further breakdown of the legal line between marriage and unmarried union."[7]

With Alexis and Joanne, July 1992

cally every feminist, including myself, and most leftists were castigating marriage as part of the patriarchal system, a remnant from the days when William Blackstone referred to marriage as the combining of husband and wife into one and that one was the husband. But the feeling of being married was one of security, security in the knowledge that you intended to stay together forever—even if that often didn't happen. So now here I am with Joanne, knowing that we will be together forever, very much wanting the state to sanction our union, and convinced that we're entitled to all the perks Marc and his new wife have.*

* The highest court in Vermont recently decided that gay and lesbian couples are entitled to the same benefits (and obligations) as married couples, but it didn't rule that the word used for these unions must be "marriage." Thus, in the spring of 2000, the state of Vermont became the first to recognize "civil unions" for gays and lesbians.

Chapter 6

THE WILLIAM MORRIS AGENCY

One summer Saturday before Marc and I separated, Gloria called to invite us to dinner at Herb and Anne Siegel's house in Westhampton. Stan Pottinger, her new beau and the head of the Civil Rights Division of the Justice Department, and she were staying there for the weekend. Herb owned a lot of Warner Bros. stock, and he was the chairman of Chris-Craft. We accepted the invitation, and early that evening arrived at a glamorous house with a long green lawn leading down to a private dock, to which a number of gleaming Chris-Craft motorboats were moored. When dinner was announced, Herb instructed me to sit next to him. Then, after a brief conversation, he started in about how like him I was, better off with as many balls in the air as possible. Why wasn't I an agent? I'd make a great agent. He reminisced about his own experience as a founder of CMA, the first incarnation of ICM, one of the three biggest talent agencies in the country. "I'll tell you what," he said. "Send a letter to Lee Stevens, the president of William Morris in New York, and tell him I suggested you write."

Late that evening, as Marc and I headed back to Bridgehampton, Herb's advice rang in my ears; I pondered it, and by August, I had sent off a letter, together with my bio, to William Morris, so sure that I wouldn't hear back that I gave the matter little thought.

My friendship with Jane Alexander, whom I'd met years earlier at the Harvard Club event, and with whom I'd frequently socialized after that, led me to a possible way out of the law firm, with

*On location in
Tucson with Jane
Alexander, who was
then, in 1983,
making* Calamity
Jane

which I was decidedly unhappy. We decided to start a production
company. It was the fall of 1981. I admired Jane, who clued me
in to the fact that decent roles for women over forty were rare.
She had all sorts of ideas for movies that she thought we should
produce.

A short time later, she invited me to join her on the set of
Calamity Jane in Tucson, Arizona. Despite the intense heat (120
degrees in the shade), it was a great five days, culminating with a
visit to Mexico during Jane's weekend off. We talked about how
we would start a production company and proceed with our own
movies once Jane returned from a mid-January vacation in Belize
with her husband, Ed Sherin. We had decided to call our new
company Altion Productions, connoting a venture that would take
us to a heavenly place.

Right after New Year's Day, my phone rang. The caller was
Jerry Talbert, head of William Morris's Business Affairs Department. He sounded like a man who had a gun to his head: "I've

been asked by Lee Stevens to tell you that we have an opening in Business Affairs. Are you interested?" I was stunned, having virtually forgotten about the letter I'd written in August. I agreed to meet with him the following week. All I could think about was how I'd made a commitment to Jane and how much I had been anticipating our producing partnership.

On the following Monday, when I arrived for my interview, I was told that Lee Stevens himself wanted to meet with me. Jerry Talbert and I ascended to the thirty-third floor and waited in silence. Finally, a tall man with the smallest (via nose job) nose I'd ever seen strode out and shook my hand, while virtually ignoring Jerry. Lee told him that he wanted to meet with me alone. Deflated, Jerry sat back down in his chair, and I followed Lee Stevens into his gigantic office. He'd been impressed with my résumé, and he knew I wanted to be an agent. But would I be willing to start in Business Affairs? They had just lost (fired, it turned out) a Business Affairs attorney (a woman, I later learned). After one year, he was giving me his solemn word of honor, I'd become a motion picture agent. Herb Siegel's words rang in my ears. I was just like him. I'd make a terrific agent. But my allegiance to Jane tormented me.

I told Lee that I'd need until the following week to give them an answer, explaining that I'd begun a new partnership with Jane Alexander, who was, in fact, a William Morris client. The day ended with another meeting, in which the chagrined Business Affairs head explained what my duties would be if I took the job. Basically, I'd have to stay on top of all television package deals, as well as motion picture deals, and make sure that contracts from buyers (studios, networks, and so on) reflected the arrangements the agents had made. It sounded simple enough, and anyway, what I really cared about was the promise of becoming an agent in a year.

They offered me a respectable salary and told me to let them know as soon as possible. I was excited enough about the offer of an actual paying job that I called Marc—even though we were "separated," we were still living together—from the lobby of the

William Morris building. He enthusiastically supported my taking the job.

On Wednesday, my plans of discussing this with Jane were dashed. I received a call from Mr. Business Affairs, Jerry Talbert. They wanted an answer from me by noon Friday, two days from then. If I didn't want the job, they had two other candidates (male) who did. My problem was that Jane wasn't due back for another week, and she and Ed had chosen to vacation on an island off Belize purposely because it had no phones or any other means of communication with the rest of the world. It was their one real vacation of the year. So the issue was for me alone to decide. After a huge amount of anguish, I decided that I would be foolish to walk away from an offer like this when I had no way of ensuring that I'd be able to earn a living producing with Jane. I wasn't happy with the thought that I'd have to tell her about my decision as soon as she got back.

Within hours of her plane's landing, Jane called, in her cheery voice, to see what was new. I must have sounded as though some close family member had died as I explained what I had done and how it all had happened. Amazingly, she was understanding. "Brendy," she said fondly, "you did the right thing. And soon you'll be my agent, so we can still work together."

My new office was small, but it had a window that opened, which would be important during the summer, when cold air-conditioning roars through Manhattan office buildings.

My education in the ways of the Industry was about to begin. I knew how to draft and negotiate contracts, which is what I'd been hired to do, but I had a lot to learn about Hollywood, its denizens and their ways of doing business. I also realized that there had then been just one woman in the Business Affairs Department and now there would still only be one woman lawyer in the whole New York office.

One day, shortly after I started my new job, a woman appeared at the door of my office and asked if she could come in. I recognized her as the secretary of a TV agent for whom I had just reviewed a contract. As she entered, she shut the door behind her.

"I was working late one night, because Dan* said that this deal was important. He was in his office, and eventually he buzzed the intercom and told me to come into his office. And then," she said, tears coming to her eyes, "he bolted the door shut. And he raped me," she gasped.

I stammered out something like "Oh, I'm so sorry. That bastard." I asked her if she had called the police.

"No."

"Why not?"

"I needed to think. I was afraid of losing my job."

"Did you talk to management?"

"Oh, yes. About a week later I went into Mr. Stevens's office. I told him what happened."

"And?"

"And he told me that if I signed this paper they gave me and never told anyone what had happened to me, they'd send me around the world on a cruise."

"Did they?"

"Yes. And they promised to demote Dan."

I wasn't sure what kind of demotion she meant, since Dan was still at the agency, making deals and bringing in a good portion of the TV Department's revenue. I knew that bastard hadn't really paid a penny for what he'd done. Nor had he suffered in any other way. Knowing him even for the short amount of time I had, I felt him to be one of the most socially degenerate people I'd ever met. A conversation with him was impossible. His tone was bullying, but he was so formidably ugly that it was more ridiculous than frightening. Until now. As far as I knew, I'd never been around a rapist before, and I was sickened by the reminder of how vulnerable women in fact are.

Finally, I addressed the frightened young woman in front of me: "I'm really terribly sorry. What can I do to help you?"

It turns out that she didn't know what she wanted, except that

* Not his real name.

she'd heard that I was active in the Women's Movement. Somehow that knowledge had drawn her to me, and maybe just telling me the story was enough. Whatever she'd signed would probably preclude her from suing the agency and the agent. But nothing she'd signed could prevent her from pressing criminal charges. I tried to explain that to her, but she was too terrified both of her former boss and of losing her job. I was glad that she'd confided in me, but I felt helpless. Worse, I was beginning to get the idea that the agency I'd just hooked up with wasn't much better than the Mafia.

True to his word, Lee Stevens made me a motion picture agent about a year after I'd started at William Morris. I moved up a floor to an office that would be decorated as I'd like. I chose a peach color for the walls and a dark-green velvet couch, and I had my own favorite ergonomically correct desk chair covered in the same dark-green velvet. An antique desk lamp allowed me to avoid the fluorescent overhead lighting.

During the months that followed, I learned more about the treatment of women at William Morris. There was only one woman on the board of this privately held company. She was a rather elderly lawyer who worked part-time out of the Beverly Hills office in an advisory, Business Affairs capacity. There were no women officers of the company, which reflected the situation in most large U.S. corporations in the 1980s.

Not long after I had moved up to the thirty-third floor, I became friends with theater agent Esther Sherman. We agreed to have dinner, and I met her in her Village studio apartment. A successful William Morris agent living with her cat in that humble, tiny space, Esther had a terrific reputation, representing artists like Athol Fugard, Howard Ashman and Edward Albee. Esther's talent for knowing good theater was reflected that year by the fact that three of her plays won Tony awards.

Not long after our dinner, I paid her a congratulatory visit in her office across the hall from mine. After hugging her and singing her praises, I couldn't help wondering aloud if they might now make her a vice president. Maybe they would even consider giving her some well-deserved shares of WMA stock. She was contemplative.

Meanwhile, Esther lined up house seats for Alexis and me to see *Little Shop of Horrors,* written by Ashman. The star was Ellen Greene, another of Esther's clients. Shortly thereafter, I went to see *A Soldier's Story,* yet another award-winning play represented by Esther, for which she also arranged house seats.

One day, Esther appeared in my office upset about her status at William Morris. I reiterated what I thought she deserved and pointed out that several men in her department with far fewer successes had achieved the rank of vice president. Looking sheepish, she admitted that she had trouble asking for recognition. I reminded her that women rarely get anything without forcing the issue. I told her that this was the time to do it, that when they most wanted her to be a member of their team—three Tonys in one year—was when she had to stand up for herself.

But Esther just couldn't muster the courage. When she died of breast cancer ten years later, she had not been promoted or recognized with shares of stock for the work she had done so well and the reputation she had built for William Morris's Theater Department.

One day I was on the phone when Loretta Swit appeared at my door. In her dramatic voice, she asked if she could talk with me. I gestured her in, ended my phone conversation, and rose to shake her hand. Smiling, she said that Gloria had sent her. She'd heard that I was a wonderful agent; she wanted a woman agent. William Morris was trying to sign her to the agency, and the only way she'd do it, she said vehemently, was if I would be one of her signing agents. I had been a fan of *M*A*S*H,* and by extension, of Loretta's, the lone female star of that popular TV series. Now she wanted to have roles that would show women in gutsy situations, and she wanted me to help find her those roles. We shook hands on that, and she left.

The next day, I signed the agency papers for Loretta Swit, happy to have attracted an important client. About a week later, I was summoned into Lee Stevens's office. A veteran agent in from

Los Angeles was there too. Lee got right to the point. Even though my name appeared on Loretta Swit's papers, I would derive no bonus from any work that she brought in. I was to pretend that I was one of her agents, although as far as the agency was concerned, I wasn't. Furthermore, if I ever said a word to anybody about this, and that included Loretta, I would be summarily fired. Loretta "belonged" to the unimpressive Los Angeles agent, who represented a fair number of sitcom stars, and that was that.

They wanted me to help find Loretta work and act as though I were her agent, when, in fact, I would get no bonus or credit for doing so. I protested. Lee warned me again that if I pursued the matter, I would be let go. Their desperate desire to represent Loretta Swit had been based on the premise that they just might be able to get a network series on the air with her as the star. And a star on a long-running sitcom not only brings in a lot of money herself but also allows the agency to package the show around her, which would mean millions of dollars, especially in the case of a successful series that goes into syndication. Syndication means profits—real ones—for the agency to commission over a period of years not just a fee based on what the network pays to air the show at first. It wasn't until years later that I told Loretta the truth, which was that I really wasn't her agent but if I'd told her earlier I would have been fired. She was appalled but forgiving; I was disgusted with myself. How low had I stooped?

It got worse and crazier. Before I started at William Morris, I had signed a contract with *Vogue* magazine, agreeing that I would write a monthly column on issues relating to women and law in the entertainment industry. My most recent column was on women and nudity in film, and I discussed the Screen Actors Guild contract as it related to the subject.

Shortly after that column appeared, I was once again called into Lee Stevens's office. This time, he advised me, I was really on thin ice. He ordered me to cease and desist from writing any more columns for *Vogue* or any other publication. Astonished, I asked him to explain his reasoning, and it went something like: "You are here to represent talent. You are not talent. Writing a column like this is something our clients do. Therefore, your writing this column is taking work away from them." I pointed out that I was writing these columns as a lawyer and I couldn't think of any feminist lawyers who were clients. He was adamant; again I backed down. I agreed that I'd stop writing columns, pointing out to him that it seemed I had no choice. I was muzzled and miserable and silenced by virtue of working at William Morris. Lee Stevens had now removed the little space, both literally and figuratively, I'd retained in which to express myself publicly on feminist issues.

There were other instances of sexist behavior at William Morris that I felt unable to fight, and angry because I couldn't. The lone woman in the Television Department at the time told me about her plight one day. She complained that the head of Worldwide Television for William Morris insisted on having TV Department meetings not in the office conference room, as all the other departments did, but at a fancy, well-known men's club near the office, in which she was not welcome.

I wasn't totally up-to-date on New York City clubs at that point, so she elaborated, telling me that not only weren't women allowed to join as members, they didn't even let women in as guests.

"I don't think he's doing this just to keep *you* out," I said. "He probably just goes there because it makes him feel more important than the rest of the agents here."

I went to my pal, who was the TV boss's personal Business Affairs adviser. Jack,* not a man fond of hard work, often enlisted me to help out with complicated deals. It was, in fact, through him that I learned that the files of the huge moneymakers for the agency were not kept in the same place as those of more commonplace clients. Instead, they were upstairs in the private files of Lee Stevens, who apparently feared that agents (and others) who might depart the agency would steal this very confidential information. I told Jack exactly what I thought of Len's† using a

* Not his real name.
† Not his real name.

men's club for TV Department meetings. I reminded him that it was a violation of Title VII of the Civil Rights Act to encumber female employees more than males, which included not being able to attend department meetings. After I left Jack pondering, I told my female television-agent friend that she had a case under Title VII. She reminded me that she needed her job. Didn't I think they'd fire her if she sued them? I told her that if they did, that was another cause of action, which would virtually guarantee her winning her suit. The trouble was that she'd still be out of a job until a court ordered her back in.

What I didn't do was confront the boss of the TV department myself. I still feel that I failed my friend, even though I had no portfolio to protect her. Because of my years "on the barricades," as my brother was fond of putting it, I had the ability to confront the Worldwide head of TV in a way that she didn't. But I too, at some level, given all of Lee's threats, must have been unconsciously scared of losing my own job. The TV boss was a man of few words; there was something about him that was steely-tough, something that made me feel that he and Lee Stevens were capable of behavior that even by now I couldn't anticipate.

Meanwhile, in 1985, out in the real world, an interesting group sprang up within the Women's Movement. At the Museum of Modern Art in New York, in which the work of only 13 women out of 169 artists was displayed in an exhibition titled "An International Survey of Painting and Sculpture," a group of women artists picketed—to no avail. Soon they formed themselves into a group called the Guerrilla Girls.[1] Each would wear a different gorilla mask (they enjoyed identifying as both guerrillas and gorillas) and assume for herself the name of a dead woman artist, keeping her personal identity secret. They showed in many different ways how badly women fared in the art world. They took action by making eye-catching posters filled with statistics about the treatment of women artists by various museums and dealers, as well as about how little women artists are paid in comparison with men. With a heady sense of humor and without the earnestness that had accompanied much of our work in the early days of the Women's

Lily Tomlin and Jane Wagner at our house for dinner, with "Kathe Kollwitz," a Guerrilla Girl

Despite her terrifying appearance, I am fond of my Guerrilla Girl friend but ashamed that most of the art on our walls was created by men—lent to me by my art-dealer brother.

Movement, the Guerrilla Girls made a striking impression, and a few museums and galleries actually paid attention. I was aware of that colorful band of women but was in no way creative enough to apply their strategy to my own battles. It occurred to me some years later that had the rest of us adopted similar tactics—not ones that had been used by women for centuries—our complaints and protests might not so regularly have fallen on deaf ears.

One female agent at William Morris, who was in the Theater Department with Esther Sherwin, bewildered me. She seemed so dumb, had no clients that I can remember, and basically was out of the office a lot. So one day in the cab I was sharing with my two women agent pals, I asked about that theater agent. They acted as though I were some kind of moron. "She's Lee's mistress. You didn't know that?"

I didn't know, always having been lousy at gossip. Maybe it started during the years when I was practicing matrimonial law, but I just don't focus on dirt, and when it's told to me, I usually forget it. I remember this piece of information now only because it struck me as perfectly in character for Lee Stevens, a married man with children who lived in the suburbs, to be having a clandestine affair with a woman whom he'd pay off with a job at the agency. I doubted that he was paying her much of a salary. But this way she could tell herself that she was an agent instead of just a mistress.

I've consistently believed that women who sell their bodies for any kind of material gain are feeding right into the way men want us: controllable and theirs for the buying. Lee Stevens was that kind of man. In the old days William Morris had staked its claim as the premiere vaudeville agency. It seemed that the present group of men running the agency was cut from the same cloth. In fact, one of my good friends, also an agent, told me that Lee had propositioned her, somehow offering her more of whatever he thought she'd like, if she'd have sex with him. She refused and, to her credit, remained where she was, an agent at William Morris with not much power and not many clients.

Although I couldn't gain access to what women were earning

compared with men at William Morris (a privately held corporation), it was a generally acknowledged statistic that in the United States women were paid 69 cents for every dollar men received. In 1970, women who worked full-time throughout the year earned $3 for every $5 (or 60 cents for every dollar) earned by men who were similarly employed.[2] By 1998, the statistic for women, in general, was 76.7 cents (a recent report in the *New York Times* had it at 74 cents) for every dollar men in the same-level positions made. But women CEOs, CFOs, COOs, and senior vice presidents only made 68 cents on the male dollar. The women I'm referring to—at a major talent agency—probably fit the latter category, so I wouldn't be surprised if women at William Morris when I was there, including myself, were making 62 cents per male dollar. Probably I didn't snoop around and get this information because of my own then unconscious fear of being found out—and fired, not to mention my reluctance to invade the privacy of my female colleagues.

Jane Alexander had, true to her word, become a client. Invariably, I would find myself closely reviewing the contracts submitted for her services. Jane came to rely on my legal input, as well as on making her deals. I enjoyed the process until I got called into Lee's office yet again. "You're not any client's personal attorney. Even when you were in Business Affairs, you spent too much time on their contracts. All you're supposed to do is see if the deal points are right. That's it," he snapped.

Lee, a former lawyer himself, had no tolerance for my reviewing, let alone negotiating, the boilerplate language in contracts. But I told him that there was no such thing as a "standard term or condition." Buyers hide things in those clauses that are far from standard. He had had enough and motioned me out of his office. He didn't give a damn what I thought, nor did he care about my professional standards.

Ignoring Lee Stevens's commands, I continued to review Jane's contracts carefully. One reason was that I so respected her own high standards for her own work that I thought she deserved the best in work being done on her behalf.

Meanwhile, I began to read material submitted by writer clients of the agency. Often they would send in ridiculous scripts, badly written, with no structure, and they'd be optimistic that the scripts would be greenlighted for production. I'd read a synopsis, ten pages, sometimes even the entire screenplay, and be stunned by the low quality of what was being sold to studios and production companies.

By early 1987, for reasons explained in the next chapter, I had decided to leave William Morris, and the powers-that-be turned out to be happy about my decision. It seemed especially fitting that only days before I left, the rumor began to spread in the office that Lee Stevens had a brain tumor. Then he was out of the hospital, making an appearance at the annual holiday party, shaved head and all. I stared at him and found that I couldn't muster a single sympathetic feeling. He gave a little speech about how his doctors had assured him that the tumor was benign and that he was fine. I doubted that. Lee Stevens had lied so much in the past there was no reason to believe him now.

Continuing on course, I needed to discuss my impending departure with various clients, including Jane. In her usual supportive way, she wished me well, adding that after my next venture, surely she and I would work together. I was enormously grateful to her for those encouraging words, and Jane and I have indeed remained close friends to this day. (Of course, her own life took an exciting turn when she became chair of the NEA.)

As the day of my departure grew imminent, I was called one last time into Lee Stevens's office. He was not alone. There he was, acting as though he'd live forever. I realized that he was in perpetual fear of being sued or misquoted, so this time sitting with Lee in his office was his trusty lieutenant, Adam.* Present also was the comptroller of the agency. It was a bit intimidating,

* Not his real name.

since all I thought I was doing was bidding a formal goodbye. But they had more in mind.

Jane Alexander and her husband, Ed Sherin, visiting Los Angeles, stopped by to see our new garden.

In return for their handing over the last payment due me, they asked for my signature on a document they had prepared. I read through it, and as stunned as they'd caused me to be before by their outrageous demands, this time they'd outdone themselves. They were asking me to sign an agreement that I would never sue the agency for sex discrimination. I shook my head in amazement. As I did so, several thoughts came to me. It wasn't clear that I myself had a case against them for discrimination. (I didn't know what my male counterparts were being paid or what their bonuses were.) And second, even if I could muster a group of women employees willing to bring a class-action suit against the agency, which I was certain discriminated on the basis of gender, I probably wouldn't qualify as a plaintiff and therefore would not be much emotional support. Rightly or wrongly, I signed the piece of paper, took their check, and left the William Morris office for good in late February.

Several weeks later, I received a two-sentence letter on William Morris letterhead stationery, postmarked March 9, 1987. It read in its entirety:

Dear Brenda:
If not for the fact that women have vaginas, there would
be no reason to talk to them. In your case, not even that
helps. Good riddance, cunt!

Your friends at the office

    I tried to figure out exactly who could have written this note. I
wondered if someone had planned it before I agreed not to sue
for sex discrimination. Then, after some comforting talks with a
few friends, I decided that I had better things to do than dwell on
the sick mind(s) behind that letter. Isn't forgetting about the bad
times, in retrospect, what most women trying to make it in Hollywood—and elsewhere—end up doing? I resolved not to compromise myself again as I had at that agency.

    Not long after I left, Lee Stevens died. I don't think too many
employees in the New York office of William Morris shed tears.
He was a man unloved by many.

Chapter 7

NAVY SEALS

In the winter of 1986, while I was still a motion picture agent at William Morris, I read a script about Ernest Hemingway that I liked by two writers. We agreed to meet.

Richard Murphy was a big guy, a little paunchy—but eager. Chuck Pfarrer was well built and much more suave than Richard. Both were funny and smart, and I liked them immediately. When I asked what else they were working on, Richard said he was writing a few other screenplays. I turned to Chuck for a response, and he laughed me off.

Several days later, Richard ambled into my office, and after some chitchat, I asked him what Chuck did for a living. Richard asked me if I'd heard of the Navy SEALs. I hadn't. He told me that Chuck was a commander of one of the teams and that they were old friends. They'd made the time to write a script together because, although Chuck lived in Virginia Beach, Virginia, where the East Coast SEALs are based, he spent a lot of his free time in New York.

The next time I saw Chuck was in my office, and in answer to one of my questions, he explained that SEAL is an acronym for "sea, air and land," and that SEALs could go anywhere and do whatever needed to be done as long as it was within 50 miles from any body of water, which included, he added jokingly, a toilet. Descendants of the old Navy Frogmen, the SEALs had been specially established in 1962 by President John F. Kennedy, who wanted the Navy's Special Forces unit to be more cunning, more

accomplished, more important and more powerful than any of
the other U.S. Special Forces, including the Delta Force and the
Army's Rangers and Green Berets. Chuck, now a lieutenant, was
eager to describe how hard it was to become a SEAL, regaling me
with stories of BUDs (basic underwater demolition) training.

After Chuck finished telling me how one of the worst parts of
BUDs training was running with telephone poles on their shoul-
ders from Coronado, California, miles down into Mexico, it was
time to leave my office and head home for the evening. The
weather had turned awful—cold, windy and snowing. As Chuck
and I approached the corner of Fifty-fifth and Sixth, I spotted a
free taxi about a block away and cried out, "Chuck, a taxi! Run!"
Calmly, he responded, "You can run as fast as I can. Go for it." I
was furious, because, of course, we missed the taxi. But later I
reflected on how unusual that brief exchange had been. How
many other guys did I know who would refuse the opportunity to
show off their running-and-getting-a-taxi skills?

As Chuck and I got to know each other better, I pushed him to
give me some details. I wanted to know when and where his last
"mission" was. He never said he couldn't tell me. He would just
subtly change the subject. I got the impression that when Chuck
and his "team" were out in the field, they reported to no one and
decided themselves how to accomplish their goal, usually without further communication with the Pentagon.

Soon I made an option/purchase deal for Chuck and Richard's
script, and we set up a meeting with the producer. But the next
afternoon, although Richard was there, Chuck wasn't. I called
and got a machine with his funny wise-guy message and crazy
music. He didn't return my call, but about a week later, when I
next spoke with him, he told me that he really couldn't talk about
why he had missed the meeting.

Shortly thereafter, I arranged for Chuck and Richard to meet
some of my colleagues at William Morris. Again, at the desig-
nated time, no Chuck. Another week passed. This time Chuck
called me to apologize. I told him we really had to talk, because I
was getting embarrassed (and annoyed) by his absences without

Alexis, age thirteen, and ex-Navy-SEAL-turned-screenwriter Chuck Pfarrer are about to venture onto Magic Mountain's upside-down roller coaster—without me.

any notice or explanation. He said he'd come by my apartment after Alexis went to bed.

When Chuck arrived, Alexis, who was not unsurprisingly still awake, insisted on meeting him. Soon they were engaged in an animated conversation about which were the coolest—in other words, to me, the most horribly scary—rides at Six Flags amusement park. Finally, Alexis headed to her room. I found Chuck the Scotch he asked for and got my Perrier, and we settled down in the living room. After a while, Chuck allowed me a peek into his secret world. To my question about the *Achille Lauro* incident, he said softly, "I was there." I realized he was serious. I had a million questions. I gleaned from what Chuck said that SEALs were climbing up the side of the *Achille Lauro* to eyeball the deck and decide if they could "take out" the terrorists without harming any civilians. (They decided they couldn't.) The only other piece of information I could get—and it was enough—was that he had been on the plane that took terrorist leader Abul Abbas to Egypt and back again when that country wouldn't let their plane land. As I thought about the dates, I realized that the *Achille Lauro* incident had occurred the day after the first of our two meetings that Chuck missed.

After he had a few more drinks, I continued my prodding. Sure enough, the Pakistani plane, which had been hijacked before it even took off right around the time of the second meeting Chuck missed, hadn't been overrun by Pakistani commandos, as the *New York Times* had reported. There were no such people. As Chuck put it, "Are you kidding?" The SEALs had been there to kill the hijackers before they could force the pilot to fly. They were implementing a new policy that prevented any plane hijacked on the ground anywhere in the world from ever again taking off. Too many lives had been lost that way already. In fact, he confessed that he'd been at another friend's funeral the day before. Between 40 and 60 percent of active-duty SEALs die in the line of duty. And there were only about 2,200 of them scattered in various places around the world. The SEALs are a small scalpel-like force and have, on numerous occasions, prevented larger confrontations, even wars. Chuck pointed out that SEALs, being a secret military group, give credit for their missions to the Delta Force or the Green Berets instead. SEALs' faces are never photographed.

Chuck would not tell me about his team except that they did counterterrorist work. But he talked some about Beirut, which seemed to have been a watershed experience for him. At one point, during the UN peacekeeping rule over that beleaguered city, Chuck and his team landed on the shore. How they got there, he wouldn't say. But he did tell me that he was immediately ordered, by an officious Marine "peacekeeper," to instruct his men to disarm. He did as he was told. They disarmed until they reached the corner. After they rounded it, ignoring the order he'd just received, Chuck commanded his men to re-arm. They walked into a bloodbath in which they would have all been killed if they had remained unarmed. Seventy Marines in Beirut died in their arms. Chuck couldn't get over how sad and stupid the whole thing was and how disenchanted he was becoming by the international politics he knew.

About a week later, Chuck and I had dinner at a restaurant near my apartment. After dinner, as we headed back, I noticed him glancing up at the fourth story of a nearby building. It was the Cuban consul general's residence. I followed his gaze and saw a camera pointing down at us, its lens following us (potential enemies, I suppose) as we moved.

By now it was the spring of 1986 and I was growing increasingly restive at William Morris. I told Chuck that since he knew how to write a screenplay, he should get out of the SEALs now, while he was still alive. He could write a movie about his experiences, actual or fictionalized. I would do everything I could to help him with the script, and when it was ready to be sent out, I would leave William Morris and produce this Navy SEALs movie. Chuck, surprised at my optimism, agreed to think about it. After all, he was twenty-nine years old, which, according to him, was old for an active-duty SEAL.

Not long after my proposition, Chuck called to say that he'd take me up on my deal. Shortly after that fateful call, I was in Los Angeles on William Morris business. One of my meetings was with the top production executives at Orion Pictures. After I discussed agency business, I mentioned that I might have a script for them in the fall. It was about Navy SEALs. As I was saying this, Mike Medavoy, then head of production and one of the two executive vice presidents of Orion, was wandering around his spacious office, not paying much attention. But Jon Sheinberg, his deputy, heard me and said, "Mike, you'd better listen to this." Medavoy, after searching for the perfect cigar, then lighting it and blowing smoke in our faces, did. He was interested, he said, in the SEALs movie much more than anything else I'd been talking about. I left the meeting promising that they'd hear from me when the script was done.

As the script got under way, Chuck and I developed a pattern. He would write all day, while I was at work. Then, in the evenings, we would go over what he'd written. My evenings were my own, because Alexis, by now, was away at summer camp. One night, Chuck, looking kind of sheepish, asked if he could stay overnight. The friend's apartment he'd been using was "unavailable" that night. My apartment was being painted, so all I had to offer was Alexis's room, which had one bunk-size bed in it, big enough for a twelve-year-old, not big enough for all of Chuck's 6 feet 3 inches. But he was more than grateful, explaining that if I could imagine what it was like to sleep all night in a closet, then I could see what a luxury her room was. He was alluding to those times when he was spying on various foreign government officials and had to hide in the closets of their rooms unseen and unheard for countless hours. Over time, Chuck made it clear to me that his least favorite SEAL activity was planting explosives underwater between a large ship and the dock next to it. That made him claustrophobic. He also hated spying because, I guessed, that too led to claustrophobic situations.

Finally, by the middle of the summer, I was certain that the script—still being revised by Chuck—could be a very successful commercial movie. If I could find an independent financier, I'd end up with more meaningful creative input—and money—than I would if I set the movie up at a studio. I called an acquaintance who is very rich and was interested in new ventures. He wanted to hear more about the project and proposed that Chuck and I come to his house for dinner.

On the appointed evening, I arrived at the door of a large Upper East Side, Fifth Avenue brownstone. A butler appeared, and after asking what I'd like to drink, he escorted me to the French Impressionist floor, where the billionaire, his girlfriend and Chuck were chatting. Eventually we sat down to dinner on yet another floor, the walls of which were covered with African art.

The billionaire seemed genuinely interested in Chuck's description of BUDs training—and in the story he was writing.

Eventually, he asked me how much money we were talking about, and I told him in the neighborhood of $15 million. We didn't have a real budget yet, because the script wasn't finished, but I doubted that I was far off. I was sure that the Navy would cooperate and save us a lot of money. After dinner and more schmoozing, we took our leave, giddy at the possibility that we'd actually secured financing that easily. All I had to do was send the script when Chuck finished it.

By now, each draft Chuck sent me was the one he hoped I would send out. There would be a cover sheet with ever more amusing sketches of computers blowing up from the strain of overwork. I was determined that the script be perfect, and finally, in October, I knew that it was as good as we could make it. I had it messengered to our potential financier.

Front-page news two days later announced a change in the tax laws that would especially affect individuals in the highest tax brackets. I didn't think much about it, because I wasn't one of them. But then I received a personally typed note from our prospect. He couldn't deal with the script now because he had to restructure his assets before the end of the year.

Coincidentally, Richard, Chuck's partner on the other script, telephoned from the West Coast. He'd heard through the grapevine that Simpson and Bruckheimer, the producers of *Top Gun,* were looking for a writer to do a script about Navy SEALs. I panicked, knowing how fast I had to move. I'd have to go the Hollywood route and forget about independent financing. I called Jon Sheinberg at Orion and told him that the script I'd mentioned the previous spring would be in his office the next day. I also told him that I was going to be the producer.

Early the next evening, as I sat eating dinner with Alexis, the phone rang. It was Jon calling to say that he'd read half the script. So far he loved it. He would finish it that night and call me the next day. Don't send it to any other studios, he said. Despite my happiness over his enthusiasm, the next morning I FedExed the script to an executive I knew at Warner Brothers and another at United Artists in Los Angeles. I realized that if Orion wanted it,

Chuck and I would be in a much stronger position if other studios did too. At 9:00 a.m. Los Angeles time I called each of the two executives to say that I had overnighted a script in which their studios would be interested.

Right after those calls, the phone rang. It was Jon. He'd finished *Navy SEAL,* the name I'd given the screenplay late one night, thought it was hot, and was giving it to Medavoy to read that evening. If Medavoy liked it, Eric Pleskow, the president of Orion, in New York, would also have to read it before they optioned it. Again, he pleaded for my patience. I told him that I couldn't hold up the script. It wasn't fair to Chuck or me. But I would let him know if somebody else wanted it.

The next day came and I got calls from the executives at Warner Brothers and United Artists. The script looked exciting, they said. They'd read it that night. But the following morning at 10:00, Eric Pleskow's secretary called. Would Chuck and I come in to meet with him and Bill Bernstein, the executive vice president in charge of deal making? I replied that we would need a few days, mumbling something about Chuck's being out of town. Then I called Chuck and we agreed that we'd meet with them in two days. We didn't tell Orion that we were stalling to give Warner Brothers and United Artists enough time to get their acts together.

The day before meeting with Bernstein and Pleskow, I heard from Warner Brothers. They were very interested, but they would partner me with a producer who had a track record the way they did with all first-time producers. I didn't want to be shoved aside and bought off with just a credit. I was also concerned that Warner Brothers always had many scripts in development, most of which didn't get produced. Still wary of Simpson and Bruckheimer, I didn't want to be on any studio's back burner, which is where one inevitably is until the picture is greenlighted for production. I thanked them for their interest, however, and told them I'd get back to them.

That night I went to a book party, and much to my surprise, there was the United Artists executive, in from Los Angeles, who said that he appreciated my getting the script to him but that he'd talked to his colleagues and that "Navy SEAL" wasn't right for them just then. I actually was relieved that I only had to deal with Warner Bros. before my meeting at Orion with Pleskow and Bernstein the next afternoon.

Then out of some knee-jerk need to be thorough, I called Jeffrey Katzenberg at Disney on Friday morning. He was legendary for being in his office at 7:00 a.m., but when I told him the subject of my movie, he said he couldn't talk about it. They were in development with a movie about SEAL kids (later called *The Rescue*). That's all he would say, but it further increased my determination that ours be the first, not the second, movie about Navy SEALs.

At 5:00 p.m. Chuck and I arrived at Orion's headquarters and were ushered into Eric Pleskow's office. He and Bill Bernstein proceeded to tell us how much they had enjoyed the script and that what they were offering was *not* a development deal. They were going to make this movie. They seemed genuinely interested in Chuck and asked intelligent questions, most of which he answered straightforwardly. To be absolutely certain, I told them again that I was to be the only producer and that I was about to turn Warner Brothers down because they had not agreed to that term. Pleskow and Bernstein pledged that they had no problem with that. Indeed, they said, I *should* be the only producer. With that, I gave them the name of an attorney I'd chosen, a former law school classmate of mine whose office was a block away. Our deals would be made and we'd be off and running!

We got into the elevator and Chuck exclaimed, "Babe, you are the greatest!" We hugged goodbye on the street as he got into a taxi and I started on a seven-block walk in the other direction to another book party. As I walked through the Manhattan streets, the song "Amazing Grace" popped into my Jewish, atheistic head, and I arrived at my destination, grinning and singing at the top of my lungs. I had done it. I'd moved into producing, a goal I'd had since before I joined William Morris. I had defied the odds. A studio was going to make my movie, and despite how awful things in Hollywood might be for women, which I'd heard from William Morris colleagues based there, I was going to be in charge of a big action-adventure film. After that, doors would open for me to do all the feminist movies I wanted to do. I was on top of the world.

On Monday morning, our new lawyer and I met. From all the negotiations I'd done for William Morris clients, I had a pretty good sense of what Orion should pay Chuck for the script and me to develop and produce it. I emphasized that I would get sole producer credit, nothing less.

The call from our lawyer after he spoke to Bernstein disturbed me for two reasons. Now that he had secured our business, his personality seemed different. He acted as though everything he was negotiating was a favor to me. First, Bernstein had not agreed that I'd be the only one to receive producer credit. Down the road, if a star or line producer insisted, Orion wouldn't break a deal over sole credit for me. They had merely said that I wouldn't be partnered with anyone else now. As for Chuck, Orion had decided that they would use a different writer for a revision of the script. Then the lawyer added that he wanted to do the production work for the movie, which meant that he'd be paid a hefty sum by Orion to do all the below-the-line contracts. That gave me the feeling that Chuck and I were not his priority. Most important, I realized within the next few days that every time I picked up the phone to ask my lawyer a question, he was obnoxious and patronizing, making remarks like "Brenda, I can't believe you don't know the answer to that."

Even though deals were negotiated for Chuck and me, I grew increasingly displeased with the lawyer's attitude. Finally I mentioned it to Bernstein, who said that he hadn't understood my choice in the first place. He agreed to hire Tom Selz, a senior partner at the New York firm Frankfurt, Garbus, Klein & Selz, to do the production for *Navy SEAL* and to negotiate my production, financing and distribution deal, which would kick in once the movie was greenlighted.

I was still at William Morris, and the annual Christmas party was scheduled for shortly before the holiday. I asked Chuck to join me in my final celebration with the folks at William Morris. As we entered, a photographer asked us to pose for a souvenir of that very happy evening. I still have that picture. Chuck is seated and I'm behind him, but instead of standing in a dignified pose, I have my arms tightly squeezed around his sturdy neck, holding on, it looks like, for dear life. I guess I was scared about the beginning of my venture into the world of producing.

Medavoy eventually called to say that he wanted Chuck and me to come to Los Angeles for a meeting with director Roger Donaldson. If Roger wanted to do the movie, they'd get a writer of his choice, but they'd want Chuck around to add material only a Navy SEAL would know. We would be staying at the Mondrian Hotel, on Sunset. So I called my good friends Lily Tomlin and Jane Wagner to say that I'd be on their turf. We agreed to a late dinner at Le Dome the first night of my stay in Los Angeles.

Chuck and I arrived, picked up our car and drove to the hotel. Later I let Chuck have the car because he had friends in Malibu and, according to the hotel's concierge, I had only a two-block walk to the restaurant. It turned out to be a twenty-Manhattan-block walk, complete with hills and in some places no sidewalks. My shoes were all wrong for that hike, and I was twenty minutes late for dinner. Lily and Jane were amused that I didn't know how to interpret distances estimated by concierges, who never walk anywhere. I was glad to be among feminist friends. Despite what must have been some disdain for my choice of subject matter, they, who knew how hard it was, toasted me for getting a movie into development.

Our meeting with Roger Donaldson was disturbing. He had just finished a grueling shoot, and apparently he had never actually conveyed a desire to direct the movie but rather had read the script as a favor to Medavoy. Basically, he didn't like it, so his comments were broadside criticisms about the characters, the story, the structure—virtually everything. I couldn't believe that I had wasted the time to watch every single Donaldson movie on video to prepare for that meeting.

Then I met with the executives at Orion. How about a woman director, I asked? They looked at me as though I were completely crazy. Maybe I was. Of the one hundred highest-grossing films of 1997—ten years later—only five were directed by a woman, and female directors had worked fewer days in 1997 than they had the year before (3,411 compared with 4,233).[1] They worked fewer than 5 percent of the total days Directors Guild members spent on theatrical films in 1997, and that represented an almost 50 percent decline from the year before.[2] (In fact, of total days worked by film directors in 1996, according to a DGA tally, women accounted for 9 percent.[3]) In 1998, women directed only 6.8 percent of the films released by major studios.[4]

"Look," I said, "if not the director, then at least the next writer." One of them blurted out, "Brenda, you've got to be kidding. Women can't write action movies." In fact, up to that point in time we hadn't been given the chance. In 1998, only 11 percent of the films released had been written by women,[5] virtually none of them action films. And ten years earlier, when I was having this conversation, the statistics for women were even worse. These utterances by the executives at Orion about what women couldn't do had the familiar ring of statements made to me over twenty years earlier at Harvard Law School. This was different, though, because I knew it was a losing battle. I let them get away with it, rationalizing that after my first movie was made, I'd have real power. But usually a person ahead of my time, why was I beginning to cave under the very sexism that I had fought so hard—and successfully—against at Harvard?

With difficulty, I regrouped. I went through lists of male directors and decided that Ridley Scott, who had made *Blade Runner* among other notable movies, was my first choice. Medavoy was amenable, and Ridley—who seemed intrigued—and I began a series of phone conversations. I suggested that his agent, Jeff Berg of ICM, get on the phone with Bernstein. Meanwhile, we agreed to keep each other posted. But then one day I got a call from Ridley's assistant, Mimi Polk, an American with a British accent just like that of her boss. From then on, she said, I was to speak only with her. My conversations with Ridley were disturbing to him (which, I realized, probably meant really to her).

Eventually Bernstein and Berg came to an impasse over Ridley's deal. After over three weeks of trying to make it work, Bernstein called and asked if I would support his decision to walk away from Ridley. It was their money, I reluctantly observed, so we moved on.

Shortly thereafter, Medavoy and Jon Sheinberg suggested Richard Marquand, another English director who had recently directed *Jagged Edge,* a suspense movie starring Glenn Close. At my first meeting with Richard Marquand, who was a short, tough-looking, arrogant guy, all he could do was tell me what was wrong with the script and how he would insist on a rewrite by a writer of his choice—if he decided to get involved. Not long after, Marquand made his interest known and I was on a plane to Los Angeles to meet with Orion executives and Marquand, as well as Gary Goldman, a writer whom Marquand liked and whose scripts I read on the plane. The Westwood Marquis has an impressive cocktail lounge, and it was there that I first met Gary Goldman, who seemed like a nice enough person, intelligent, scrawny and Jewish.

When I got back to New York, I learned that Marquand had agreed to direct but was demanding producer credit in first position (in front of my name), in addition to director credit. I told Tom, my lawyer, that if Marquand was going to get producer credit, then I wanted a production credit above the title: after the "Orion Pictures presents" credit, the next one would read "A Brenda Feigen Production." Tom was dubious. This was never given to first-time producers. Then I insisted on my name being in first position in the "produced by" credits. Happily, I won both credit battles.

One day early in the summer I stopped by the Armory on Park Avenue to watch Oliver Stone shoot *Wall Street's* art auction scene. My brother, Richard, an old friend of Michael Douglas's, was in the scene. When I arrived, Oliver Stone, whom I'd met at a party in the Hamptons several years earlier, came up to say hello and asked me if I would go home, change into a silk suit and come back to be an extra in the scene they would be shooting that evening.

During one of our many breaks, Richard informed Michael that I was producing a movie about Navy SEALs. Michael volunteered that Lewis Teague, who had directed *Jewel of the Nile,* the sequel to *Romancing the Stone,* would be a good director for my movie. He neglected to add that Lewis had come on board that movie as they were about to shoot and that he had done whatever Michael wanted throughout. I told him that we had already hired Richard Marquand but thanked him for the suggestion.

We were in the sweltering Armory (no air-conditioning) for eight hours, shooting a scene that lasted about three minutes in the movie. Although I ended up on the cutting-room floor, I pocketed my paycheck of $96.96 (which included extra pay for the smoky conditions) and said my goodbyes. My role as an extra had been a once-in-a-lifetime, albeit tedious, experience.

As the summer drew to a close, I was spending more time at the house Vicky and I were renting in Sag Harbor. Alexis was with us, having returned home from camp with lice, poison ivy and the usual loss of clothes, shoes and weight from the "yucky" food, about which she had endlessly complained.

Gary Goldman was in the final stages of finishing his draft of the script. Chuck had helped him with the dialogue, so it read the way real Navy SEALs talk, funny and obscene. (I also heard that Chuck had Gary pumping iron in his spare time.) The plan was for Gary to send the draft to me and to Marquand at the same time but wait to send it to Orion until it met with our approval. He didn't follow the plan. It was the Wednesday before Labor Day weekend, and he decided to overnight-pouch it to me care of the New York Orion office, overnight mail it to Marquand in London—and give it to the guys at Orion on Thursday. That way, he reasoned, we could all read it over the long weekend. I arranged for someone at Orion in New York to get my copy on a jitney bus out to Bridgehampton so that I would be sure to receive it.

The next day, Alexis, Vicky and I waited for the bus at the Candy Kitchen (great ice cream, quaint place) which was on the same corner as the bus stop. I thought it was nice of them to sit there with me as jitney after jitney came and went. Three hours into this, by which time I had stopped running out the door of the Candy Kitchen every time a jitney arrived and was sitting on a bench outside, a bus pulled up, the driver holding my package in his hand. The three of us returned to our little house on the bay—I to read my script, Alexis and Vicky to watch two videos they'd selected when we stopped for Chinese food on the way home. I shut as many doors as I could to keep out their noise and began to read. That was Thursday night.

On Friday morning, we were relaxing by the bay and preparing for lunch with a much-beloved senior colleague of Vicky's whom we had invited. It was time to eat, and we were waiting only for Alexis to be dropped off after a play date with her friend, when the phone rang. It was Gary Goldman. I assumed he wanted to hear my reaction to the script. But instead his tone was grave. Vicky later related to me my end of the conversation as she'd overheard it: "What do you mean he can't read it?" Long pause. "You mean he just fell over?" Pause. "Well, how bad is it?" Pause. "Wait a minute! Are you telling me he's in the hospital? Who'd you just talk to?" "He's had a stroke! . . . How bad a stroke?" And then apparently I ended the conversation with "Oh my god, I can't believe it. He just came back from a vacation in the Greek Islands!"

Richard Marquand, age forty-nine, had had a major stroke and was unconscious, and the doctors said there was little chance that he'd survive. If he did, he'd be a vegetable. I'd turned ashen, Vicky told me later. I apologized to our guest and went inside to call Bill Bernstein in Rye, New York. After his initial shock, he got down to business. The partners—Pleskow, Medavoy, Arthur Krim, who was chairman of Orion's board, and he—would discuss whether to continue with the movie on Tuesday. There was no point in their reading Gary's draft.

I couldn't have felt more helpless. It was almost one year since Chuck and I had made our deals, and now Orion was going to decide whether they still wanted to make the movie. They were out of pocket about $300,000, by my calculations. Maybe that was enough to keep them going, because there's a rule of thumb in the business that the more a studio sinks into the development of a movie, the more likely they are to make it. But I wasn't optimistic. Because to Orion the director is all-important, our chances weren't good. Vicky's friend, polite throughout lunch despite my inability to focus on anything but my own problem, took his leave later in the afternoon. I apologized profusely for my rudeness and spent the rest of the weekend in an anxious funk.

By this time, the Orion executives had arranged for me to move out of their fancy Fifth Avenue offices into the Twentieth Century Fox building, on West Fifty-seventh Street. They needed what had been my office for someone on the Orion staff. So on that Tuesday after Labor Day, I sat in my new office nervously waiting for the phone to ring. Finally, in the early afternoon, Bernstein called to say that they had decided to go ahead with the movie. I should call Medavoy and talk about the next step. I almost fainted with joy.

I called Medavoy. "Uh, Brenda, there's a director I've been thinking about. He's attached to a project with another producer here, but we're not going forward with that one." I asked whom he had in mind. "Lewis Teague," he responded tersely. I couldn't believe it. The very guy that Michael Douglas had recommended. I agreed to a meeting with Lewis in New York. I also asked my assistant to rent all of his movies for me to watch that night and the next. I was so overjoyed at the prospect of still having a movie in development that virtually any director would have made me happy. I called Chuck and Gary and told them the good news.

That night I watched *Jewel of the Nile* and was impressed with the airplane rolling through the city streets. I watched another of

Teague's movies and thought how similar it was to *Jaws*, just not as good. But I was determined to make it work with this guy.

Lewis and I met at the beginning of the following week. He seemed innocuous, not too bright, but eager to make *Navy SEAL* (as it was still titled). What was odd about even our first conversation was that whenever I said anything, there would be a long silence before Lewis replied. And he had a quizzical look on his face, as though he didn't quite understand what I was saying. When I spoke with Medavoy the next day, I couldn't articulate any problems I had with Lewis; his movies were okay *and* Michael Douglas had said he would be good for my movie. I conveyed the same reaction to Bernstein, who was delighted that he'd be able to close a deal for Lewis's services for half of what he'd been willing to pay Ridley Scott.

As soon as Lewis's deal was firm, they scheduled another "creative" meeting in Los Angeles, and out I flew. This time it was to hear how much Lewis hated Gary's script. He didn't like the one Chuck and I had worked on either. I wasn't surprised by what he said, knowing that directors are usually egomaniacs who always want their own script to be the one they shoot. What Teague wanted was for the SEALs to have to get Stinger missiles out of the control of Arab terrorists who were planning to blow up a planeload of innocent civilians. Medavoy asked Lewis to suggest a writer, and after a long enough pause to make everyone nervous, he came up with Kevin Jarre, represented by William Morris and known for his ability to write *Action*. It seemed futile for me to ask to read anything this new suggestion had written. Kevin was hired, and his draft was due at the end of February 1988.

I had been doing some serious thinking. Alexis, now thirteen, had expressed her unhappiness with traveling to Marc's every other weekend and every Wednesday night. I would routinely pack her into a taxi with her dog Popcorn, her dwarf parrot Mango, clothes and schoolbooks, only for her to travel ten minutes across the park and unload. She had come up with an idea. She would stay with me for three weeks and then go to her dad's for the next three weeks. Marc was fine with this plan, but at first the thought horrified me. How could I not see her for three weeks at a time? She reassured me that we could have dinner in between. But I knew Alexis, and the question was when she would make the time. That was the catalyst for my new idea. Feeling too removed from the process, and not having even met our latest writer, I decided that instead of paying rent for my office in New York, Orion should pay for a place for me to stay in Los Angeles, and I'd fly back to New York every three weeks. That way I'd be ready for pre-production, which was scheduled to start as soon as Kevin's script was in.

Bernstein and Medavoy okayed my proposal, which was that I would be in Los Angeles by the beginning of March, when Jarre's draft would be in. Alexis had approved my plan, pleased that Marc and I had taken her wishes seriously. I had even already arranged for her to spend her spring break, which would start in a few weeks, with me in Los Angeles. I planned to take her to Disneyland, maybe even Magic Mountain with Chuck. My apartment, which Jane Alexander had found for me, not far from her own, was across the street from the beach. I knew Alexis would love that.

I arrived at LAX in the early afternoon of March 5, 1988, picked up my rental car, and drove to my new apartment, which was all I could have wanted. Soon I was swimming laps in the pool beneath my patio, from which I could also see both the ocean and the mountains. The air was glorious, and in the evenings it was filled with the scent of night-blooming jasmines.

On Monday, I strode into Orion's offices all set for my first day in a new office. But as soon as I found Medavoy, I learned that the Writers Guild had just called a strike, and predictions were that it would last six months. As I thought about my options, they narrowed down to precious few. One was that I return to New York, on the assumption that the predictions were right. The thought about giving up the apartment, into which I had just moved so many of my clothes and other personal effects, was distressing. The other option was to stick it out and assume that this

strike, like others that had hit Hollywood in recent years, would
end, because the issues seemed far from crucial. Anyway, staying
would also give me an opportunity to learn my way around Los
Angeles. Furthermore, I would meet more people and maybe
even test some new movie ideas out on Orion, which could do
everything but work with writers. And finally, Alexis was so looking forward to her visit with me in several weeks. I decided to be
optimistic and stay.

Since there was no rule that I couldn't *talk* to a striking writer,
I got Kevin Jarre's home number from Orion and left a message.
Eventually, he called back, and we set a date for dinner. On the
phone, he sounded like a fairly average, young, self-important
writer, and we met in a romantically lit restaurant on the beach in
Santa Monica. He was dressed in jeans, a white T-shirt, a black
leather jacket and a baseball cap. He didn't take off the jacket or
the hat during the entire evening. I did my best to avoid any mention of the script, so I wouldn't run afoul of the rules of the WGA
strike. The conversation limped along, not only because he was
so much younger but also because he seemed to think he was
really cool and I didn't. I did ask how long after the strike ended
he'd have the script ready. I wondered if he had really stopped
and was working on a spec script, as I'd heard so many writers
were. Kevin was noncommittal, but it was clear that he wasn't
writing our script and that he strongly supported the strike.

Within a few days, I received a long-awaited call from Captain
Mike Sherman, the Chief of Naval Information in Los Angeles.
He would run interference between us and the Pentagon and
essentially be the one who would decide what kind of support, if
any, the Navy would give our movie. He told me that the security
clearance I had requested had been approved. Lewis, Chuck and
I could visit Coronado, where BUDs training takes place, and
meet some SEALs on active duty the following weekend. I ran
into Lewis's office, excited finally to be able to bring a smile to his
face. But when I told him, there was a very long pause, coupled
with a sour expression. "You're not going," he said softly. I tried to
comprehend what he was saying and gasped, "What are you talk-

ing about?" His answer was that he didn't want me or any other woman around. Dumbfounded, instead of shouting, as I might have twenty years earlier, after a minute of staring at him, I turned and walked out of the office, heading straight for Medavoy, who I was sure would tell Lewis where to go. Wrong. Medavoy told me that the trip to Coronado wasn't important enough and that I should let it—and them—go.

I left the office that night not having called Captain Sherman back. What power did I have to force my way? If I went, Lewis wouldn't and he needed to see the place to make the movie. I felt isolated and humiliated. When I told Chuck, he responded with a pointed witticism about Lewis and his balls, but beyond that he didn't offer to refuse to go if I didn't, and what's worse, I didn't ask him not to go. That's where I made my mistake, I figured later. I could only surmise that Chuck didn't like to buck authority unless it was really important. He was merely a lowly first writer on the project, already replaced by two different writers. Settling for an active role only as a technical adviser must have been hard for him.

As is my wont when I'm upset, I retreated into myself. Vicky, of course, I did tell, and she thought the whole situation was outrageous, but she was three thousand miles away. One fact was clear: I experienced a sense of isolation in Los Angeles like none I'd ever felt before. This was the 1980s, a period in which many feminists were separated from one another, pursuing individual goals or just trying to earn a living. What was also happening to me was that where earlier I'd been feisty all the time, now those moments were becoming fewer and farther between. I kept on going, but it wasn't with the same enthusiastic feeling as I'd had when I'd first set up the movie. I was being kept in "my place," but I was afraid to scream and shout about it, because here I really could be told to get lost. They could, consistent with any producer's contract, pay me my fee and tell me to go home. In the old days at Harvard, they couldn't throw me out of school for making a fuss, and in fact the traits I'd displayed there were treasured in lawyers. But not in female producers, I was now learning.

About four months into the strike, which seemed as though it would never end, the WGA announced that it would permit independent producers (but not studios) to sign agreements, which would allow writers employed by them to resume their work. I soon persuaded Orion to let not only Seal Team Productions—my company—sign but also all their other producers who had movies in development. Now we could get going.

What seemed to be a turn of fortune didn't impress Kevin Jarre very much. Medavoy tried to contact him, and maybe Lewis did too. Finally, the strike was settled. Another few months went by before we got the script, the arrival of which was announced by a call from Kevin's William Morris agent. The script was *so hot,* it should be shot as is, *without a word changed. The* best action script he'd ever seen.

By the next morning, all of us had read it. In addition to a large amount of gratuitous violence, there was one really sexist line that I determined to fight. The starring female role was that of the best investigative journalist when it came to matters about the Middle East. But the script described her as "a cunt at the end of two long legs." I hoped that the more civilized members of the Orion team would agree that line had to be deleted.

A meeting was scheduled in the conference room for late morning, and everyone except Lewis had pretty much the same overall reaction to the script. It was exciting, but we wanted to know more about the characters. Lewis seemed unable to understand the criticism, saying that he disagreed but not explaining his reasoning. Then I spoke up: "The line about a 'cunt at the end of two long legs' has to go." The only person who defended my position was a gay male creative director upon whom Medavoy relied heavily for script notes. Medavoy didn't respond to what I'd said but instead muttered that we'd have to find another writer to flesh out the characters. The meeting was over.

I had liked the movie *Hoosiers.* The characters were well drawn; the tone and action good. So I suggested that Angelo Pizzo, who had written the screenplay for it, be our next writer.

*At dinner with
Orion's Mike
Medavoy and his then
wife, Patricia, during
the pre-production
phase of my movie*

After he was set as our fourth writer and we talked about the starring roles, which we agreed had no depth, he got to work.

By now the 1988 Orion Christmas party was upon us, and
Medavoy introduced me to his very pretty wife, Patricia, saying
that he thought we would hit it off. Patricia apparently had
recently "produced" the Democratic National Convention, so we
shared an interest in politics, and we established that we both
played tennis. She invited me to their house on Coldwater to play
the following Sunday. That was to be the first of many social Sun-
days with Patricia and Mike.

To Patricia I confided my feelings about having been forbidden
to visit Coronado. She told me that it was horrendous, that Mike
had never mentioned anything about it to her. But she also said
that she thought it was important that I do everything I could to
ensure that the movie get made, because if I ticked off the direc-

tor and he walked, that would be the end of it, she was sure. I had
already decided that I respected Patricia's political instincts. Out
of the ashes of the Gary Hart presidential campaign, she had
begun Show Coalition, a group that attracted major politicians
and other dignitaries to Hollywood. I joined and soon after found
myself at a small lunch honoring Madeleine Albright, whose
knowledge of world affairs impressed me immediately.

Out in the real feminist world, there were actions happening.
The next big one planned was in 1989, a march on Washington
for choice. We would protest any further laws reducing a
woman's right to choose, which had been rampant when it came
to federal employees (over which Congress had jurisdiction) and
women receiving Medicaid. Patricia and I decided to go together,
although we were part of the much larger group organized by the
Hollywood Women's Political Committee (HWPC) and several
other pro-choice groups. We held placards and wore white with
the traditional yellow and purple banners across our fronts. It was
a heady experience because so many thousands of women
showed up from all over the country, some by train, bus and car;
others, like us, by plane. The unpleasant part was marching
through clusters of anti-choice moralists who held jars with
fetuses in them. When they tried to gather on the steps of the
Supreme Court, the police moved them away. Determined to
avoid fistfights, they also tried to get us to march somewhere
besides where the anti-choice people had positioned themselves.
It all worked out, and I found myself on the lawn in front of the
Capitol, chatting with my old friend Judy Collins right before she
sang, in her amazing voice, "Amazing Grace."

A very similar experience would repeat itself—for choice—
three years later, when I ventured back to Washington with
another new friend, actress Meredith Baxter. The only difference
was that on the second trip, Meredith and I—together with her
family—got separated from the HWPC crowd, as did lots of
other marchers. Despite the logistical problems causing our Los
Angeles group to seem smaller than it really was, the sentiments
were just as strong as they had been over the past years.

The plan for my movie was to start production in the fall of 1989. It was spring, and Angelo hadn't yet handed in his draft. Mike and I were now talking about finding a line producer, the person responsible for the movie's budget and for getting all the "stuff" that's actually needed to make the film. It had to be someone who knew how to deal with the unions, and Mike wanted someone who had worked abroad, because the movie would be shot, at least in part, in a country that looked like the Middle East.

After talking with Eric Pleskow and Mike, as well as checking everyone's availability, I narrowed to two the list of possible line producers. One was an Israeli who'd made movies all over the Middle East and promised to bring the movie in at $20 million. That commitment was made without his drawing up a budget or even going over Orion's in-house budget. I liked Yoram Ben-Ami, but I wasn't sure what kind of standards he had if the only issue was sticking to an arbitrarily set budget. The other candidate, preferred by Medavoy, was Bernie Williams, who had line-produced Orion's *Dirty Rotten Scoundrels,* a movie shot in the South of France. Bernie seemed smart. And somehow he made me feel important in a way that Lewis never had. He persuaded me that it was senseless for him to promise what it would cost to make the movie until he'd done his own budget. He also felt sure that Orion would agree to whatever he came up with, because they knew how efficiently he worked. I was distracted by his metal teeth.

Then Bernie gave me an ultimatum. Either I agree to share my producer credit with him or he wouldn't do the picture. It was a repeat of Marquand. Another little Napoleon type threatening that he was going to get his way or I wasn't going to get him, which meant, he maintained, the end of the movie. I told Bernie that I'd think about it over the weekend. When the phone rang relatively early on Sunday morning, it was Bernie calling to confide in me that Lewis was inept, that Lewis would never get the movie made without him. He knew how to handle this studio, and he'd worked with incompetent directors before. Bernie maintained that he and I really needed to be partners. If he was going to put his all into this picture, as he would have to, he deserved to walk up to the podium with me as we collected our Best Picture Oscar. Actually, even I had never deluded myself that *Navy SEAL* would be Academy Award material, although I did hope it would be a big commercial summer movie.

On Monday morning, I told Medavoy that Bernie had my vote, and the deal making started after Medavoy complimented me on my wisdom in deciding to share my producer credit. After all, Bernie wasn't going to get a production credit like I was, above the title, and my name would appear before his in the roll after the title. But when I heard that Bernie's line-producer fee was bigger than my "creative"-producer fee, after all the time and energy I'd put into this project, I was upset. Again, I decided to let it go, in the spirit of getting the movie made. Later, I learned that it was commonplace in Hollywood for women doing the same work as men to earn less. In fact, Meryl Streep, several years after my experience, stated publicly that when a female star, including herself, is hired to do a picture, the male star always makes sure that his salary is higher. Had I heard her story before Bernie's deal was made, I would have demanded that my fee be raised to match his. The problem was my lack of leverage. They could always tell me to leave and go home. And Bernie had figured out how to get my endorsement: pretend to be on my side 100 percent and put Lewis down in the process.

Meanwhile, despite the Coronado fiasco, I was still in frequent communication with Captain Sherman. My goal was to get Navy cooperation, because without it, we wouldn't be able to use either the SEALs' Coronado base or their Virginia Beach base— with all their ships and other colorful stuff—as locations. I told Captain Sherman that I'd show him the script as soon as it was finished. I dreaded the idea of his seeing Kevin's draft—too many shootings and too many buildings and people blowing up.

Sitting in my office one morning, I was surprised to see Lewis standing in the doorway. In an icy tone, he declared that I was never, ever, to speak to the writer unless he authorized me to. At first I couldn't understand what had made him so upset. Then I realized that Kevin, not even our most recent writer but Lewis's choice, must have told him about our dinner months and months earlier. My response was defensive: "Lewis, all I did was have dinner with Kevin. We did not discuss the script." He pushed further, ordering me not to talk to the writer at all. But now he'd gone too far. "Lewis, I am the producer, and I have every right to talk to writers and anyone else I choose. You can't stop me." He glared at me, unable as usual to think of a quick response. Then he said flatly that he could stop me, and he left. This time I didn't go to Medavoy. I had lost faith that he would be on my side.

By now, Bernie's deal was done, and strange things began to happen. I would go to his office to discuss something and get brushed off. Whatever he was doing, he kept it to himself. The only time Bernie really talked to me, after his deal was signed, was to tell me that he couldn't and wouldn't get the budget down to less than $23 million. He wouldn't show me his budget, however, so I couldn't figure out why that was so or whether there was anything that could be changed. He also said that he wanted to film the Middle East portions of the movie in Spain. He had arranged a trip for himself, Lewis and Guy Comtroix, our art designer, to visit various cities there. When I said I wanted to go, he said I wasn't needed. This time, I went to Medavoy, and his reply was that there was no money in the budget for me to scout locations. I protested that my travel should have been budgeted. Again, "No."

Shortly after that I was in the hallway of the floor where Medavoy's office was located. As I walked by, I saw through the open door everyone—all male—affiliated with my movie sitting around the conference table. No one had told me about the meeting, and from the way things had been going, I was sure it was intentional. I was furious, and as I walked down the hall, I noticed that Eric Pleskow, Orion's president, was alone in the office he used when he was in Los Angeles. He motioned for me to come in, and I did, obviously upset. I told him that as we spoke, a meeting about my movie was taking place in Medavoy's office. He told me that I should be in the meeting and offered to tell them to let me in. On the one hand, nothing would have given me greater pleasure; on the other, the idea of sitting in a room full of men who had made it known that I wasn't wanted was abhorrent.

I felt the way I did as a Jew in Chicago on New Year's Eve—a pariah, as far as they were concerned. Patricia's words came to me: "Just let the movie get made. Then you'll be able to do what you want." I told Pleskow that both Lewis and Bernie were making it impossible for me to work with them. I guessed that probably the best thing I could do was stay away. He tried to jolly me up with a story about another producer and some other Orion movie. I felt like crying and screaming at the same time. I now realize that the process, albeit a gradual one, was about my becoming a nonperson with respect to the movie I had created. And there was absolutely no reason except that I was a woman. Worse, I still couldn't summon up the righteous indignation that had been my salvation at Harvard. There I had no option but to fight a blatantly sexist institution, and I had nothing to lose by doing so. Now I was really afraid that they would send me home and it would be the end of my career in the film industry.

As I left Eric's office, I noticed Angelo Pizzo, our writer, in the hallway, probably on his way back from the bathroom. I seized the moment to ask how the script was coming along, hungry for information from anyone who knew anything. Then I realized that if Lewis came out of Medavoy's office and saw me talking with Angelo, he'd have another one of his tantrums. So like a bad school child, I beckoned Angelo to talk with me around one of the corners, out of view of Medavoy's doorway. He wanted to know what was going on, so I told him that Lewis got upset if I talked to a writer. He seemed amused, like he'd love a good fight, as he purposely pulled me out to the center of the hall, visible to anyone who came along. All I could say to him of any substance was that I wanted the part about the "cunt at the end of two long legs" out. It was already gone, he reassured me. I ended the conversation quickly and scurried off, feeling like a rat in the night. I wanted to fight back, but despite my years in the feminist trenches, I couldn't think of how to do it—and this was 1989!

Angelo's script was delivered on time. He'd been given a month to make the characters real, and the job was done. I liked his draft. By now, the only conversations I was having with Bernie were ones in which he wanted something from me, in particular whether I knew if the Navy would cooperate with the movie. It would save us millions. As much as I was eager for the support, I also enjoyed the fact that I was the only person Captain Sherman would talk to. Then Bernie wanted me to agree to his giving the king of Spain several hundred thousand dollars—to buy him off—so that we'd be sure to get the "Spanish Armada," which consisted largely of old U.S. warships, as well as a submarine that was crucial to a big scene in the movie. The Navy would never let us use an American sub, Chuck had told me all along, because they're almost all nuclear-powered and classified as top secret.

Now that Angelo's script was finished, it was time to attach stars. Shooting was scheduled to begin in September, and we had only the summer for the two stars to get into what should look like Navy SEAL shape. I'd arranged with Chuck for him to have a group of SEALs, no longer on active duty but in the Reserves, available to train one on one with the actors on our "team." And I'd talked to Rochel Blachman, the head of Business Affairs, about hiring a special trainer for the two male stars. She proceeded to find one who would charge about $600 per week. Now we needed to find the stars.

Medavoy and I went through a list of actors. Then I started calling agents at the major agencies to ask who would be available in the fall. In the middle of my calls, Medavoy buzzed me. He liked the idea of Charlie Sheen. I told him that Charlie wasn't even attractive, let alone sexy. He seemed out of shape, and he acted like a punk, too cool for his own good. But Medavoy insisted, saying that the Japanese went to movies to see him, and that was one territory we needed. In fact, Medavoy had already talked to Charlie's agent, and he was available. Again, I felt superfluous. I proceeded to focus my energy on choosing the other male star, as well as the female costar.

Negotiations began with Charlie's lawyer, Richard Hume. He

demanded $2 million as Charlie's fee. I protested that he wasn't worth it, but Medavoy ignored me, agreeing to that fee plus a percentage of adjusted gross. One of Hume's comments in the margin of Charlie's contract was an emphatic "No" next to the paragraph about our providing a trainer. Charlie wanted to select his own, and that person would get $1,800 per week. I went into Rochel's office steaming. "Not only is he ugly, but there's no way we should spend that kind of money on his body." She looked at me as though I were being naïve. His lawyer, she told me, had made this a deal breaker. "If he doesn't get a trainer of his choice, he won't be in the movie?" I asked. Again I was floored by another instance of the male sense of entitlement.

Orion gave in to all Charlie's demands, and he was our star. The good news was that his deal was pay or play. That meant we were making the movie. It had been officially greenlighted!

A long time later, I learned that the deal-breaker "trainer" provided a lot more than training. Hence his high "deal-breaker" price. Much later, a hint of Charlie's involvement with Heidi Fleiss (prostitutes and drugs) occurred when we were trying to do publicity for the release of the movie in July 1990. Charlie refused to go on television talk shows, because he didn't want to be asked about his "girlfriend," who allegedly had been a prostitute.

Eventually, Michael Biehn and Joanne Whalley-Kilmer were cast in the other starring roles. By this time, Orion had procured production office space on Tennessee Avenue. I drove over there and was shocked—again—that the first two parking spaces had Lewis's and Bernie's names on them. I introduced myself there to the two women who were our casting directors, and after we exchanged some niceties I left for my Century City Orion office. Again, I approached Medavoy. Where was *my* office on Tennessee? He just looked at me, as if to say, You don't get it, do you? and then he did say, "You don't have one over there. I think you make Lewis nervous."

Later in the summer, I ran into Roz Heller, a producer and a sister member of the Hollywood Women's Political Committee. Answering her question about whether I had a good line producer, I said I thought so: "Bernie Williams . . ." Cutting me off, she shrieked, *"Bernie Williams!* Why didn't you ask me?" I'd forgotten that he was the line producer on her Madonna movie. Roz kept repeating how awful he was and what a terrible time she had had with him on her movie. I was dismayed. Clearly, because this was my first movie, I should have made a point of calling the people I knew in Hollywood who had produced movies before. In retrospect, I think the reason I didn't was my embarrassment that I was having such a bad experience.

Three weeks before production was to begin, I received a call from Captain Sherman. He and his SEAL superiors in Coronado and Washington could live with the latest draft of the script. We would receive "limited government assistance." I asked him to translate. "That means that we'll let you shoot in Virginia Beach. You may film, but not use, U.S. Navy ships, submarines and aircraft on the base. You may not shoot the faces of any active-duty SEALs." Actually, that was more than I'd expected, given Chuck's constant refrain that the Navy's help wouldn't be worth a damn. I rushed to Medavoy's office to tell him. He, too, was pleased. Then I realized that we hadn't talked about my transportation to, and lodging in, either Virginia or Spain. His only response was that I'd better talk to Lewis about that.

So that night, I called Lewis. After he grunted hello, I told him that I needed to finalize my plans for traveling to Virginia and Spain, as well as reserve a hotel room. Again, a painfully long silence before Lewis launched into a tirade that began with, "You're not going to Virginia or Spain. And if *you* do, *I'm* not going to be there." I started to express my anger, but he shouted into the phone, "Everybody hates you." The words rang in my ears. I have a strong personality, but "hate" me! The only people, besides the Orion executives and Bernie, connected with the movie whom I'd met were Guy Comtroix, the art designer, the various writers and the casting women, all of whom I had liked immediately and felt sure had liked me. Well, maybe not Kevin Jarre, the tough-guy writer. I had never met the stars or any of the crew. I couldn't figure out what Lewis was talking about.

In Medavoy's office the next morning, I was close to tears. "Mike, this is my movie. I have every right to be there. Producers go on location." "Brenda," he said, "you can't go, because there's no money in the budget. We've stepped up to Bernie's $23 million, but that's it." I argued that surely there was something else that could be cut. I even took issue with the fact that they were paying Bernie so much more than me. And then I asked him whether my transportation and lodging had ever been in any of the budgets Bernie had drawn up and refused to let me see. The answer was no.

I was being shut out of my own movie. I had done nothing wrong, and it hurt so bad that I couldn't think of anything else to say. The silence was broken by Medavoy, who had moved on to a new subject. "We'll have the contract from Loeb & Loeb for you to sign on Monday." Orion, which financed its movies as negative pickups,* needed my signature as president of Seal Team Productions, the company through which Orion ran all the contracts and the company I'd used to get around the Writers Guild strike. Now Seal Team Productions would borrow $23 million from Bank of America, represented by Loeb & Loeb, which had, coincidentally, merged with Hess, Segall, where I'd worked ten years earlier. The loan to my company would be backed by Orion's line of credit, and they would pay the bank back after the movie was made. But in fact I didn't feel, right then, like borrowing the money for them. I was very angry.

At home that night, I just sat there. I was too embarrassed even to tell Vicky, and the thought of telling Alexis, who was already fluent in Spanish and had been pressing to visit me in Spain, was awful. But somehow I pulled myself together, and by Saturday I had told both Vicky and Alexis that I wouldn't be going to Virginia or to Spain. The lumps in my throat were hard to swallow. Vicky was outraged at Orion, Lewis, and the whole Industry, while Alexis, although I know she was as empathetic as she could

---

* That is, by getting the production money before the movie is shot by preselling it to foreign exhibitors, after initially borrowing that money from a bank.

be, was probably at least equally upset that she wouldn't be able to spend Thanksgiving in Spain, where we'd planned to celebrate her fifteenth birthday.

I was in the office on Monday when I received a call from Rochel Blachman, in Business Affairs. They were expecting the contract to arrive about 4:00 p.m. from Loeb & Loeb. They would need me to look at it immediately—if I wanted to—and then go over to Loeb & Loeb to sign multiple originals of various supporting documents, together with the contract. Four p.m. came, and then at 5:00 p.m. there was a call that the messenger was leaving their offices, which were four blocks away. It took him until 5:45 p.m. to get to me.

I was a good enough lawyer to know that I shouldn't sign anything I haven't read—even though my lawyers had—so I settled in. It was a long contract. Rochel called to ask if I was ready to leave about fifteen minutes after I'd received the contract. I told her I'd call her when I'd finished reviewing it. She reminded me that my lawyers had already approved it and that a team of Loeb & Loeb lawyers was waiting. "Let them wait," I replied. "They should have thought of that while they were taking all day to finish the contract."

Bleary-eyed by the time I'd reached the last page of the "boiler-plate" language, nonetheless I woke up fast when I read the third paragraph from the end. There, in tiny type, was a sentence saying that if I had received any payments more than three years before the date the contract was signed, all provisions in the contract regarding my pay and credit were null and void. I read that paragraph three times. Then I called Rochel. I referred her to the offensive language. When she tried to defend it, I interrupted to tell her that since it meant I would be entitled to no producer's fee or credit, we might as well hang up then and there. I wasn't signing. We got off the phone, and I called Tom Selz, my lawyer, in New York. It was about 9:30 p.m. East Coast time.

My question was whether he had actually read the contract that he'd approved my signing. He hesitated and then, sounding fearful, replied that their associate had gone over it. I told him that had been a mistake and read the offensive language to him. He sounded stunned, then defensively tried to tell me that Michael Hausman, a well-known producer client of theirs, had always signed Orion contracts that included such language. I told him that Michael Hausman, an aging hippie line producer who rode around on a motorcycle, was not someone whose legal acumen impressed me. I didn't care what he had signed. Either Tom would get them to delete the paragraph or I was going home and not signing. Tom asked me to conference Rochel in, which I did. At that point, he started shouting at her, defending the position I had just taken with him. Rochel stood firm. I told them I was hanging up. I'd stay in the office while they worked it out—for a while, at least. Rochel said she'd have to try to find Bill Bernstein in Rye, New York. "Whatever," I said, picking up the trades and starting to read them. And the great thing about that moment was that I was enjoying the taste of power for a change.

A little while later, Tom called. Bernstein had agreed to change the language. I'd be paid my full fee and get the credits as agreed. I hung up, put on my jacket, and headed toward the elevators, where Rochel was waiting, looking duly chastised. When we arrived at Loeb & Loeb, about ten lawyers—of all ranks, ages and sizes—were waiting, looks of relief visible as we entered the room. I changed and initialed that paragraph in all the copies, and finally signed the contracts.

As Rochel and I were leaving their offices, she said she heard that I wasn't going on location and that she thought it was outrageous. To her, it was obvious that the sole reason was because of my gender. The only woman in the company with any real power got it, and for a moment I didn't feel so alone. I thanked her for her empathy and wished that she had more power so she would be able to influence Orion's decision-making processes, at least about my going to Spain. And I forgave her for her blinding devotion to Orion in defense of that ridiculous paragraph in the earlier draft of my contract.

September came and production started. Everyone at Orion knew that I was the producer and I wasn't on location. By then,

Bernie and Lewis weren't speaking. Every day at 3:00 p.m., Orion had dailies. Since *Navy SEAL* was one of several movies they had shooting at the same time, I had to wait in the projection room until my movie was on the screen. (It's not proper for a producer of one movie to view the dailies of another.) Medavoy had been trying to convince me that I'd get more out of watching dailies than trudging around behind Lewis or Bernie on location. I was almost able to persuade myself that he was right.

During the first week, even though I hadn't seen many dailies in my life, I could tell something was wrong. Lewis had insisted on a director of photography of his choosing, and the scenes were dull and lifeless. Finally, on about the seventh day, Medavoy called me into his office. "We have to talk," he said. This will be a first, I thought. "Seriously," he added. I waited. And then he told me they weren't happy with Teague. Medavoy asked me to check with my sources at the agencies, without telling them why, and find out which directors were available to begin work immediately. He seemed troubled because he knew I knew he'd been wrong all along about Lewis.

"You finally get it," I couldn't resist pointing out.

I started making calls to the heads of the big agencies in town. All of them had someone who could start in several weeks if the project was right, but I'd have to tell them what the movie was before they'd cooperate further. When I relayed those results back to Medavoy, he told me that maybe his going to Virginia, where they were shooting, would help. Because Orion wouldn't pay for even one week of the set being closed while another director was brought up to speed, he was giving up finding another director. "Penny-wise and pound-foolish," I kept thinking.

When Medavoy came back to Los Angeles, he called me into a meeting before dailies. His remedy to the Lewis problem was to get the best director of photography they could find. John Alonzo, a highly respected cinematographer, had been hired, and Lewis's choice canned. As much as I wanted to believe that the DP would be the solution, I knew that Medavoy had taken the chicken's way out. If he had allowed me to tell the agents the truth, I still believe, we could have found a terrific director—more expensive, but worth it.

Fortunately, the dailies that were coming in now looked infinitely better. Alonzo knew how to light a scene so that the sky and the ocean were actually different shades of blue. The movie was a lot prettier, but the reports we were receiving from the set were troubling. It sounded as though the cast and crew were about to mutiny. At one point, I heard that Lewis had lost total control and that Bill Paxton, playing the role of a maverick SEAL called God, had ended up writing and directing a whole new golf course scene. At another point, I heard that the nine SEAL technical advisers—Chuck and his ex-SEAL friends—had worked for thirty-six hours without a break. They were in the first unit, playing roles ranging from CIA operatives to Naval Intelligence Service officers. They were the stunt doubles for the actors. And they were also the stunt people when we just needed guys to perform difficult exercises, like those in the BUDs training scene.

In Spain, there were seven units working full-time in an attempt to finish the movie before the holidays. Lewis was largely being ignored. People were doing their jobs without his direction.

One day, when we were watching dailies in the screening room, the Orion executives—all guys—started laughing. The scene was of Billy Paxton, the team's sharpshooter, in deep weeds showing off his sharpshooting skills to Joanne Whalley-Kilmer's character at the request of Michael Biehn's character. Instead of doing the scene as it was written, Lewis had given Billy a young partner, who was crouching in the weeds next to him. There was nothing funny about it, but the guys kept hooting in disgust, while I worried that Lewis was really losing it. The scene made sense only if the viewer was to infer a gay relationship.

Another day, we were watching dailies when all of a sudden Medavoy growled loudly, "Goddamnit. He'd better have covered that scene with an outside shot." It turned out that, at considerable expense, Guy Comtroix, the art director, had procured a houseboat, which was where Michael Biehn's character lived and which said something about the kind of guy he was. But instead of having Joanne Whalley-Kilmer's character visit him on the deck of the houseboat, so the audience could see that it *was* a houseboat, Lewis had shot the scene inside, making it look like any apartment anywhere. Medavoy called the location in Virginia from the screening room and ordered Lewis to reshoot the scene the next day outside on the deck.

Bernie, of course, was making his presence felt. I had heard that he'd called Medavoy and threatened to quit unless Orion came up with another big chunk of money for him. Bernie knew that if he left, the whole movie would fall apart. So Orion apparently paid him more to do what his contract already required— stay and complete his job.

Meanwhile, I found a lot that needed to be done stateside. First, the logo had to be cleared. The Navy hadn't trademarked their BUDs logo, but we wanted our own for merchandising, T-shirts, and whatever advertising we might need it for. So there were meetings with artists and lawyers, all engaged in the task of tweaking the insignia—enough so that Orion could own it but not so much that it wouldn't resemble the real BUDs insignia. Then the music had to be determined and the music supervisor selected. After that I directed my attention to merchandising and met with Data East, a big Japanese computer/video game company, to develop a game based on the movie. A deal was made, but the details would have to wait until Data East could see the final version of the movie. And finally, Orion hired a woman named Debra Davis to do publicity for the movie. Debra and I got along famously, and one of our tasks was to figure out a way that the SEALs could help with the movie's promotion, because this was the first time the Pentagon was letting the public see them up close and we wanted to take advantage of that.

The shooting finished miraculously close to schedule, and Don Zimmerman, the editor, went to work, ferociously determined that the movie be ready for the following summer. In April, ShoWest was having its annual Las Vegas convention, at which studios and other distributors displayed a few minutes of each of their upcoming films. Then the exhibitors decided what would play in their moviehouses over the summer. Two days before the convention, I hadn't yet been invited to go to Las Vegas. When I raised the subject with Medavoy, this time the answer was "Of course you're going." A first-class round-trip ticket was delivered to my office that afternoon. Two days later, I was picked up by a large limousine, and when I reached the Las Vegas airport, I stopped at the slot machines. I lost two quarters, won five and decided to quit while I was ahead. Another limousine was waiting to take me to the hotel.

The heart-shaped king-size bed with a mirrored ceiling above it might have been great if I'd had somebody in my life and with me, but the only activities available to me then were to unpack and go downstairs for a round or two of blackjack. I stayed for about an hour and won eighty dollars, which was a lot for me, especially since I was at a five-dollar table. Finally, I saw some folks from Orion, and off we went to dinner.

Orion's big moment came the next morning. There were at least three thousand exhibitors crowded into the hotel's largest ballroom. Up on the stage were all the people responsible for Orion's summer and fall movies, including Kevin Costner with a crowd from *Dances with Wolves*. The stage was divided into two halves by an aisle in the middle. On one side sat Michael Biehn, Lewis, and assorted other cast members, as well as all kinds of people from other Orion movies. On my side were Charlie Sheen, Bernie and more cast members. At the podium up front was Orion's head of marketing and publicity, Joel Resnick.

Finally he got to my movie. I was feeling proud, but then he misstated the movie's name, calling it *Navy SEALS* instead of *Navy SEAL*. I remembered that someone had handed Joel a piece of paper just before he started to introduce himself. As I was pondering this, Joanne Whalley-Kilmer made a late stage entrance, came up to say hello, and in a soft whisper asked me where Michael was. I said, "Over there," nodding toward the other side. "Where's Lewis?" she then queried. I said, "Right behind Michael." "Oh no," she said. "I'm not going near him." With that she managed to find a seat on our side of the aisle.

After Orion's presentation, I went up to Joel. Before I could even ask what was up with the name, he volunteered that in the middle of the night, Arthur Krim, the chairman of Orion's board, had decided that no one would understand *Navy SEAL*. He liked *NAVY SEALS* as a title better. I didn't mind the new name, but the problem was that Arthur Krim had decided to use his muscle at a really bad time. Now there could be no *NAVY SEALS* game. It would take too long for Data East (or any other company) to redo the packaging.

Traditionally, the director is allowed three screenings before "typical" audiences so that he (or she) can adjust the movie depending on the reaction. The first screening was in a blue-collar shopping mall miles from Los Angeles. This would be the first time that the Orion executives and I saw the ending, and we were all shocked by it. Honoring the main Arab terrorist, thousands of Arabs chanted anti-American bullshit as his corpse was carried on a platform, raised above their heads, through the streets of Beirut. We couldn't figure out what Lewis's political message was, nor did we care. It was an almost unanimous decision—Lewis was the only dissenting vote—that the scene was out and one of the other three possible endings that they'd shot would be substituted. I realized that if Lewis had been prevented from shooting that scene, I could easily have traveled to and from locations and there would still have been tons of money left over. Where had Bernie been?

When I went down to Coronado to attend a special screening for SEAL officers from both coasts, I was introduced to some very big-deal SEAL officers, one of whom notoriously had affairs with young SEAL wives while their husbands were off on missions. (He was in a position to know how long the teams would be away.) The screening began after both Chuck and I said a few words of introduction and the lights dimmed. The SEALs loved the movie, which they showed by throwing beer bottles at the screen and hooting. Sometimes they would shout out the dialogue before the actors had even said anything. They speak their own language, which Chuck, helping the other four screenwriters, certainly got right.

Meanwhile, Orion had agreed to my having a small private screening for my friends and Alexis in New York about a week before the movie was to open. After that, it was back to Los Angeles for the premiere, which was also an exhibitors' screening. I anxiously took the seat that Patricia and Mike were saving for me next to an "eligible" male friend of theirs. To my delight, the standing-room-only audience seemed really to enjoy the movie.

Opening night of the movie was a time of high anxiety for me, as it is for all producers. Debra Davis, the publicist, and I drove around from theater to theater, making sure the posters for our movie were prominently displayed. As we made our rounds, I realized that all the other studios had arranged for the ticket sellers to wear their buttons (Disney with its *Arachnaphobia* buttons, for example), in an effort to send a subliminal message to ticket buyers. Orion had no plans to spend any more money on publicity, so Debra and I hauled from the trunk of my car plastic drinking bottles emblazoned with our *NAVY SEALS* logo and the movie's name (originally intended as gifts for me and my

The SEAL team of NAVY SEALS posed for a promotional photo. Stars Charlie Sheen and Michael Biehn are in the front row.

friends) and asked the sellers to put them in the windows of their booths. Most agreed, but I felt as though Debra and I were the only ones promoting the movie at the time when promotion was most needed.

I arrived home that night to find a telegram from Lily Tomlin and Jane Wagner, congratulating me and wishing me a great opening weekend. It had been almost four years since my long walk to dinner with them at Le Dome on my first NAVY SEALS business trip to Los Angeles.

One day not long after the movie opened, I received a call from the Gersh Agency, which represented Lewis. This particular agent started out pleasantly enough, but then he got to the point. He wanted to be sure I was saying nice things about Lewis. I said I would tell the truth to anyone who asked. He flew into a rage and threatened to sue me. I dared him to and hung up.

Lewis had a hard time finding work after NAVY SEALS, I heard. One day, while I was out for lunch, I received a call from a William Morris friend and agent, Joan Hyler. I returned her call as soon as I got back to the office: "I was going to ask you how it was—working with Lewis," she said, "but now it's too late." I replied that the experience had been truly terrible, but she'd already committed her client, Rutger Hauer, to an HBO movie that Lewis was directing. "Too bad," I replied. "You should have given me a chance to return your call." Months later I received a call from Joan confirming that I had been absolutely right. Rutger had had a horrible experience. "Even big, macho Rutger," I mused, smiling.

Then about two years later, I met Kathleen Turner at the Cirque de Soleil. She had costarred with Michael Douglas in Romancing the Stone. I said I had a question for her.

"Okay," she responded quizzically.

"How did you like working with Lewis Teague?"

She responded in her throaty, theatrical voice, "It was perfectly horrible."

But this tale is not about Lewis Teague; it's about the fact that no other men really supported me, as the producer of NAVY

SEALS. (There weren't enough women to count.) I was too upset to fight; I wasn't the "Feisty Feigen" of Harvard Law School days, but instead someone intimidated into playing by their rules so I'd be able to work in this town again. I now know that this happens to women all the time in Hollywood, and it doesn't matter that there are a few more women today with the power to greenlight movies.

Several years after *NAVY SEALS* had been released, I was in New York and met an old friend from Prague for lunch at the Russian Tea Room. She had a "sort of" compliment for me. Medavoy had told a well-respected producer she was seeing that I was "one of the smartest cunts in the business." I didn't feel flattered. No matter how smart I was, I was still a cunt.

So there I was—a woman who entered the movie business with a lot of experience (albeit not much as a producer) and a lot of knowledge both about the business and the Industry. And I was treated badly and unfairly. Many women want to be producers, and my advice is that they have to be tough and say no from the start to any attempts to treat them as inferior. The fact that they're getting a credit and a fee is no reason to shut up and stay home. Strong women make a lot of guys uncomfortable. And those guys may well threaten to walk, just the way Lewis and then Bernie did, if they don't get their way. If I had to do it again, I'd call them on their threats. I still feel ashamed for not standing up to them.

Until my own experience, I hadn't really realized how bad things are for women in Hollywood. What I wanted most after *NAVY SEALS* I couldn't get: a deal at a studio, any studio, that would allow me to develop and produce movies with strong positive roles for women. Instead—and as might be expected—Chuck, who was rewritten by four different writers, immediately got a big three-picture writing deal at Universal and an offer, I heard, actually to direct a movie as well.

Chapter 8

HOLLYWOOD

Making *NAVY SEALS,* I had been immersed in an all-male film environment. Rarely was anything in the outside world discussed. It was all business. Often I had wondered if they watched the national news or read anything but the trades—*The Hollywood Reporter* and *Variety.* I couldn't help but make all sorts of comparisons between New York and Los Angeles.

On the East Coast, the men I knew talked about world issues. In Los Angeles, a different dynamic is at work. Most of the men there talk only about—and live only for—the Industry. Many of the East Coast men were married and apparently monogamous; if they had extramarital affairs, it was quietly. But in Los Angeles, everyone knows about the married men who screw around, including their wives. In one of Liz Smith's columns, she discussed the possibility of Bill Clinton's moving to Hollywood. And at the end, she concluded, "Bill Clinton would be an asset in a show-biz world where sexual peccadilloes and sly dodging are not considered high crimes but a way of life." Possibly to save face, maybe to keep their husbands, the Hollywood wives (as distinguished from many New York and Washington wives) comply by having every possible alteration made to their bodies—from face lifts to tummy tucks and liposuction. Movie stars go to crazy extremes. One movie star had ribs removed so that she would look even more anorexic than she already did. Not only do actresses want men to want them, they want jobs, and that means preserving a youthful image. Once they no longer can pass for thirty-something, they either give in and play grandmothers or they decide to try their hand at directing (which is a good thing, but they should be able to get acting roles too).

Men in Hollywood drive cars that project testosterone-driven, hell-bent masculinity—and lots of money. Recently, I saw a black stretch Hummer limousine and imagined Brad Pitt or even Leonardo DiCaprio in the back. In general, though, Porsches and Ferraris seem the cars of choice right now for the men, representing to their owners rich, phallic power: "My thing (car and/or penis) is better, bigger and faster than yours." This kind of guy, on both coasts, usually smokes cigars, basically daring women to put up with their odor, although there are young women who, despite studies showing how carcinogenic cigars are, think it's cool to smoke them themselves. The wives of these men almost all drive various top-of-the-line sport utility vehicles, which, although necessary for real soccer moms, who do the family grocery shopping and shlep their kids to school and sports, seem only to be the latest fad for Hollywood wives.

In 1995, *You'll Never Make Love in This Town Again,* written by my partner, Joanne, was published by Dove. Gloria had been asked to write an introduction for a manuscript about prostitutes, but before she would lend her name to it, she felt that what she read needed a complete rewrite. She also recognized that the book needed a feminist consciousness and that Joanne was the perfect person for it. The book was all about prostitutes who spend time with movie stars, and it became an instant best-seller. When it was finally time for me to read Joanne's book, I had trouble, because not only were the men disgusting—the desire of many of the men for toilet sex was beyond my worst imaginings— the women were naïve and drug-addicted. A big part of the problem was that they enjoyed the money and the gifts and, in fact, were willing to put up with just about anything—usually to support their drug habits.

Joanne took the feminist position that the comparatively powerless women, most arriving from Hick Town, U.S.A., with dreams of becoming starlets, are sexual slaves, in this case victims of the worst kind of power-hungry, egotistical men—movie stars like Sylvester Stallone and Jack Nicholson and producers like Robert Evans (*Cotton Club*).

Joanne followed that book with a sequel in 1996, *Once More with Feeling,* which was more of the same—just different men. What these books do is illustrate that powerful men, especially those with money and not much reason to think seriously about anything, will spend their time making their own personal pornography in which young, vulnerable women become objectified and even abused.

There were threats of lawsuits from some of the men, but they evaporated. It had become a badge of honor to have made it into Joanne's book. Some who weren't in it, I heard, were dejected because they felt either that they hadn't been deemed important or famous enough to make the cut, or that they weren't "manly" enough to engage in the kind of kinky sex only prostitutes will provide.

What johns want is disconnected sex—no obligations, no emotional involvement. They go home to their wives (at least the ones who can keep a wife) and pretend to be normal husbands. And the wives have too much invested in these Hollywood marriages to ask questions, let alone start fights or threaten to leave. These men probably don't use condoms with their wives. The odds are good they don't with the prostitutes either. Therein lies a possible death sentence.

Before I got to Hollywood, I didn't know that so many men went to prostitutes. In fact, men I knew in the East thought having to pay for sex was a sign of their own inferiority. But much later I learned that men pay prostitutes not only for sex but also to go away. While enjoying the absolute power they're wielding over a woman, they don't even need to utter a word. These men cannot do this with their wives, because even the most oppressed Hollywood wife, hanging in there for the good life, would demand at least minimal emotional connection with her husband.

I had made friends with some of the wives of the men I'd worked with in Hollywood, but in general I'd found that the wives of male studio executives aren't allies in our fight to get more feminist content on the screen. In fact, many of them feel threatened by the word "feminist." They want to travel the world with their husbands, wear designer clothes and jewels of their choice, work as much or as little as they want or not at all, or have a "career," which is always secondary to whatever is going on with the husband.

The schizophrenia caused by being a wife is reflected in the names by which they are known. Not long ago, I received an invitation to a lavish baby shower. The hostesses were ten *major* Hollywood wives, every single one of whom identified herself on the invitation only by her husband's name, even though, in their daily lives, many use their birth names and all, their own first names. To be important enough to host that party, however, they used the names of their husbands, the ones with the real power. And, of course, all of these women *were* wives—not a single or divorced woman among them.

As I looked at the very made-up faces of the women in that room, I realized, as I had many times before, that these wives' lives are really just glorified forms of prostitution and that their primary relationship to their husbands is economic. The major difference between prostitutes and wives is that the latter have children to justify their marriages to men, most of whom, everyone knows, also have affairs, keep mistresses or go to prostitutes on the side. In fact, prostitutes seem to be rampant in Hollywood. An intelligent, married male writer was writing a script for a producer but it wasn't working out to the latter's satisfaction. As the writer was sitting in the producer's office one day, the producer pulled out a cigar box. "If you write the story my way," he said, "you can have any one of these you want." Opening the cigar box, he revealed nude pictures of a number of beautiful women, several of whom the writer recognized to be fairly well-known actresses.*

---

* Joanne Parrent, *Once More with Feeling* (Los Angeles: Dove Books, 1996), p. xii.

Not much seems to surprise the denizens of Hollywood. Once I heard that a well-known married producer sexually abuses very young children. Then the same bit of information was given me by a totally different source. If I'd heard it, so had other people. The same man keeps getting work, which translates into people not caring. They just accept the fact that certain men are pedophiles; others use prostitutes and/or drugs, and still others have affairs and/or physically abuse their wives. Whatever their preference is, it's either kinky enough to turn the others on or it's behavior thought to be the other guy's personal business. As long as he delivers on the job, they don't care what he does—even if his actions get as bad as late producer Don Simpson's (*Top Gun*) notorious drug use, which eventually, after he'd abused countless women with his sick, sadomasochistic practices, led to his death.

Most women in Hollywood, be they executives or wives, didn't find it offensive that Jeffrey Katzenberg, when he was head of production at Disney, took a group of men, all powerful executives, on an annual rafting trip down the Colorado River. (I don't know if he is continuing that practice now that he's at Dream-Works SKG.) Women were not invited. Katzenberg's guests clearly were conducting business; most wouldn't know how to let a day pass without consummating some sort of deal. And at the very least it solidified relationships so that deals would flow naturally after that. It's so reminiscent of what I was fighting back in the sixties at Harvard Law School, and it certainly smacks of the old Harvard Club days, with its no-women policy.

Here in Hollywood, keeping women out is a sport to be enjoyed (although it's really actionable sex discrimination). On the other hand, male politicians in Washington get black marks if they are members of male-only clubs, just as they do if they join all-white clubs. There is a political consciousness there—at least about private clubs, if not sexual affairs—that doesn't exist in Hollywood.

The attitude of men toward women in Hollywood is to suffer us and to elevate us when absolutely necessary so as to appear progressive. At the 1997 Women in Film Crystal Awards lunch, I heard Joe Roth, head of production at Disney, declare that discrimination against women in Hollywood has become a nonissue. He was sitting next to Diane Keaton. Goldie Hawn, Bette Midler and Diane were being honored for their roles in *The First Wives Club*. After Roth introduced Diane and sat down, what she had to say was a total contradiction of what he'd said. After stating that there are few decent roles for women in general, she announced that she wanted to help ensure that women, especially those over fifty, got roles in movies. Those are the kinds of scripts she was looking for as a director and certainly, given her age, as an actor.

Joe Roth didn't seem to be listening to Diane, maybe because his own wife, Donna, had produced a hit movie, but did he (or she) ever wonder whether she had the opportunity to make that movie because her husband was head of the studio? In fact, that's how it is with a lot of women producers here. Either the husband gets the wife an office and some sort of deal at the studio the husband runs, or he has influence with some other powerful male. The fact that many of the successful women in Hollywood even today, married or not, have slept their way to the top is depressing. Despite feminism, this phenomenon continues.

As for women directors in Hollywood, the statistics in the previous chapter speak for themselves, but so do the attitudes expressed in news stories.

In a *Los Angeles Times* front-page story on September 25, 1997, captioned "Shooting for a Role in a Male Film Genre," statistics were printed regarding how hard it has been for women to get jobs directing action pictures. When I saw the headline, I remembered the day I suggested to Orion's Mike Medavoy and Jon Sheinberg that we find a woman who could direct *NAVY SEALS*. They had laughed at me, but seven years later, a big-budget ($50 million) action picture, *The Peacemaker*, was directed by a woman, Mimi Leder, whose next picture, a sci-fi thriller, had a budget of $75 million. Of course, more is at stake than there would be for any male director. As Penelope Spheeris, who directed *Wayne's World* and *Beverly Hillbillies*, bluntly put it, "Let's hope it [*The Peacemaker*] does well, because if it doesn't we're screwed."[1]

According to the same *Los Angeles Times* article: "Looking across all film genres, including the character-driven dramas with female stars that some in Hollywood call 'chick flicks,' women make up a fraction of the directing world. Fewer than 2,300 of the 11,000 Directors Guild of America members are women."[2]

Much more on the subject came out in a January 1999 *New York Times* article. Penelope Spheeris, for example, has found the going rough since *Wayne's World* (1992) made her the first female director of a movie that earned more than $100 million at the box office. As she put it, "For me, this is the only issue: how women are treated. It says just about everything about the way this industry works, what it values. But no one wants to really face it."[3]

Action films are essentially off-limits to women in Hollywood, except for two (Kathryn Bigelow and Mimi Leder) who have connections to powerful men in town. Steven Spielberg has suggested that the formulaic quality of action films may not appeal to women. "You don't need touch, or feel, or taste. It's very mathematical."[4] (I was a math major!) And there are women who actually help to perpetuate the stereotypes. Lynda Obst, a veteran Hollywood producer, believes that women are willing to work less frequently in order to "make personal movies. They come to the business more for reasons of expression than for careerist reasons."[5] Apparently, Obst doesn't think women need to work the way men need to, or that they want, or care about, their careers.

Martha Coolidge, who directed *Valley Girl* and *Out to Sea*, calls Lynda Obst's reasoning "ridiculous": "There are women like me who like to work. Period. Sure, we want to make the films close to our heart. So do guys. But while you're waiting for that, you want decent work. John Frankenheimer [another director] said to me recently, 'You don't learn anything from not directing movies.'"[6]

Betty Thomas, who directed the film *Dr. Dolittle*, which earned more than $150 million domestically, commented that with big-budget movies "there's a feeling out there that it's a war that you have to win or die. And in a war, the director is the head dude. I guess it's harder to imagine the general as a girl."[7]

Kathryn Bigelow, who was married to director James Cameron, has another opinion that feeds the sexist attitude of the men with power in town: "A lot of women just aren't interested in making movies that involve a lot of flying rocks and explosions. . . . Some women may not be tenacious enough to cope with the enormous pressure that comes with trying to get big-budget projects off the ground. . . . It takes everything you've got. Women may just not be able to wait it out."[8]

For some reason Bigelow seems to think that she herself, unlike most women, is tenacious and able to wait it out. Why she attributes to other women character defects that she isn't plagued with can probably be attributed to the fact that she is part of a very small elite who can make these action movies. It eliminates the competition.

But looking only at action pictures gives an inaccurate sense of how bad matters are for women. All but one of the big-budget, so-called women's pictures of 1998 were directed by men.

Lynda Obst had something to say about that too. She insisted that she tried "desperately" to find a woman to direct her film *Hope Floats* but that "none of them was completely right," so she chose Forest Whitaker, a black man, who has, she said, "the directing sensibility of a woman."[9]

Three weeks after the article in which these women were quoted appeared in the *New York Times,* a letter by B. Ruby Rich, the former director of the film program at the New York State Council on the Arts and the author of *Chick Flicks: Theories and Memories of the Feminist Film Movement,* appeared in the Letters to the Editor section. She wrote that "it's a relief to see *The Times* print what every woman in the industry will only say off the record: if you don't look like anybody's son, it's hard to get your movie made." And her conclusion was that "the combination of a free market and Hollywood's male clubbiness has created a devastating situation for American women directors. It's a waste of talent that we can ill afford."[10]

After reading that depressing *Times* article about women filmmakers in Hollywood, I was hopeful that women fared better in the independent film world, which was just wrapping up its 1999 Sundance Film Festival. But alas, there staring me in the face in the same section of the *New York Times* was the headline of another piece: "Even in Independent Film, A Suit Is a Suit Is a Suit."[11] The question posed in bold typeface was "Nobody doubts that independent film is a boys' club; the question is, how exclusive?" The author, Manohla Dargis, the film editor of *LA Weekly,* had strong opinions:

> It isn't fashionable to talk about the alarmingly low number of American women directing independent features. In fact, the tendency is to insist that things are nowhere near as bad as they seem. . . . It's the sort of collective denial practiced by women and men alike that results in those preternaturally optimistic women's film panels . . . the endless special editions of magazines that haul out the usual suspects like Jodie Foster as evidence that, really, women don't have it so bad. . . . The truth [is] that independent film is no more hospitable to female directors than Hollywood is. If anything, sometimes it's worse, a boys' club where few girls are allowed.[12]

Dargis pointed out that matters are getting worse. There were four female directors who won the Sundance Grand Jury Prize for the dramatic competition during the 1980s, but in the 1990s there were none. And Tom Ortenberg, copresident of Lion's Gate Films (a respected independent film company), frankly agreed: "It would be dishonest to say that there was no boys' club." Even he is "constantly shocked by some of the stuff" he still hears about women in the business.[13]

Again, there are women detractors—women who, it seems clear, don't want other women to succeed and are intent on perpetuating the stereotypes. Polly Platt, a longtime producer of both independent and studio movies, calls directing "really, really, really a difficult job. Women are generally nurturing, that's why they have become producers rather than directors, they tend to pour oil on troubled waters."

While Polly Platt may be confused, the author of the *New York Times* article, Nancy Hass, who teaches journalism at New York University, isn't. She concludes:

> Without question, the prototype for the independent American movie director remains overwhelmingly male: The monomaniacal visionary caught between genius and madness who sacrifices everything to direct. The choice for female directors is clear. Either to accept that male model, and risk being damned for behaving the same way your male counterparts are rewarded for behaving every day, or try to forge a new path. The danger with the latter choice is that you just might get jeered off the set.[14]

Some women filmmakers focus on remakes like *Little Women*, but movies like that don't add anything to what the culture already has absorbed about the role of women, be it two hundred years ago or today. And those are the kinds of pictures women writers, directors and producers are most often encouraged to make. It seems that the only women who manage to break out of the mold of safe pictures, aside from the two action directors connected to powerful Hollywood male directors, are huge stars like Barbra Streisand. When she decided to produce a movie, starring Glenn Close, based on the story of a lesbian army officer discharged for saying she was a lesbian, she had the power to get it made on network television.

In the late 1960s, what distinguished Harvard Law School, for all its sexism, from Hollywood was that the former had an image as an intelligent, liberal organization, which required that it appear receptive to change. The same is true of other establishment operations against which I butted my feminist head in New York. They want to seem enlightened. In Hollywood, there is no such desire. None of the guys in power are particularly interested in change, or even in appearing to be interested in change. Rather, they want to preserve the status quo and keep the supply of money and other perks flowing their way. They seem to get it about gay men but not about black or Hispanic executives. And there are only a few minority actors.* At one moment in time— on the heels of the success of the movie *Waiting to Exhale* and the biopic about Tina Turner, as well as the TV miniseries *The Women of Brewster Place*—I thought they understood that audiences of all ethnicities and both genders would go see movies about black women. That was short-lived, and *Beloved,* which received negative reviews, didn't help at all.

Just after I arrived in Hollywood, I decided to try to make a movie about the involuntary sterilization of young black girls in the South. CBS was interested and signed me to produce, and I hired writers to do a script, based on one of the true stories that Gloria and I had unearthed after I had taken on representation in 1973 of a new client who had been involuntarily sterilized in North Carolina. More stories had surfaced about the subject after we announced that case—and this one, I knew, would make an important TV movie. I took a trip with the writers—a husband-wife team—to Alabama to meet the Relf sisters and their family. But when the finished script was delivered to CBS, the executives there started to get cold feet. Finally, after much hemming and hawing, they 'fessed up. Even though they'd spent a lot of money on the writers, rights fees, travel and other expenses, they decided that the typical TV audience wouldn't be interested in the story unless I could get Oprah Winfrey to star as the social worker who tried to help the girls. The problem was that Oprah's deal was with ABC, so she wouldn't star in a CBS movie. I persisted, pointing out that a number of other well-known black actresses had expressed interest, including Lynne Whitfield, who had the dialect of the black Alabama family featured in the movie down pat. It didn't matter. CBS decided not to make the movie, leaving me free to set it up elsewhere. I could still make the movie if

---

* The NAACP has recently begun a protest against the scarcity of black actors on television.

only there were some entity "brave" enough to produce a TV movie or low-budget feature (and that included paying back CBS for all its prior expenditures) on this controversial subject.

Another minority group, lesbians who are out, is very small: television's Ellen DeGeneres and her movie-star girlfriend, Anne Heche, are about it. Despite fears that she'd never work again, Anne's career continued as she starred opposite Harrison Ford in *Six Days and Seven Nights*. She left her former agents and became a client of Mike Ovitz's Artists Management Group, which will, no doubt, find plenty of work for her. Meanwhile, she and Ellen worked together on the terrific three-part HBO movie *If These Walls Could Talk 2*—stories of three lesbian couples, one in the fifties, one in the seventies and one, contemporary. Other lesbians remain closeted, probably because they fear that they would never again be cast in romantic roles opposite male stars. There are a few out lesbians who are executives and agents, but they don't tend to promote material involving lesbians.

Washington, D.C., is a town to which Hollywood is frequently compared, because it, too, is a one-industry place and everyone knows and socializes with folks they work with on a daily basis. But Washington is forced by its being the capital of our country to appear politically correct, so men there are more sensitive to criticism. Senators had to appear to welcome women onto the Judiciary Committee after the Clarence Thomas fiasco. Clinton had to appoint women to high positions in his administration and to federal judgeships because the time had come—and it was both politically appropriate and morally right.

Men in Hollywood judge each other exclusively by how much money they make and how much power they wield, not by anything about morality. Men in Washington care most about power and the semblance of proper behavior. But the most powerful of them all, the president of the United States, had clandestine adulterous affairs and then was impeached by the House for engaging in perjury and the obstruction of justice by lying about them.

Fortunately, neither Dick Morris nor former Senator Bob Packwood could keep his job once word on him was out. A major difference between Hollywood and Washington is that in Washington politicians try to hide bad behavior, because if they don't they won't get reelected.

What one-industry towns like Hollywood and Washington have in common is an intense focus on the power of individual men in that industry. And this intense focus leads to easy comparison of one man with another, which in turn leads to insecurities, about salaries and material possessions or different kinds of perks, including the parties to which one is invited. In a place like New York, however, home of a number of vital industries, from Wall Street to the media, from book publishing to ballet, from the art world to opera, power brokers congregate socially not because they are all in the same industry but because they find each other amusing or interesting and because they want to be around people who are different from themselves but in their own way just as powerful. The fact that a world-renowned violinist, like Itzak Perlman, or opera singer, like Jessye Norman, lives differently from the way Donald Trump does is to be expected, and if it's not as grand a way of life, no one respects him or her less. If anything, the talent of those musical artists is more highly regarded than Trump's money made for its own sake, with no particularly redeeming social value.

By 1995, I had developed a plan for continuing a career in Hollywood. An old acquaintance from Harvard Law School, George Vradenberg, was the number-two man at Twentieth Century Fox, under Rupert Murdoch. I scheduled an appointment with George, and at the agreed-upon time I was escorted into the usual huge office of a top studio executive. He was all hugs and friendliness and then, after a bit of reminiscing about the Law School, I told him that I wanted to start a division within Fox that would focus on movies with strong, positive roles for women. I added that I had talked with a number of women in Hollywood, including movie stars, who had expressed their enthusiastic support. George said he thought it was a good idea but he needed ammunition, and I should give him a list of names of actresses, managers and agents who supported the idea of such a division.

I spent hours on the phone with managers and agents, as well as well-known women stars and directors. The letter I wrote to George contained direct quotes from a long list of female artists and their representatives. A week had gone by with no word from George when Joanne and I were on the Fox lot for a meeting about one of our projects. I asked her to wait in the car while I ran into George's office to see if he had a response to my letter.

It was late in the day, so George was there and alone. He didn't apologize for not getting back to me. He simply said that he liked the idea, but then came the bombshell. He wouldn't take it to Peter Chernin, then head of the movie division, who would ultimately have to decide whether he wanted another subdivision making movies of the sort I wanted, unless I agreed that they had no obligation to hire me to run the proposed entity. I was not only taken aback, I was furious. Trying to hide my strong emotions and act like a professional, I explained that the idea for this new division was mine alone and that by its very nature it required a feminist sensibility to run the division and choose the kinds of projects I was talking about. George then pointed out that I couldn't copyright an idea. If I wanted him to discuss it with Peter Chernin, I would be taking my chances about whether they would hire me to run the division if they, in fact, proceeded with it. If I didn't want him to talk with Peter, that would be the end of it. No division for movies that would appeal especially to women at Fox. Once again, in Hollywood, I was squeezed between my beliefs—in this case that the right kind of movies should be made—and the possibility that in going forward I myself would not be treated fairly. I said that I wanted to talk with my lawyer before I decided what to do.

The next day, I called my old friend Peter Dekom, one of the best lawyers in town. Peter advised me that even though you can't copyright an idea, in California I would have a claim to be compensated for the proposal I'd made to Fox if they hired someone else besides me to run "my" division. When Peter called George on my behalf, to my dismay George repeated to Peter exactly what he had said to me.

Peter told me that I would have to decide. If I gave them the go-ahead on their terms, that would be the end of any lawsuit if they hired somebody else. Because I knew George from law school, I decided to take my chances. I was optimistic—in retrospect foolishly—that George was just being a careful lawyer (instead of yet another horrific studio executive).

George, of course, wanted my decision in writing, so I said in a letter to him that he should talk to Peter Chernin about my idea and that I wanted to establish the understanding that they would not hire anyone else until I had the opportunity to meet with Chernin. Only now, as I write this book, do I realize how likely it is that George Vradenberg never intended to mention my name to Peter Chernin. Maybe he decided instead to take credit for my idea himself. I never heard another word about the subject from George Vradenberg, and I never was called to a meeting with Peter Chernin, although I made several efforts to contact him directly. What I did get was the shock of reading, shortly thereafter, that Fox was starting a new division to be called Fox 2000. It would be headed by a woman producer who had made movies in the past that indicated she would not produce the kinds of movies I wanted to make or had intended for the new division.

That executive, as well as other female heads of production, so far, seem to have the same sensibilities as their male counterparts—not surprisingly, there is really not a feminist among them. I shouldn't be shocked. Men in power are going to find women—when they feel they must find women at all—who won't challenge their own values or ways of doing business. For example, two women, Lisa Henson and Janet Yang, produced the movie *The People vs. Larry Flynt* (see the next chapter). When Gloria and other feminists blasted the movie, Lisa's and Janet's reactions were vitriolic. Lisa Henson, a Harvard-educated woman with an enlightened family upbringing who has directly benefited from our bashing our older heads on various glass ceilings, should have had a strong sense of how much the Women's Movement has contributed to her own life. Why did she, with Janet Yang, make a distorted film like *Larry Flynt*? Again, the answer is that these women don't want to rock the boat. Now that they have power, they don't want to change anything about Hollywood. As if to reinforce my point, Helen Hunt, who had just won the Academy Award for Best Actress, was quoted as saying that there are so few good roles for women in feature films (even if you win an Academy Award) that she would keep her day job in the sitcom *Mad About You*.

In February 1991 I met actress Meredith Baxter. We decided to develop movies together about women. One we called *Witch-Hunt*, based on the real-life purge from the Parris Island Marine Corps Base of all the lesbians there, was especially compelling. Meredith and I parted ways in May 1992 still without a screenplay—thanks to Rita Mae Brown's agreeing to do one but never turning anything in. When I met Joanne, she decided to write the script herself. It turned out to be terrific, and I mentioned our project to Barbra Streisand when I saw her at a reception. Her response was that you have to be a star to get material like that off the ground in Hollywood.

Just before I moved to Los Angeles to work on *NAVY SEALS*, I had met director Penny Marshall. The production offices of her next movie, *Big*, were in the same Fox office suite as my own on West Fifty-seventh Street in New York. I had just come across some really interesting material about the first women's baseball league, having met in Los Angeles a woman with a connection to one of the players in that league, started just after the United States entered World War II. The woman had given me a videotape of the actual women playing baseball, and that video was called *A League of Their Own*. I was also sent another tape, *Diamonds Are a Girl's Best Friend*, as well as a batch of printed material. Sure that the story of the league would make a terrific movie, I ventured into Penny Marshall's smoke-filled office and told her that I had a project I wanted to produce and that she'd be great as the director for it. At her urging, I told her all I knew about the All American Women's Professional Baseball League.

We agreed that I would check out interest in Hollywood, so on my next trip there, I pitched the project to Amy Pascal, who was then an executive and is now the Chair of Columbia Pictures. She watched the videos, got all excited, and told me that she thought they'd really want to make the movie. She just had to run it by Dawn Steel, who was then head of production at Columbia. I was delighted that all the decision makers were women.

By the time I arrived back in New York, Penny was off somewhere shooting *Big*. About a week later, Amy Pascal called to say that Columbia was passing on the project. So I made a list of other industry executives for the baseball project. A few weeks later, back in Los Angeles, I set up some more meetings, one of which was at Fox. Nothing came of those meetings. When I returned to New York, I learned that Penny had completed production and was in Russia on a vacation, for the summer.

In September, at a party in Los Angeles, I was chatting with a screenwriter whom I'd met while *NAVY SEALS* was in production, and I mentioned the baseball story. He looked at me, apparently surprised, as he divulged that Penny Marshall had just set that movie up at Fox. She would direct and some man I'd never heard of would be the producer.

The information I'd been given became a reality, which festered inside me for a long time. Finally, I took a friend's advice and found a lawyer. One of the best litigators in the city, referred by Pierce O'Donnell, who had successfully sued Paramount on behalf of Art Buchwald, accepted the case on a contingency basis. He agreed that it was a winner. (By the time *A League of Their Own* came out, the studio releasing it had become Columbia—Fox had put it into turnaround to them—and Amy Pascal was the executive on the movie.)

After a long time and a deposition the other side took of me that lasted three days, my lawyer got a call. They wanted to settle. I wanted to go to trial, but my lawyer urged me to accept their offer.

Feminist Majority founder Peg Yorkin (second from right) celebrates her sixty-fifth-birthday party in April 1982 at the Century Plaza Hotel in Los Angeles. The guests were a mix of Hollywood stars from Peg's "old" life (she had been married to producer Bud Yorkin) and feminists who populated her new life. With Peg and me are actor Harris Yulin and friend.

It still saddens me to think about *A League of Their Own.* It was a picture I would have loved to produce. The world may think that Penny Marshall is thoughtful on women's issues; in reality, she screwed another woman just the way the worst male directors do.

For a long time, I've wanted to make a miniseries about the Women's Movement. Joanne wrote a terrific treatment, using as her story the friendship among three of the movement's leaders and the events that occurred starting in the late 1960s. Once she finished the treatment, I scheduled meetings with various television companies and networks. We received interest from a male executive at Warner Bros. television who had an eleven-year-old daughter. He appreciated how many doors the movement had opened for her. But the networks' general response was that the subject matter was too "political." The executives then at Lifetime, a cable network supposedly for women, were put off by the fact that the leadership of the movement appeared too "elitist" for their primarily blue-collar viewers. Next, we had a series of upbeat meetings with a feminist woman executive at a major TV production company, but then she left her job and the company she moved to wasn't interested in the Women's Movement. So after more than seven years of trying, we still don't have any real hope that we'll get a movie off the ground about the most profound revolution of the twentieth (and of the twenty-first, probably, as well) century.

Change in Hollywood and the product coming out of it will happen when there is a massive influx of feminist sensibility. This can come from men as well as women. I have some hope that Alexis's generation will have a better time than mine. I would say that without a doubt Alexis's friends are all feminists, and with women like her and her friends, men their age have little choice but to think of women as being their equals. (Fifty-two percent of Alexis's law school class at Berkeley was female!)

Alexis has very clear opinions of the movies she wants to see, and although her taste sometimes differs from mine, never does she enjoy a movie with a weak, sappy traditional woman in it. That's not her reality, and she very much likes movies about real people. Her contemporaries are coming to Hollywood and making movies. If my contemporaries have raised children with feminist values and who want to see strong women in movies, we may have a chance to watch different kinds of stories on the screen by the next generation. Meanwhile, of course, I retain hope about what I'll be able to accomplish, but I've always been called eternally optimistic.

Chapter 9

PORNOGRAPHY, FEMINISM AND THE FIRST AMENDMENT

The ERA seems to have died a slow death and today interests few people. Abortion rights have progressed in the United States to the point at which now, while women can usually get legal abortions, the focus is on keeping doctors who perform them and other health care workers from being gunned down, as well as preventing new erosions in laws we've attained to protect a woman's right to choose. While abortion is a straightforward issue, ensuring that women can actually exercise their rights is still a challenge.

Another subject, that of pornography, has bothered me and other feminists since the early days of the Women's Movement. In 1971, when I was national vice president of NOW, rumors in New York began to spread that snuff films had made their way to Times Square. Produced in South America, they depicted the most horrible acts of violence toward women; what the viewers saw on the screen was allegedly the actual chopping-up of real women. I was asked to go see one myself and report back to both New York NOW and National NOW my reaction and, especially, whether I thought we should picket the theaters showing these kinds of movies. The officers of both groups had chosen me because they wanted my First Amendment take on what we should do.

I corralled a member of New York NOW into accompanying me to a Times Square theater. We agreed to catch the earliest show in the morning, hoping that there wouldn't be anyone else there. Aside from a few old winos scattered around in the darkness, we had the place to ourselves.

As with all porn films, the acting was terrible and the story incomprehensible. After an angry, abusive buildup, I watched, horrified, as the woman was grabbed, dumped and chopped up in a meat grinder. To determine whether a dummy was used instead of the real actress, I sat there staring at the screen, watching for scene changes, nauseated and horrified but determined to do my assigned job. Finally it was over, and all the way back to my office, feeling sick, I pondered what to advise NOW to do in the face of this horror. I was positive that it was a real woman who had been mutilated and killed.

By the time I made the first phone call to the presidents of National and New York NOW, I had decided that if we publicized this movie at all, by picketing it or writing letters to the *New York Times,* people who would otherwise not know about it would want to go see for themselves. This would create an audience that the movie would not otherwise attract. More snuff films might be made, leading to the deaths of more women.

In a conference call with various local and national officers of NOW, I was adamant. There were a few dissenters who felt strongly that NOW should picket the movie. But I succeeded in persuading the other officers of NOW that we should be quiet about it so that this truly obscene and vicious "movie" would disappear from the theater soon. In fact, that was what happened.

During the snuff-film days, I was bothered about coming down on pornography because of my First Amendment knee-jerk reaction. But the issue for me was far from resolved. Some claim to be confused by the distinction between erotica and pornography. No feminist suggests that erotic movies, in which we women are happy, even lusty, participants, should be banned. When we're not obsessing about free speech, our objections to pornography, as distinguished from erotica, aren't based on prudish morals but rather on depictions of women enjoying, or voluntarily engaging in, brutality directed at them. In the pornography industry, women have no power. In fact, if we did have power, some of us might make films that appeal to women's erotic interests. It is not we who make pornography that demeans women and makes us the object of men's often violent sexual fantasies.

After the snuff-film experience, the next time I wrestled with the issue of pornography was over lunch in a small Japanese restaurant near Wall Street with Susan Brownmiller and First Amendment lawyer Victor Kovner. Susan and I were casting about for a way to get magazines like *Hustler* and *Penthouse* away from the fronts of newsstands. We were both sick of walking by large sidewalk displays of naked women with legs spread. Victor's idea was to require those magazines to put brown wrapping paper across their fronts to hide these pictures while still allowing the publishers and sellers to display the magazines' titles. Somehow, that wasn't enough for me and Susan, and the idea was dropped.

Even though our concerns had focused on pornography, there was not a clear distinction between that and "obscenity." So after the snuff film and the above-mentioned magazines had become part of contemporary American culture, the wait began for the Supreme Court's decision in *Miller v. California.*[1] It would determine what was and wasn't obscenity. Finally, in that case, the Court settled on what it apparently still thinks is the best definition of obscenity:

> The basic guidelines for the trier of fact must be: (a) whether the *average person,* applying contemporary *community standards* would find that the work, taken as a whole, appeals to the *prurient interest;* (b) whether the work depicts or describes, in a *patently offensive way,* sexual conduct specifically defined by the applicable state law; and (c) whether the work, taken as a whole, lacks serious literary, artistic, political, or scientific value.[2] [Emphases mine]

In those days—the early 1970s—we had collective faith that the *Miller* decision would have a greater impact on society than it in fact has had. We felt that perhaps this ruling would be a way to get rid of magazines such as *Hustler,* which clearly has *no* literary, artistic, political, or scientific value. What we didn't factor in was the number of men who used such magazines as perhaps their only sexual outlet, creating a market demand to keep the offensive material on the stands throughout America. This market demand, in turn, lowered "community" standards to gutter level.

One writer called the standards set out in *Miller* "hopelessly subjective and vague," worrying that books or movies *with* literary, artistic, political or scientific value would be censored, even though *Miller* spoke directly to that point. But there were problems with *Miller.* For example, the phrase "average person." Surely every one of those male justices on the Court knew that an average woman is very different from an average man. Women are usually depicted in material challenged as "obscene" or "pornographic" in humiliating, submissive positions and situations that might encourage men viewing that material to treat women in the same ways. Pornography that depicts sexual violence against women in a way designed to turn men on may appeal to the average man's prurient interests and be not at all offensive to him, while to the average woman it might well be "patently offensive."

If we consider what an average *person* (woman/man) thinks about a particular work, while applying contemporary community standards, the next question is, what is a *community?* Clearly it's not synonymous with "state." As the *Miller* Court itself said:

> It is neither realistic nor constitutionally sound to read the First Amendment as requiring that the people of Maine or Mississippi accept public depiction of conduct found tolerable in *Las Vegas* or New York.[3] [Emphasis mine]

So in defining "community," the Court recognizes the city of Las Vegas, not the entire state of Nevada. Just as Times Square in New York City is known for the exhibition of the worst kinds of pornographic movies, there is also freedom in other communities in that city *from* such pornographic material. It seemed that

Miller allowed for what is known in First Amendment jurisprudence as a "time, place and manner regulation" of pornographic/obscene material, as opposed to an outright prior restraint on all such material. "Time, place and manner" refers to a standard by which courts will allow otherwise obscene material to be sold—in a certain, usually bad, part of a city, on magazine racks in the back behind the reach of minors, and in many instances wrapped in cellophane. An outright prior restraint, which has been rejected by the Court, would mean prohibiting material defined somehow as obscene before it even reached the stands. Some have argued that limiting pornography to one section of a city is unfair to poor, usually minority, residents who invariably live in or near the neighborhoods to which pornography is relegated.

What, then, *is* a "community"? Usually it's a group of people who live in one geographic area and who are presumed to have similar tastes. To me, an altogether different kind of community should be considered—namely, the community of women. Why should the Court give more respect to the sensibilities of citizens of a particular city or section of a city than it gives to half the citizens of our country? Possibly women from different geographical areas have different standards for what they think is obscene, but the odds are good that women will agree with one another more than they will with most men about what is offensive. If, for example, a movie is about raping and maiming women, and women, as a group, feel that movie portrays sexual conduct in a patently offensive way, then the next inquiry should be whether there is any serious literary, artistic, political or scientific value that would require First Amendment protection. If an average female member of the community of women would think that the work has no serious literary, artistic, political or scientific value, then the jury, in an obscenity trial brought against the maker or distributor of that movie, should be instructed to consider the average *woman's* reaction as the test it should use—along with considerations, if necessary, of the geographical community—to determine whether the material should be regulated. To do otherwise is to impose on the entire community, including women in local communities or nationally, the average *man's* view of what he finds patently offensive (which may not be much). In other words, the jury would be applying the lowest possible standard.

If obscenity law gets us nowhere, then women might have reason for hope from the Court's ruling, twenty years after the *Miller* case, in favor of the female plaintiff in a sexual-harassment case.[4] As discussed more in the next chapter, in that case, writing for the majority, Justice Sandra Day O'Connor declared that the applicable standard prohibits a "working environment" that a "*reasonable person* would find hostile or abusive" (emphasis mine), one that "unreasonably interferes with an employee's work performance." Clearly here Justice O'Connor was looking at what a reasonable woman would experience as a hostile work environment, because the plaintiff was a woman and the kind of harassment she experienced was the kind most often perpetrated on women by men (despite Hollywood's two feature films on the subject—*Fatal Attraction* and *Disclosure*—which depicted men as victims of predatory females). In the same way, the most common kind of obscenity is made by men for men, using women as victims—or "fuckees," as several feminist experts would say. Obviously, a "reasonable" or "average" woman determines what is sexually offensive very differently from the way a "reasonable" or "average" man does.

Maybe the problem stems from the Supreme Court's requirement that in cases involving governmental-based restrictions, the government must show a "compelling interest" in regulating *protected* speech. This requirement means that a reasonable or slight interest in such regulation is not enough, because such speech is considered a "fundamental right" guaranteed by the Constitution. It therefore becomes important that any regulation of speech is "narrowly tailored" to serve the underlying interest behind the need for such regulation.[5] It also means that special efforts must be made to limit the offensive material, because banning it runs afoul of what we cherish about the First Amendment—its guarantee that we can read and view what we like. While I believe that a "regulation" of pornography could be precisely drawn and "narrowly tailored," virtually nothing has been found obscene under the *Miller* test. It left too many outs. Because it did, feminists, including myself—at least for now—have more or less given up on its helping us in our fight against violent pornography.[6]

In the late 1970s, long before Diana Russell's book and serial rapist/killer Ted Bundy's confession (both discussed later in this chapter), I participated in a colloquium entitled "Violent Pornography: Degradation of Women Versus the Right of Free Speech," held at NYU and sponsored by its *Review of Law and Social Change.* During that colloquium, I made a number of suggestions—one, echoing my position today, was that if we are to have community standards establishing what is obscene, they should be set by women, since women constitute the "community" most affronted by pornography.[7] I also stated in the same colloquium that the community-standards rule, if applied geographically, doesn't really work for magazines—I now add movies, videos and the like—that are distributed nationwide.[8]

Before that symposium I had asked myself, What about creating a new tort? If a woman, as a result of some man's "reading" violent pornography in a pornographic magazine, were to be injured, either psychically or physically, if a woman were to be raped or otherwise battered because a man is turned on and decides to mimic something he's read or seen, shouldn't that woman have a cause of action both against the batterer *and* against the magazine publisher and distributor, which would, no doubt, have deeper pockets? Wouldn't the mere existence of such a tort have a chilling effect on both the potential rapists and the magazine publishers, newsstand owners and others involved in pornography? *I* thought so. It wouldn't actually prevent them from peddling their wares, but it might cause them to think twice about publishing and selling them. I had concluded by 1978 and still maintain, after many years of contemplation and concern about First Amendment issues, that the producers and sellers of pornography should be liable for inciting rape and other violence.

Another civil liberties attorney present at the same symposium, Ephraim London, thought it would be permissible to "draft an ordinance which would prohibit the display of material to people who did not want to see it."[9] This would give ordinary people rights that seemed to me might be paramount to the First Amendment rights of pornographers.

By the mid-1980s, Professor Catharine ("Kitty") MacKinnon and Andrea Dworkin had drafted a bill advocating that pornography be treated like any other form of sex discrimination. A few jurisdictions adopted it, and one of the antipornography ordinances drafted by Kitty and Andrea was tested all the way up to the Supreme Court, where it failed to pass constitutional muster.[10] The proposed ordinance set forth an explicit definition of pornography: "the graphic sexually explicit subordination of women, whether in pictures or in words."[11] In fact, in MacKinnon's book *Only Words*,[12] she elaborates on that definition of pornography: "Pornography is masturbation material. It is used as sex. It therefore is sex. Men know this. . . . With pornography, men masturbate to women being humiliated, violated, degraded, mutilated, dismembered, bound, gagged, tortured, and killed. . . . What is real here is not that the materials are pictures, but that they are part of a sex act."[13]

Germaine Greer in her book *The Whole Woman* seems to agree: "Women are not the point of pornography. Pornography is the flight from woman, men's denial of sex as a medium of communication, their denial of sex as the basis for a relationship, their rejection of fatherhood, their perpetual incontinent adolescence. . . . Fear of commitment is inseparable from indulgence in pornography. Masturbation is easy; relationships are difficult. Relationships interfere with masturbation."[14]

Interestingly, the remedy that MacKinnon and Dworkin included in their proposed legislation was that anyone injured by someone who has seen or read pornography has a cause of action against the maker or seller of that pornography. It's very much like the remedy that would flow from the tort theory I proposed at the NYU colloquium years earlier. Both focus on the *harm* pornography causes.

Some feminist scholars take issue with MacKinnon and Dworkin's definition of pornography, even though they oppose pornography. For example, Professor Drucilla Cornell feels that MacKinnon's definition of pornography is "dangerously over-broad," citing language from the latter's original ordinance: "the sexually explicit subordination of women graphically depicted." Cornell defines pornography more narrowly as "the explicit presentation and depiction of sexual organs and sexual acts with the aim of arousing sexual feeling through either (a) the portrayal of violence and coercion against women as the basis of heterosexual desire or (b) the graphic description of woman's body as dismembered by her being reduced to her sex and stripped completely of her person-hood as she is portrayed in involvement in explicit sex acts."[15]

Cornell, while reconfirming the legitimacy of MacKinnon and Dworkin's move from an offense focus to a harm focus, wants to exclude "indirect" expression and written pornography.[16] Probably worrying that any prohibition of the written word no matter how heinous is a prior restraint and thus a violation of free-speech rights, Cornell, I feel, misses the point. A detailed description of a rape or other molestation can easily have the same effects as a picture. Anyway, both libel and false advertising are restrained before they're written, and these restraints aren't considered a violation of the First Amendment.

Cornell also wants to limit the definition to mainstream heterosexual pornography, because she says that lesbians, gay men, bisexuals and transsexuals have contested the idea "that their sexuality, including as it is represented in their own porn and erotica, can be reduced to heterosexual definitions and fantasies of homosexuality."[17] I disagree with this limitation and wonder why Cornell wants to protect heterosexuals but is willing to let all others struggle (probably in separate groups) to come up with their own definitions of their own pornography. To me, the graphic depiction of one woman (or man) sexually abusing another woman (or man) is likely to be pornographic, regardless of gender.

There are a few women who come to the defense of violent pornography—and still insist on calling themselves feminists. For example, Nadine Strossen, the president of the board of directors of the ACLU, wrote a book about pornography and how it should be protected—on First Amendment grounds, of course.[18] Strossen has taken totally gratuitous actions to denounce feminists, among them putting a photograph of Andrea Dworkin's head on the body of a large pig.

Strossen, who calls herself an anticensorship feminist, sees two major problems with attempts to outlaw pornography. The first is that she thinks it's indefinable, existing only in the eye of the beholder, and labels feminists who are antipornography "pro-censorship feminists," which we're not. The second problem to Strossen is that outlawing pornography puts dangerous power in the hands of government, which historically has used antipornography laws against women. To Strossen, we "pro-censorship feminists" take the position "that women are not free and independent agents in the realm of sexuality or sexual expression and that we need to be protected."[19] She's correct. We won't be free and independent agents until we share equal power with men in our society. Furthermore, we do need protection from those men, turned on by violent pornography, eager to mimic, with the nearest female or child target, whatever they last saw that gave them a hard-on.

I have consistently taken the position that publicly protesting pornography is appropriate (except during the snuff-film episode, when my position was based solely on not wanting to call attention to the horrific, dangerous movie I'd seen). So on December 8, 1990, I sent a letter to Sonny Mehta, president of Vintage and Alfred A. Knopf (both Random House imprints); S. I. Newhouse, then owner of Random House; and Alberto Vitale, then president of Random House, expressing strong feminist disapproval of Vintage, itself an imprint of Knopf—my very own publisher—for publishing Bret Easton Ellis's *American Psycho*. While they no doubt felt that this novel deserved to be published and not be censored, I felt strongly that it should not have been published at all, let alone by such a respected house. My feminist colleagues and I saw no redeeming value in a not very good novel that graphically depicted, for example, one woman being killed and chopped into "meatloaf."

I sent a copy of that letter to both the *New York Times* and the *Los Angeles Times*. It read:

> With respect to Bret Easton Ellis's *American Psycho*, it is painfully clear that despite more than twenty years of our speaking out against outrages perpetrated on women, the liberal male establishment still doesn't get it. Sonny Mehta would not have been so quick to buy the [book] if [its] protagonist had dismembered and tortured a black or Jewish man. You, as male publishers, fail to see that violence against women . . . is not acceptable. When Knopf published John Updike's *Witches of Eastwick* we kept silent, perhaps out of some misplaced sense that John Updike is, after all, a "great" American author whose women characters were merely unlikable—and unrealistic. Now you've gone too far, and we are calling for a boycott of all books published by you, including *American Psycho*, which deal with women in this, or any other, hateful way.
>
> The issue is not one of censorship. Every day, you, as publishers, make decisions for all sorts of reasons about the books you will and won't publish. This time, as far as we're concerned, you made the wrong decision, and we are exercising our constitutional right to object and tell you that we are appalled by your poor taste, bad judgment and inability to hear what feminists for at least twenty years have been saying about violence toward women, what causes it and what it causes in return: American psychos.

This letter was signed, not only by me, but by Gloria Steinem, Kate Millett, Robin Morgan, Andrea Dworkin and Phyllis Chesler, all feminist writers who care a great deal about the First Amendment. Sending that letter was the least we could do in the face of a decision by a major publishing house to publish a book like *American Psycho* in which the author wrote of real atrocities against women with such gusto.

It was only in a recent *New York Times* article about the movie based on that tawdry book that I read about how, apparently, the book was intended as satire.[20] Of what? I wondered. Was the article on the movie version a snide effort to rewrite history, to tell us that we should have found pornographic material funny, and that if we did not, we weren't as smart as we thought we were—or should have been? After all, the movie's director, Mary Harron, is a Canadian who went to Oxford; her writing partner, Guinevere Turner, is also a woman. This, of course, only demonstrates once again that women who want to get ahead in the film industry invariably play the game by men's rules without regard to the consequences to women. Perhaps, because women get so few jobs in Hollywood, the film's producer, Edward R. Pressman, and its distributor, Lions Gate, felt they could quell feminist protests against the movie by hiring women. It is likely that the fact that two women were involved in creating a movie painful to watch had only the effect of generating more publicity for the film. It didn't seem that protests were necessary, given the negative reviews the movie received, and we didn't want to arouse curiosity.*

Right after I mailed the letter to the executives at Knopf, I happened upon a statement that had been issued by the ACLU in 1977, expressing concern that organized group activities like boycotts can result in removal of materials to which members of the public may wish access.[21] Thus to the ACLU, if a boycott is successful, it may constitute a First Amendment violation, because it will have effectively removed materials to which at least some members of the public may wish access. Perhaps they were worried that some crazy guy who today gets off on seeing women

---

* The review in the *Los Angeles Times* timed to the movie's release on April 14, 2000, concluded: "The bottom line is that this film is 100 minutes spent with an unpleasant, unmotivated, disconnected psychopath . . . who enjoys hacking folks into pieces and storing body parts in a freezer. Which is . . . 100 minutes too many." The *New York Times* critic observed that "*American Psycho* remained a one-joke satire of materialism and soullessness" (April 14, 2000).

chopped up might be deprived of seeing more of the same in the future. He should be able to seek relief, per the ACLU, under the First Amendment. To me, the ACLU's equating a private boycott with a prior government ban erodes the organization's credibility and helps destroy its relationship with feminists, who have also counted on the ACLU to protect *their* civil liberties.

The absurdity of the ACLU's position was highlighted during the 1996 Academy Award campaign. The movie *The People vs. Larry Flynt* was released at the end of that year. For some misguided reason, the ACLU Foundation of Southern California decided to honor that movie's director, Milos Forman, "as a First Amendment advocate and an artist of unsurpassed creativity, ability and courage." The ACLU took out a full-page ad in *Daily Variety* announcing the award, the apparent purpose of which was to invite readers to attend the ACLU's next annual fund-raiser, the Torch of Liberty Dinner—in May 1997—honoring Forman. But the ad appeared in February, just before Academy Award ballots were due. Clearly, the ACLU wanted the movie to win some awards so that they could show off their own "courage" in supporting such a movie—and at the same time get more people to their fund-raiser, maybe even recruit more members.

But far from being wooed to attend the dinner, several of us feminists noted two somewhat aberrant sentences in that ad: "We abhor . . . all attempts to suppress the discussion of ideas. Censorship can be carried out by private pressure groups as well as by the government."[22] So in a letter to the editor of the *New York Times,* published a few days after the ad appeared, Gloria Steinem maintained that in condemning "private pressure groups" who were speaking out against *The People vs. Larry Flynt,* "the ACLU has bought the Orwellian argument of a $10 billion a year pornography industry . . . that using free speech against pornography is a danger to free speech." She went on:

> Feminists and others who have pointed out the movie's fraud in its portrayal of Flynt's life, *Hustler's* content, and pornography itself are providing additional informa-

tion on which people can make their own decisions, whether movie-goers or Academy Award voters. This is not the same as preventing entrance to theaters, as the right-wing does at abortion clinics, or even calling for a boycott, though that would also be within First Amendment rights.

Gloria concluded her letter with the hope

> that one truth—which is rendered invisible by the movie as well as by the ACLU—becomes visible as a result of this controversy: It's possible to be against pornography *and* against censorship.[23]

I talked with Gloria about calling Ramona Ripston, executive director of the Southern California ACLU. While my normal tendency would be to debate Ramona in some public forum, Gloria's concern was that Ramona understand what we feminists were saying, because if she did, she couldn't help but agree with us. Gloria faxed me a note pointing out: "It's as if the ACLU had made the decision to honor D. W. Griffith for 'The Birth of a Nation' before it opened and then condemned as enemies of free speech those who used their free speech rights to point out its inaccuracies."

Soon, Ira Glasser, executive director of the national ACLU, chimed in. He wrote a letter to the editor of the *New York Times* at the end of February spouting the ACLU's First Amendment party line and defending the ACLU's "right to point out the danger such boycotts pose in limiting freedom of expression." I assume that the boycotts to which he was referring—because they were the only actions about which I'd heard—were Gloria's letters and an unsigned ad in *Daily Variety* expressing distaste for the movie *The People vs. Larry Flynt.*

I'd known Ramona Ripston for twenty-five years, going back to my days at the ACLU Women's Rights Project, and when I finally reached her on the phone, her argument was that the ACLU thought the movie was a good vehicle to make their point that all speech (in this case, *Hustler*) deserves to be protected. In fact, she admitted that she hadn't seen an issue of *Hustler,* while at the same time she maintained that the movie didn't glorify Flynt. I wondered aloud how she could know if she hadn't followed his career or even, as she also admitted, read articles about the real Larry Flynt? My own eyes, in fact, were opened by a piece in the February 1997 issue of *Penthouse* (which is almost as bad as *Hustler*), written by one of Flynt's former bodyguards, Bill Rider. It revealed the true depths to which Flynt had sunk. Referring to Flynt's frequent manic episodes, one in particular in 1983, Rider stated that based on a recording he'd made of a conversation between Flynt and his wife, Althea, Flynt described his own behavior in a way that could only be paraphrased as molesting his twelve- or thirteen-year-old daughter Theresa. During that same period, Flynt threatened to give AIDS to a number of employees. (And this was before he hired private investigators to check out the sex lives of Republicans in the House during the impeachment proceedings against President Clinton.)

I doubted that anyone at the ACLU paid any attention to Tonya Flynt, who spoke out at a press conference against her father, calling him "a pornographer, a pimp, and a molester of children." Tonya testified that "on many occasions, [my father] would touch my breasts or grab me between the legs. One time he came into my bedroom, took my panties off, and fondled me." On another: "He penetrated me with his fingers. He made me touch his penis. He had oral sex with me and made me have oral sex with him. I hadn't celebrated my thirteenth birthday when he did this to me." Tonya also emphatically stated that her father "doesn't give a damn about freedom of speech, all he cares about is making millions of dollars out of the sexual exploitation of women and children."*[24] Hardly was Flynt the attractive character portrayed by Woody Harrelson in the movie celebrated by the ACLU and heralded by many in the inner circles of Hollywood.

* In Tonya Flynt Vega's book, *Hustled,* Larry Flynt's denial (in a letter to his daughter) of these allegations is included. He signs off with "I will ensure that you will never benefit one penny of my estate. I don't want to . . . see you or speak to you as long as I live."[25]

My chat with Ramona Ripston didn't make a dent. She claimed that private pressure chills Hollywood producers. Condemning us for the bad box office the movie experienced after Gloria and others started their letter-writing campaign against it, Ramona and the rest of the ACLU actually said that we feminists are so well organized that we have the power to stop women around the country from going to a film that we find offensive. As I later said to Ramona, would that we were so powerful.

Meanwhile, as Gloria was holding her own in editorials and letters to editors, one Thursday morning I received a call from a producer of *Judge Judy*, a syndicated television show. Would I be willing to debate Larry Flynt himself the following Tuesday on their show? Located in Los Angeles, they could messenger me a copy of the current *Hustler* and a recently published biography of Larry Flynt. I was intrigued, and I agreed, even though I'd never opened an issue of *Hustler*. I also received a call from the *Judge Judy* people to inform me that Alan Isaacman, Larry Flynt's lawyer, who graduated from Harvard Law School a few years after I did, would be appearing with Flynt.

The next evening, I sat in a dark theater with my lighted pen and notebook, watching *The People vs. Larry Flynt*. Woody Harrelson, in the starring role, was a good-looking, fun-loving kind of guy and, playing Flynt, fell in love with Courtney Love's character, Flynt's real-life wife, Althea. In the movie, "Althea" was depicted as in her late teens, early twenties. She was wild and crazy but nothing like the real Althea, who was a fourteen-year-old prostitute and drug addict when she married the real Flynt. Harrelson's Flynt had no children; in fact, he'd never been married before. The real Flynt, when he met the real Althea, already had several children by other women, and one of these children was Tonya. I had read enough about the real Larry Flynt before I went to the movie to know that what I was viewing was a work of fiction. The fact that the real Larry Flynt had endorsed this fiction as his life story didn't make it acceptable for the studio releasing it to call the movie a true story and to deceive the public about what that story really was.

Next, I set about gathering information that I could use to attack Flynt and *Hustler* on feminist grounds. I spoke with Kitty MacKinnon and feminist sociologist Diana Russell, who had written the self-published book *Against Pornography.**

Dr. Russell, whose book Gloria had sent me, demonstrated clearly how a picture is worth more than a thousand words. Although they were black and white, her copies of color pictures and cartoons that had appeared over the years in various issues of *Hustler* were horrifying. The only experience that was worse was when I opened *Hustler* magazine itself, sent by the *Judge Judy* producers. Color photographs of women's open, vulnerable vaginas being penetrated by all sorts of male paraphernalia, including huge penises, dominated the pages. There were punctured clitorises and black women's genitalia that were meant to look as if they gushed, oozed and reeked. I looked in horror at a cartoon of a grinning father, forcing himself into his young teenage daughter, his tongue in her ear, as she tried to make excuses to her friend on the telephone about why she was busy that evening. And then, worst of all, there was the picture of a male construction worker standing over a naked woman, her legs spread. He had a jackhammer between his legs, and it was going straight into her vagina.

All this made me more determined to make our case forcefully on the show. I spent the entire weekend preparing what I would say. I even arranged for psychologist Wendy Stock, a friend of Diana Russell's, to send me, via same-day United Airlines, big color blowups of photos straight from *Hustler,* which she uses when she gives lectures on pornography. As I pulled them from the huge protective envelope in which they were wrapped, I saw such painful, shocking images that I knew I had to show them during the debate. FCC rules about what could be shown on a syndicated daytime show would be *Judge Judy's* problem.

---

* This book was self-published so Dr. Russell could take full responsibility for defending herself against possible obscenity charges (from the photos she included) and not put that burden on another publisher, if one were interested in publishing the book.[26]

That weekend, I typed an opening statement and my main arguments about how and why *Hustler* is bad for women, as well as blacks, Jews and just about any group that didn't fit Hitler's (and Flynt's) notion of the master race. I learned that proof has been accumulating that the depiction of violence, for example, does cause the viewer to copy and act out the same senseless acts. Psychologist Jennings Bryant testified to the Texas attorney general's Pornography Commission[27] about a survey he'd conducted involving six hundred telephone interviews. Respondents were asked if "exposure to X-rated materials had made them want to try anything they saw."[28] Two-thirds of the males reported "wanting to try some of the behavior depicted."[29]

In 1984, Jennings Bryant, together with Dolf Zillman, had studied the effects of what they refer to as "massive exposure to pornography"[30] (4 hours and 48 minutes per week). They found that consumers "graduate from common to less common forms of pornography . . . to more violent and degrading materials . . . because familiar material becomes unexciting as a result of habituation."[31]

Meanwhile, Dr. Russell, discussing pornography as a cause of rape,[32] concludes that exposure to pornography

1) Predisposes some males to desire rape or intensifies latent desire
   a) by pairing sexually arousing stimuli with portrayals of rape,
   b) by becoming sexually aroused by self-generated rape fantasies,
   c) by sexualizing dominance and submission,
   d) by creating an appetite for increasingly stronger material;

2) Undermines males' internal inhibitions against acting out rape desires
   a) by sexually objectifying females,
   b) by increasing belief in rape myths,
   c) by increasing acceptance of interpersonal violence,
   d) by increasing trivialization of rape,

e) by increasing sex-callous attitudes and hostility to women,

f) by increasing acceptance of male dominance in intimate relationships,

g) by desensitizing males to rape and violence against women;

3) Undermines males' social inhibitions against acting out rape desires

a) by diminishing fears of social sanctions,

b) by diminishing fears that peers will disapprove;

4) Undermines potential victims' abilities to avoid or resist rape

a) by encouraging females to get into high rape-risk situations,

b) by creating a pornography industry that requires female participation.

By his own admission, the first three factors clearly influenced serial sex killer Theodore Bundy, executed on January 24, 1989, for the sex slaying of a twelve-year-old girl. Raised in a "good Christian" home (no smoking, drinking, and so on) with two parents, he claims to have encountered, as a boy of twelve or thirteen, in the local grocery store, soft-core pornography. Then he started going through neighbors' garbage to find pornography of a harder nature.

In an interview with Dr. James Dobson, Ted Bundy himself declared on the day before his execution that "the most damaging kinds of pornography are those that involve violence and sexual violence." Bundy went on in the same interview to say

> I've lived in prison for a long time now. And I've met a lot of men who were motivated to commit violence just like me. And without exception, every one of them was deeply involved in pornography, without question, without exception, deeply influenced and consumed by an addiction to pornography. There's no question about it. The FBI's own study on serial homicide shows that the most common interest among serial killers is pornography.

As for nonprisoners, he added,

> There is loose in their towns people like me whose dangerous impulses are being fueled day in and day out by violence in the media, particularly sexualized violence.

Another man, Thomas Schiro, convicted of the rape and murder of a twenty-eight-year-old woman, had been examined by a psychologist who, testifying at his trial, stated that Schiro had been exposed to hard-core pornography depicting rape and simulating murder from the time that he was six years old. Another expert testified that continual exposure to hard-core pornography creates "a person who no longer distinguishes between violence and rape, or violence and sex."[33]

Reading all this, I wonder why there hasn't been a single lawsuit asking a court to keep pornography away from convicts in jail for rape (making the fair assumption that they'll be released in an unrehabilitated state). I'm not sure that people convicted of violent crimes should be allowed to watch more violence on TV. But even in my most optimistic moments, I know that my wonderings won't lead to any real policy change until more people become educated about the effects of pornography on women.

Responses from men defending pornography shortly after a *Los Angeles Times* article was published in early 1995 had a repetitive and illogical theme: "If we do not allow films that are pornographic, then critics will use these same arguments to ban films that do have redeeming social value."[34]

Most of us can distinguish pornography from erotica. But the real truth is that most of us know when one gender is being used, dominated and made submissive, let alone harmed, for the sexual pleasure of the other. As Justice Oliver Wendell Holmes once said, when attempting a definition of obscenity, "I know it when I see it."

So over that weekend I had educated myself, and I went into the office early Monday morning to type up my notes. But when I pushed the blinking button on my answering machine I heard the grave-sounding voice of the *Judge Judy* producer asking me to call as soon as possible. When I reached him, he told me how embarrassed they were to have to cancel the debate. Larry Flynt had pulled out after they told him who his opponent was. I wondered if Alan Isaacman, his lawyer, had looked in his Harvard Law School directory, found me and decided that I'd be too tough to compete with. Was Flynt afraid to debate a feminist? Had he anticipated a religious attack and did he now realize that he was unprepared for what must be coming? Did they know that Gloria and I were friends and that I had read each of her increasingly acerbic letters to the editors of various newspapers following the battle between the feminists and Flynt? Not wanting all my preparation to be for naught, how about, I asked, getting Oliver Stone, the producer of the movie, to debate me? As Tonya Flynt had said at the press conference, "*Hustler* says it's funny and sexy to molest little girls. . . . And Oliver Stone says that *Hustler* is about freedom and liberation. That's a dangerous message."

I'd even take on Milos Forman, the director, who had sworn he had never seen an issue of *Hustler*. I'd be glad to debate Janet Yang or Lisa Henson, the two female producers, or even Mike Medavoy, my old friend of few words, whose new company, Phoenix, was also one of the movie's producers. The *Judge Judy* producer said he thought that all my ideas were good, but that they had booked a different show as soon as they heard from Flynt (which must have been at dawn). He tried to humor me by promising that they would call me soon to appear on another show.

Meanwhile, Hollywood couldn't get enough of the uproar surrounding *The People vs. Larry Flynt*. On February 17, 1997, the *Los Angeles Times* reported that between the third and fifth weeks in the movie's release: "With the Steinem/NOW campaign in full swing, the weekly box-office receipts dropped from an average of $4,311 on 1,233 screens to $1,705. Last weekend 'Larry Flynt' made an average of $1,201 in just 500 theaters. It's dead. Mission, apparently accomplished."

In the same *Los Angeles Times* article we were told by Sherlee Lantz (the wife of Milos Forman's agent, Robbie, but described in the article as a "former New York theatrical casting agent and long-time friend of Forman's") that "Milos is in deep shock, depression and disillusionment." This may have been because Forman came here from communist Czechoslovakia in 1968, and now he's "being set up for criticism from people on his side of the political spectrum." I wonder why no one told Milos Forman that all sides, in America, have the right to invoke their freedom of expression, including feminists. Finally, the women who had participated in the making of *The People vs. Larry Flynt*, Janet Yang and Lisa Henson, weighed in, again in the *Los Angeles Times*, criticizing feminists for their attack on their movie.

After a female Hollywood screenwriter wrote a piece stating her own disgust with the *Larry Flynt* movie, Gloria followed with a letter to the editor of the *Los Angeles Times*, asking, in summation of weeks of consciousness-raising, why "a $20-million-plus Columbia/Phoenix [publicity] campaign [is] evidence of sincerity, while a few voices raised in protest are 'an orchestrated [and, therefore, bad] effort.'"

To me, orchestrated or not, our calling attention to the fraud that *The People vs. Larry Flynt* was did pay off, and the movie died a quiet death. We experienced a refreshing victory, rare in recent years.

Chapter 10

SEX DISCRIMINATION AFTER *FRONTIERO*

After the *Frontiero* decision, in 1973, many of the gender discrimination cases were brought by male plaintiffs, and Ruth
Bader Ginsburg thought that would make it even clearer to the
all-male Justices what a double-edged sword gender* discrimination was. But in *Kahn v. Shevin* that strategy backfired.[1] The case
got all the way to the Supreme Court before we heard about it
and decided again to intervene.

Kahn v. Shevin challenged a Florida law under which widowers were not allowed a $500 property-tax exemption automati-
cally given widows. The justification for this was to make up to
women the discrimination they had suffered while their husbands were alive and making more money than they were. Ruth
was unhappy that this case reached the Court, because, while
she said she believed in affirmative action, this exemption wasn't
tailored narrowly enough to remedy a specific wrong. It would
make for bad affirmative-action case law. She and I agreed that
many widows were entitled to help, but so were some widowers,
and thus we wanted this Florida tax exemption to be extended to
widowers, not withdrawn from widows. No matter what, men
and women had to be treated in the same way to avoid keeping
women in their place primarily as wives and mothers.

* Ruth now preferred this word over "sex," having been urged by her secretary to consider the effect of the repetitive use of "sex" on the then nine elderly male Justices.

The Court, however, didn't see matters our way, and in a set-back to the cause of equality, it held that such an exemption was a proper and sufficient way to redress the less-than-equal treatment that widows had suffered while their husbands were alive. *Kahn v. Shevin* muddied the waters terribly about what is appropriate affirmative action to remedy past discrimination. And almost nineteen years later, during Ruth's confirmation hearings, she declared that she actually "hated" that case.

In July 1973, Ruth and I had been asked by the U.S. Commission on Civil Rights to do a study of all the federal statutes that distinguished on the basis of gender. Once these laws were located, we were to decide whether the distinction mattered, and if it did, what our suggestions for change were. With the help of one of Ruth's Columbia Law School classes, we finished our report in about six months. Several months later, our encyclopedic findings were published in book form.[2] Though it was exciting to see the results of our work, it was also depressing, because it confirmed how much sexism was still embodied in many sections of the federal code.

There were a number of Supreme Court cases that Ruth had briefed and argued and in which the ACLU's Women's Rights Project participated as *amicus curiae* after I left the ACLU to start Fasteau and Feigen in July 1974. These cases include one in which women were exempted from jury duty in Louisiana unless they filed a written statement that they wanted to serve;[3] another in which widowers, but not widows, were denied insurance benefits for themselves and their children;[4] yet another in which a widower was denied survivor's benefits because he hadn't been dependent on his wife for more than half of his support, while a similarly situated widow would have received the benefits;[5] and a real doozy in which all female employees of the Los Angeles Department of Water and Power were provided less take-home pay than all similarly situated male employees, because women "on the average" live longer than men.[6] In each case the Court struck down the discriminatory treatment—whether it was of men, women or both.

The law in the area of gender discrimination was evolving throughout this period. One case in particular received a lot of publicity because it struck down an Oklahoma statute allowing eighteen- to twenty-one-year-old women but not men to buy 3.2 beer.[7] In Ruth's *amicus* brief she noted that while "on its face" the statute discriminated against men, "upon deeper inspection . . . the discrimination is revealed as simply another manifestation of traditional attitudes and prejudices about the expected behavior and roles of the two sexes in our society, part of the myriad signals and messages that daily underscore the notion of men as society's active members, women as men's quiescent companions, members of the 'other' or second sex."[8]

But there were not always happy endings. One case in which Ruth failed to influence the Court was brought by a woman who wanted to be a prison guard in a maximum-security male penitentiary.[9] The Court held that although the height and weight requirements imposed by the Alabama statute were not job-related, the regulation prohibiting women from guard jobs in these institutions fell within the bona-fide-occupational-qualification (BFOQ) exception of Title VII.[10] The Court found that from the evidence

> Alabama maintains a prison system where violence is the order of the day, inmate access to guards is facilitated by dormitory living arrangements, every correctional institution is understaffed, and a substantial portion of the inmate population is composed of sex offenders mixed at random with other prisoners, and that therefore the use of women guards in "contact" positions in the maximum-security male penitentiaries would pose a substantial security problem, directly linked to the sex of the prison guard.[11]

The ACLU's argument in the brief, written by Ruth, was that

> the BFOQ exception to Title VII does not justify barring *all* women . . . from employment . . . in male maximum

security prisons. Any BFOQ application . . . should be
narrowly confined, for a broad reading . . . would cast a
shadow upon a large body of well-reasoned precedent.[12]

In defense of this position, Ruth's brief went on to state that

> [e]vidence [including] expert opinion on prison admin-
> istration support[s] the proposition that qualified
> women can work successfully as line correctional offi-
> cers in male prisons, including those which house max-
> imum security inmates. . . . [P]rison administrators
> retain the right to require women applicants to demon-
> strate their individual suitability for the demanding
> work of a prison guard. . . . The valid *privacy interest* of
> male prison inmates can be accommodated by selective
> work assignments among correctional officers rather
> than by refusing women employment altogether.[13]

Interestingly, in the 1990s seven female prison guards, all then
or formerly employed at Folsom State Prison, which houses more
than 7,000 maximum- and medium-security male inmates supervised by 1,017 corrections officers, 171 of whom were women,
filed a class-action lawsuit in federal court claiming sexual
harassment and discrimination at the predominantly male facil-
ity.[14] Who was doing the harassing? The women's complaint contained allegations of numerous specific acts of sexual
harassment, *not by the criminals* they are trained to guard, *but by
their fellow officers and superiors* on whom they are trained to rely.

In one of Ruth's last cases before she was appointed to the
D.C. Court of Appeals, she successfully challenged a Missouri
statute granting any woman, on request, an automatic exemption
from jury duty.[15] This was the kind of case she loved to bring,
because it went directly to the issue of traditional sex-role stereo-
typing.

Before assuming her seat on the D.C. Court of Appeals, Ruth,
in an article in the *North Carolina Law Review,*[16] observed that
the Court "has formally reserved judgment on the question

whether, absent ratification of an equal rights amendment, sex, like race, should rank as a suspect classification."[17] By this time, the Supreme Court had begun to articulate a new heightened "intermediate" standard of review of gender classifications in *Craig v. Boren*,[18] where the Court found Oklahoma's purported interest in traffic safety—thus, no sale of 3.2% beer to males— serious enough to warrant greater consideration than administrative convenience.[19] Under this new "intermediate" standard, the Court required that sex-based classifications "must serve important governmental objectives and must be substantially related to achievement of those objectives."[20] That standard would evolve even further once Ruth took her seat on the Supreme Court on the first Monday in October 1993.

The only opinion from Ruth regarding gender discrimination when she was on the D.C. Circuit involved a female general manager of the Congressional food-service facilities.[21] Ruth wrote, for that court, that the woman could sue for violation of equal protection even though Congress had exempted its own staffs from Title VII coverage.

Not much progress was made in the 1980s. While the Supreme Court did recognize the right of men to a nursing school education at an institution maintained by the state for women only,*[22] it had earlier declined to condemn a state statutory rape law penalizing males but not females[23] and draft registration limited to men.[24]

With respect to the standard of review, the most important gender-discrimination cases, beginning with the case against the Citadel, have been decided by the Court in the 1990s. A young female applicant sued because the Citadel, which received fed-

---

* In a 1997 speech to the Women's Bar Association, Ruth noted that Justice O'Connor's 1982 opinion in *Mississippi University for Women v. Hogan* (requiring the admission of men) was 5 to 4, while the vote to strike down men-only admissions in Virginia fourteen years later was 7 to 1. "What occurred in the intervening years in the Court, as elsewhere in society?" she asked. The answer, Ruth continued, lay in a line from Shakespeare that Justice O'Connor had recently spoken while playing the role of Isabel, Queen of France, in a local production of *Henry V:* "Haply a woman's voice may do some good" (*New York Times*, May 26, 1999).

eral funds and was a military school, didn't admit women. After she brought her case to court, the school was ordered to admit women, and for the first year the young woman who had been the plaintiff in that case was treated exactly the same as the guys, including being ordered to get a crew cut. She was assigned a private room in the infirmary while the school figured out how to build a dormitory for female students. The victory was there; we'd won. And then all of a sudden, the young woman dropped out of school. Probably, the pressure of being the only female was just too much for her. By then, however, another case was making its way up to the Supreme Court. The Virginia Military Institute (VMI) was also all-male. And again there was a young woman, this one even more determined, who wanted to attend and was being denied admission solely because of her gender.

When I learned that the U.S. Supreme Court had decided to hear that case, I was delighted. This would be an open-and-shut decision for Ruth. And in the spring of 1996, Ruth herself, writing for the majority of the Court and striking down the men-only admission policy, stated that there has to be an "extremely persuasive reason" for the government to maintain a policy or statute that discriminates on the basis of gender. I chortled as I realized that Ruth had figured out a way around the "compelling state interest" language; the words "extremely persuasive" sounded awfully similar. Only a plurality of the *Frontiero* Court in 1973 had agreed to elevate the scrutiny applied to gender distinctions to the same level accorded race distinctions. Now, with the *VMI* case, we apparently had closed the gap, not only with respect to constitutional levels of scrutiny but also with the standard that would have been applied had the ERA been ratified. As Ruth herself told students at the University of Virginia, "There is no practical difference between what has evolved and the E.R.A." But she added, "I would still like it as a symbol to see the E.R.A. in the Constitution for my granddaughter."[25]

The "extremely persuasive" standard makes moot the question of whether sex is a suspect classification. An example of the application of the "extremely persuasive" standard: a woman suing the federal government because she wants to be a Navy SEAL—or even easier, she wants a clear promotion path to become one of the joint chiefs. In order to assure herself that she won't be passed over, she needs as much combat experience as any male with whom she might compete for the joint chiefs job. That is maximum combat exposure, and women are still kept out of most kinds of combat duty, in all branches of the services. Thus, she sues to get into a combat position from which women are now excluded. The case gets to the Supreme Court, and the Court decides that there is maybe an important, certainly a rational, reason for her being barred from said combat. But she is able to argue successfully, because of Ruth, that there is no extremely persuasive reason for keeping her from a combat rat hole just because she is female. In other words, is there an extremely persuasive reason to discriminate against her and keep her from traveling the career path of which she has dreamed? Or is it just that women should be protected from whatever goes on among men alone in bunkers? That hardly is serious enough to compare it with the damage done her if she isn't allowed to rise in the military ranks as men do.

That Ruth would make new law was never in doubt. That it happened so quickly shouldn't come as a surprise either. But knowing my own tendency toward optimism, I checked out my hunch about the significance of her decision in the *VMI* case with Herma Hill Kay, then dean of Berkeley's Boalt Hall Law School, who cowrote (with Ruth) the first sex discrimination casebook. Smiling broadly, she agreed with me and acknowledged how clever Ruth had been to circumvent the old "suspect" language and substitute new words with the same meaning. This was before I knew that Ruth herself, during a talk to students at the University of Virginia, had said there was no practical difference in the meaning of the words "compelling" and "extremely persuasive."

Meanwhile, the ERA seems to be a moot issue. I have been told by various U.S. senators that we don't have the two-thirds vote necessary to get a proposed constitutional amendment out of the Congress. By 1994, I had learned from Senate Majority Leader George Mitchell that in fact there weren't enough votes in the then-Democratic-controlled Senate to pass the ERA, even before the Republican landslide that November and Newt Gingrich's ascension. The ERA has not been reintroduced because no one I know can stand another defeat over an issue that is so clearly a symbol of true justice.

Reproductive freedom was another front on which we were waging war. In 1972, a year before the landmark abortion-rights case *Roe v. Wade*[26] was decided, the ACLU's Women's Rights Project took on the representation of a Catholic servicewoman who refused to have an abortion and didn't want to lose her job.[27] In our brief, Ruth argued that an Air Force regulation requiring all women officers to be discharged as soon as they became pregnant was unconstitutional sex discrimination because it treated pregnancy far more harshly than it treated other temporary disabilities. Ruth wrote in that brief that the "exaltation of woman's unique role in bearing children has, in effect, restrained women from developing their individual talents . . . and has impelled them to accept a dependent, subordinate status in society."

She went on to note that "individual privacy with respect to procreation and intimate personal relations is a right firmly embedded in this nation's tradition and in the precedents of this Court."[28]

At Vassar in 1963, I was in the bathroom one morning and heard the sound of someone vomiting in the stall next to me. It struck me that whoever it was must be pregnant. No one talked about it, but one classmate disappeared from our dorm for about a week. Then she returned, and that was that. I myself was terrified of getting pregnant. When, at age nineteen, I started having sex with my boyfriend, I warned him that we'd have to use "everything," which basically meant that he used a condom and I, a diaphragm—at the same time. Only much later did I learn that acting on my fear in this way actually heightened my chances of getting pregnant, by making one or the other device more likely to break. The pill wasn't widely available until I reached law school a few years later.

Then, of course, in 1973 *Roe v. Wade*[29] made constitutional history. The ACLU Women's Rights Project had nothing to do with *Roe*, which had been brought by a lawyer in Texas just as the Reproductive Freedom Project was beginning. Essentially that case established a privacy right allowing women, in most situations, to obtain abortions. And that privacy argument has over the past twenty-seven-plus years been used in other areas of the law, including gay and lesbian rights, where much still needs to be done.

Abortion is about a woman's right to control her own body. To Ruth, the fight for the right to choose abortion was really also about equality under the Fourteenth Amendment's Equal Protection Clause. It took until Ruth's confirmation hearings for me to realize how much she would have preferred that the Court in *Roe* had relied more on a Fourteenth Amendment right to equal protection than the much more slippery constitutional right to privacy, which Justice Blackmun (and the majority of the Court) found embodied in the First, Fourth and Ninth Amendments to the Constitution. It was 1997 before I finally understood Ruth's reticence about the decision in *Roe v. Wade,* as I read a cover story on her in the *New York Times Magazine.*[30] Ruth had delivered the Madison Lecture at NYU Law School in 1993, and in it she asserted: "If the [*Roe*] Court had merely struck down the extreme antiabortion restriction at issue in the case, rather than presuming to devise an elaborate trimester scheme that governed abortion restrictions in all states . . . the decision might have been far less controversial and the political momentum for liberalizations [of state abortion laws] might have continued."[31]

Whether Ruth is right about the decision in *Roe,* I don't know. I'm glad the Court carved out the privacy right that it did in that case, but I sense that there may be something to Ruth's political—and constitutional—instincts.

It has been said that Ruth waited until it was clear that the Equal Rights Amendment was defeated before articulating her theory, in a speech on April 6, 1984, at the University of North Carolina,[32] and set forth in an essay in the *North Carolina Law Review*,[33] that abortion restrictions are a form of sex discrimination.

Ruth's central thesis[34] is that antiabortion laws, like employment discrimination against pregnant women, are based on "stereotypical assumptions" about women as caregivers. She expressed concern that using the scientific approach geared toward the viability of the fetus in questioning the right for a woman to elect to terminate her pregnancy by an abortion, relied too much on the scientific data and technology available in 1973 when *Roe* was decided.[35] By now, much smaller fetuses than those considered just barely viable in 1973 have been kept alive on various high-tech life-support systems. And Ruth surmised that probably by the year 2000, fetuses just recently conceived *could* be supported outside the mother's body. If a pregnant woman, under *Roe,* was unlikely in 1973 to be granted an abortion in the third trimester because most fetuses are viable by then, it's difficult to imagine what cutoff point might be established when a woman's uterus is replaced—sooner or later—by some sort of high-tech incubator. I agree with Ruth that a Fourteenth Amendment equal protection argument would, in the future, engender more respect for a woman's wishes to terminate her pregnancy than would the more amorphous privacy right established in *Roe.*

Privacy as the cornerstone of the right to abortion is also raised by University of Michigan Law Professor Catharine MacKinnon. She rejects the idea that sex is a private matter, because it might lead to the conclusion that the government has no legitimate concern with what happens to women behind the bedroom door, where sex, according to MacKinnon, is often like rape.[36] Drucilla Cornell, professor of Law, Political Science and Women's Studies at Rutgers University, maintains that abortion "should be protected as a right necessary for the establishment of the minimum conditions of individuation for women. . . . The right to abortion," she clarifies, "should not be understood as the right to choose an abortion, but as the right to realize the legitimacy of the individual woman's . . . bodily integrity."[37] To deny this right "would mark [women] as unequal."[38] Again, the focus is on the woman rather than the abortion. While I agree that the right to have an abortion is necessary in order for women to preserve their bodily integrity, I also believe in the importance of the right to choose abortion, and I would categorize that right as fundamental, guaranteed under the Due Process Clauses of the Fourteenth and Fifth Amendments—just as, for example, all children are guaranteed the fundamental right to an education.

In any case, because of *Roe,* at the ACLU we were inundated with calls from all over, women wanting abortions and being denied them, because they were too young, or their husbands objected—or they were too pregnant. This gave added impetus to the idea of beginning the Reproductive Freedom Project, as an offshoot of the Women's Rights Project.

The treatment of pregnant workers has evolved significantly in the past quarter century. In 1974, the Supreme Court held that a state-operated disability income protection plan could exclude normal pregnancy without offense to the equal protection principle.[39] And a few years later, the Court ruled, as it had earlier in a constitutional context, that women unable to work because of pregnancy or childbirth could be excluded from disability coverage without regard to Title VII.[40] The rationalization used by the Court was that all "non-pregnant persons," women as well as men, were treated alike.

After this decision, Ruth, still a professor at Columbia Law School, coauthored an op-ed column in the *New York Times* in which she asked, "If it is not sex discrimination to exclude pregnant women from standard, fringe benefit programs, is it sex discrimination to fire pregnant women, refuse to hire them, force them to take long unpaid leaves or strip them of seniority when they return to work?"[41] Ruth urged Congress to reject the Court's interpretation of Title VII. Perhaps as a result of her comments, the Pregnancy Discrimination Act (PDA), which included discrimination on the basis of pregnancy in Title VII's definition of sex discrimination in the workplace, was passed by Congress in 1978. But this wasn't exactly what Ruth had in mind. Never wanting to emphasize what is unique about the reproductive system of women, Ruth noted the "boomerang effect" of special pregnancy benefits for women, who are invariably less likely than men to be hired anyway. Thus, she looked favorably upon a legislative alternative, the Family and Medical Leave Act,* which creates child-rearing benefits that can be claimed by men or women.

Finally, on February 2, 1999, in the first sex discrimination case brought under that act, a jury awarded $375,000 to Howard Knussman, a Maryland state trooper who was refused an extended leave to care for his newborn daughter because he was male. In December 1994, after being told that he would be considered AWOL if he did not return to work, he returned, and he filed suit in April 1995, charging violation of the Family and Medical Leave Act and of his constitutional right to equal protection under the law. Besides damages, the Knussman lawsuit asked for twelve weeks of compensatory parental leave and the issuance of a formal state police policy regarding parental leave.[42] Trooper Knussman and his wife had a second daughter several years ago, and he took the full twelve weeks paternity leave after her birth. I can't imagine that any feminist would disagree with the outcome in that case—or with Trooper Knussman's right to bring it.

Discussion among feminists about the Pregnancy Discrimination Act and the Family and Medical Leave Act was really a precursor to a great divide that would arise within the feminist legal community. "Difference" feminists would start to argue that pregnancy should be viewed as a unique condition, not legally comparable to anything that men experience, and that women and men must be treated differently in order for women to be equal. Special treatment for pregnant women is justified because

---

* Signed into law by President Bill Clinton on February 5, 1993, it applies to employers of fifty or more employees and guarantees them an up-to-twelve-week unpaid leave of absence.

only women get pregnant, and thus the treatment of pregnant women and women who have just given birth can be compared with nothing else. To these "difference" feminists, men and women cannot be "similarly situated" for purposes of evaluating such policies. Meanwhile, "equalist" feminists argued that pregnancy should be treated as a temporary occupational disability, comparable to other temporary disabilities, such as a broken arm or curable cancer.

The 1987 *Calfed* case[43] highlighted the philosophical difference between these two jurisprudential camps. Lillian Garland, a black woman employed as a receptionist, took a leave from her place of work, the California Federal Savings and Loan Association Bank (Calfed), to have a baby. She had trained the person who was to fill in for her while she was out on leave, but when she returned she was told that her job had been permanently assigned to her replacement. In fact, Calfed's general policy was to decide on an ad hoc basis whether "disabled" people would get their old jobs back. Garland sued them in a California state court under the California statute, which mandated that employers grant "pregnancy disability" leaves and then allow the formerly pregnant women to return to their jobs, regardless of the company's policy toward others with disabilities.

The bank didn't respond but brought suit in federal court on constitutional grounds that California law conflicted with the Persons with Disabilities Act, a federal law. The PDA requires that pregnant women be allowed disability leave only if others are granted disability leaves. In other words, under the PDA, pregnant women can't be discriminated *against,* whereas California law requires companies (for example, Calfed) to treat pregnant women in a more favorable way than they might treat otherwise "disabled" employees.

Calfed argued that the California law was a violation of both the U.S. Constitution and Title VII of the Civil Rights Act. The case got all the way to the U.S. Supreme Court. Briefs flew back and forth, and as they did, the line between "difference" and "equalist" feminists became clearly drawn. The California

Women's Law Center wrote the brief for Garland, defending the California provision on the grounds that (pregnant) women—the only ones who give birth—are entitled to special provisions so that they may take necessary (and unpaid) leaves and return to their jobs after their babies' births, during which periods the jobs would remain unfilled. The ACLU was on the defendant Calfed's side,* arguing that pregnant women should receive disability leaves as all other disabled people did, male or female, and that to do more would be to confer a special benefit on pregnant women, which would constitute discrimination against men, precisely because only women can get pregnant.

The Supreme Court (with Thurgood Marshall writing for the majority) declared that Title VII governed, but that it too would cover the plaintiff in this case. He viewed the PDA as not restricting states from doing more for pregnant women than the PDA alone would. In other words, in a states'-rights kind of argument, his position was that federal law could not limit the benefits already conferred on women by state law.

So California singles out pregnant women for special, preferential treatment. Some "equalist" feminist law professors, like Georgetown's Wendy Williams, think that "conceptualizing pregnancy as a special case permits unfavorable as well as favorable treatment of pregnancy."[44] To judge by her statement about "boomerang effects," one would have to conclude that Ruth might be in this camp too.

It's hard to ignore the possible political consequences of granting special benefits to pregnant women. When we wouldn't let an amendment banning women from combat be added to the ERA, it was because we knew that if we accepted preferential treatment, we would never achieve equal power. To Professor Williams, "treating pregnancy as a special case divides us in ways that . . . are destructive in a particular, political sense as well as a more general sense. On what basis," she asks, "can we

---

* Interestingly, Ramona Ripston, the Executive Director of the Southern California Civil Liberties Union, individually signed the *amicus* brief *for* the plaintiff.

fairly assert . . . that the pregnant woman [fired by a company in Montana, which had passed a law forbidding employers from firing women who became pregnant] deserved to keep her job when any other worker who got sick for any other reason did not?"[45]

Williams goes on to note:

> As our experience with single-sex protective legislation earlier in this century demonstrated, what appear to be special "protections" for women often turn out to be, at best, a double-edged sword. . . . Implicit in the PDA approach to maternity issues is a stance toward parenthood and work that is decidedly different from that embodied in the special-treatment approach to pregnancy.[46]

Whereas the "enlightened" approach, back in the 1970s, often provided mandatory unpaid leaves of absence for the pregnant woman commencing four or five months before and extending for as long as six months after childbirth, that practice was now seen as sexist. As Williams points out, "Such maternity leaves were firmly premised on that aspect of the separate spheres ideology which assigned motherhood as woman's special duty and prerogative. . . . Maternity leave was always based upon cultural constructs and ideologies rather than upon biological necessity, upon role expectations rather than irreducible differences between the sexes."[47]

In my opinion, "difference feminists" are delaying the day when fathers are expected to take time off from work to care for newborns. "Equalist" feminists want to avoid sex-role expectations, so the clash between them and the "difference" or "special treatment" feminists has come to a head. It would be one thing if the only leaves we were talking about were medical leaves based solely on women's physical recovery from childbirth. In some cases, such leaves might last a week; in others, like mine, six weeks. After that, there is no reason, except a stereotypical one, to prefer the mother over the father when it comes to caring for infants. Nursing mothers might justify longer leaves, but then the question arises of how long those leaves should last. I know of women who have nursed their children for two years, but I can't imagine any employer holding a job open for that long. Breast pumps are probably the only solution to this dilemma.

Right after the abortion and pregnancy cases began to flow into the ACLU, other related issues within the broad area of reproductive freedom started coming to my attention. One day, a twenty-one-year-old black woman was shown into my office. She introduced herself as Nial Ruth Cox, who lived and worked as a nurses' aid in Suffolk County, New York. Pulling out of her handbag a small piece of dog-eared paper, she asked me to read it. On it were the words "bi-lateral tubal ligation." I asked Nial Ruth if she knew what the words meant. Visibly shaken, she said she thought so. I wanted to know everything, so I asked her to start at the beginning of the story.

She had been a seventeen-year-old girl living on welfare in North Carolina with her mother and eight brothers and sisters when she discovered that she was pregnant. Sometime later the local hospital sent a social worker to her mother, warning her that if she didn't sign the form they'd just handed her (without saying what it was), the entire family would be thrown off welfare. The mother, who couldn't read or write and who obviously felt that she had no choice, put an "X" where her signature was supposed to be. Her minor daughter, Nial Ruth, knew nothing about that incident. She carried the baby to term and entered the local hospital to give birth. When she awoke from the general anesthetic they'd given her, in addition to learning that she had had a little girl, she found bandages on her stomach. The hospital nurses and doctors told her nothing, and she left the hospital a few days later with her new baby.

Now she was living and working on Long Island and was engaged to a man whom she'd been seeing for quite a while. They had been having frequent unprotected sex, and she hadn't become pregnant. Finally, no longer willing to keep her head in the sand, Nial Ruth got on a Greyhound bus headed for North Carolina. She went straight to the hospital where she'd given birth and asked for her medical records. Their response was to show her the form her mother had "signed" and then give her the piece of paper, which she'd just shown me. She left the hospital and got back on the bus for the return trip home to New York.

This was my first introduction to what was a widespread practice—the involuntary sterilization of poor black girls in the South. Shortly after her visit, we accepted Nial Ruth's case, and working with the Southern office of the ACLU, in Atlanta, we drafted and filed a complaint in the federal district court in North Carolina, naming as defendants the doctor, the hospital and the social workers who had coerced Ruth's mother's signature. We then had a big press conference about the lawsuit, which led immediately to my receiving two other calls, one from a young woman in Georgia, another from two women in South Carolina.

The issue in all these cases was the same: Because the women and their families had no money, various state agencies made sure that they were permanently sterilized. It gave new meaning to the phrase "freedom of choice" and, together with all the abortion cases people wanted us to bring, allowed us to proceed with, and seek funding aggressively for, the new Reproductive Freedom Project. I now had a different batch of cases and issues to oversee; the staff of lawyers and assistants I supervised in New York exceeded twelve, and ACLU lawyers working with us around the country exceeded one hundred.

There had been some concern at the ACLU that starting this new project might jeopardize the funding of the Women's Rights Project. Lots of people approved of equal rights; no one knew how many approved of the freedom to choose abortions—or as it was called in those days, "abortion on demand." Surprisingly, in fact, more money poured in earmarked for the Reproductive Freedom Project than for sex discrimination cases in general and for lobbying for the ERA in particular.

A producer from *60 Minutes* called one day not long after we announced the case to ask if Nial Ruth Cox would be willing to

appear on the show. They had decided to do a segment on involuntary sterilization. Nial Ruth agreed to talk about her story on network television. I would appear with her to deflect any questions that might compromise her lawsuit.

Nial Ruth Cox and I after the press conference where we announced the filing of the lawsuit against the doctor who performed the sterilization operation, the hospital, the family's welfare caseworker and past and present members of the North Carolina Eugenics Board, which included the state's attorney general

On the appointed day, I arrived at the CBS studios for the taping, but as the time grew near to start, Nial Ruth was nowhere in sight. While I was fretting that I might not have been clear in the directions I'd given her, Mike Wallace charged into the room. He was agitated because Nial Ruth wasn't there and loudly shouted, "CPT, goddamnit!" I didn't know until later what that meant, so I didn't respond. I was just glad when Nial Ruth came hurrying in a few minutes later, right before the taping was scheduled to start. Her train in from Long Island had been delayed on the tracks, so she couldn't even call to say she'd be late.

Mike Wallace calmed down when he saw her, and the interview went so well that I barely had to intervene. For someone with an eighth-grade education from an impoverished Southern all-black town, Nial Ruth was eloquent. She concluded by stating simply that as a result of her not being able to have children, her fiancé had broken their engagement. She hadn't told me that; it made me sad and even angrier.

As I was becoming aware of how widespread the problem was, Gloria decided that *Ms.* should do an article about involuntary sterilization. So she and I agreed to tour the South together. I was thinking about class-action suits in several states and wanted to urge women to become plaintiffs. Usually, it is improper for lawyers to seek out clients (a practice called champerty), but the rule is not supposed to apply if you don't profit in any way from cases you generate.

Gloria and I arrived in Mississippi to meet with Fannie Lou Hamer, the late, great civil rights leader. When we told her our purpose, she looked us straight in the eye and said, "Girls, you don't begin to know what goes on here. They did that to all of us." We were astonished that a leader of Fannie Lou's stature had had this terrible "operation" performed on her and she had never complained. Of course, for her and others of her generation, the time periods in which to sue under the relevant statutes of limitations had expired.

In North Carolina, we met a young black woman lawyer who, affiliated with the ACLU there, was helping me on Nial Ruth Cox's case. We also met with another of my clients, a young woman in Georgia. She was fourteen years old when she was scheduled to have an appendectomy. Her grandmother, with whom she was living, was illiterate, and this time the social worker threatened to throw the grandmother off social security if she didn't put her "X" on the line, so that the hospital would have "permission" to perform a bilateral tubal ligation on her underage granddaughter while they were performing the appendectomy. This client would never have any children.

After visiting about five different states, we had enough for Gloria's article and I had more possible plaintiffs than I could handle. What I hadn't expected was a call I received shortly after we returned to New York. It was from my new lawyer friend in North Carolina. She told me that she'd been suspended from the practice of law for six months, having been accused of champerty by the North Carolina bar. Apparently, the state bar people in North Carolina didn't care that she wasn't going to make any money. They had probably never heard of *pro bono* work on behalf of blacks, women or poor people. I felt partly responsible, worried that Gloria's presence had led to a story in the local paper, bringing attention to that lawyer's involvement and causing her suspension.

The federal district court in North Carolina eventually issued its ruling in *Nial Ruth Cox v. The State of North Carolina:* The state statute of limitations precluded her from bringing the suit, because it had started to run from the date that Nial Ruth had been sterilized, not from the date on which she found out what had happened to her. We couldn't get the court to agree that it was unfair to have required Ruth to bring a lawsuit before she knew she would never be able to have children. No one in the hospital had told her anything, and no one, not even her mother, had told her about the form on which the "X" had been placed. When I told Nial Ruth Cox the bad news, she took it philosophically, as though she had never thought she might win.

To me, the Nial Ruth Cox case was about a woman's right to control her own body, and it was about racism. A much larger percentage of black women than white were involuntarily sterilized in the South, because racist doctors and hospitals there simply didn't want more black babies, who were likely, in their opinion, to end up on welfare. But bad people don't just live in the South. In California, the practice of sterilizing non-English-speaking Hispanic women was apparently widespread. A woman in labor would be asked to sign a "consent" form that she couldn't read. In pain and certainly under duress, most of the women signed—and never had any more children.

Coming full circle, at the end of 1997, I received a call, prompted by Gloria, from Brazilian TV. They wanted to interview me for my views about a woman who was offering crack-addicted mothers $100 to get sterilized. My position was that thanks to federal regulations, passed in 1979 largely because of our work in the area of involuntary sterilization, anyone who performed the operation on these women addicts would violate the regulations that require consent from someone capable of giving it. A crack addict with a $100 bill dangled in front of her would not be considered legally capable of giving her voluntary consent.

In 1992, Clarence Thomas burst onto the scene with his nomination by George Bush for a seat on the highest court. His confirmation hearings started, and soon Anita Hill became a household name. While Thomas, exuding a shifty-eyed dishonesty, seemed morally indignant at the charges leveled by Hill, she seemed like a woman bound by moral duty to come forward and testify about his sexually harassing behavior. But the senators on the Judiciary Committee either weren't listening to her or they didn't think what she was saying was important. Clarence Thomas was confirmed.

The facts became clearer to me after I read *Strange Justice: The Selling of Clarence Thomas,* by investigative reporters Jane Mayer and Jill Abramson,[48] and then spent an evening in Los Angeles with the authors on their book tour. Unlike the senators on the then all-male Judicial Nomination Subcommittee of the Judiciary Committee, they had conducted a thorough investigation. They had talked with the women whom Senator Joseph Biden, the committee chair, had decided it wasn't worthwhile to ask to testify. These women not only confirmed what Anita Hill had testified to (she had told one of them about his remarks and come-ons as they were taking place), they also reported that several other women had complained about Thomas's imposing himself on them. One of them said that his remark about the pubic hair on the Coke can was familiar around the EEOC offices. Another told of her shock when she went into the kitchen of his D.C. apartment to find herself facing a graphic and, to her, obscene *Playboy* centerfold. And there was the video-store owner who confirmed, by producing a receipt, that Clarence Thomas was a regular renter of porn, his favorite being *Big Mama Tama.* But rather than take this information seriously, the members of the committee ordered the FBI to cease and desist from any investigation into these kinds of matters.

As Senator Barbara Mikulski of Maryland, then the only female Democratic senator, forcefully stated, "What disturbs me as much as the allegations themselves is that the Senate appears not to take the charge of sexual harassment seriously."[49]

For example, Ted Kennedy's silence, coupled with his constant fidgeting, indicated how eager he was to proceed to a vote. Like many of the other male senators, Senator Biden seemed to believe that what men do in their private lives doesn't impact their public lives. But women felt that Thomas's behavior toward Anita Hill and the other women at the EEOC working under him could hardly be termed his private life. Meanwhile, Paul Simon, a Democratic senator from Illinois, took the position right after *Strange Justice* was published that had he known during the hearings what he learned later from reading the book, he wouldn't have voted for confirmation.

George Mitchell's role in Clarence Thomas's confirmation was curious. Mitchell was the Senate majority leader and in charge of timing floor votes. But rather than insist that all evidence be heard, he, along with Biden, continued to maintain that Hill's charge was not serious enough to postpone the full Senate vote. Pat King, a black professor of law at Georgetown University and a former classmate of mine at Harvard Law School, was a member of a small delegation of women who visited Mitchell privately to try to convince him that it was in the Democratic Party's interest to delay the vote and allow the Senate, as well as the American people, the right to hear evidence from others who might corroborate Hill's charges against Thomas. But she recalled that Mitchell just kept saying, "My hands are tied. I can't do anything."[50] Of course he could, I thought when I read this. He just didn't want to. Who knew what skeletons he had in his own closet?

As for blacks speaking out against Clarence Thomas, several have come forward. Karen Grigsby Bates, who writes from Los Angeles about modern culture, race relations and politics for several national publications, blasted Thomas in the *Los Angeles Times*.[51] She took issue with his statement "I am not an Uncle Tom" by saying that is exactly what he is: "A black person whose primary concern is being well thought of by white people often to the detriment of himself and other blacks." She compared him unfavorably with Professor Charles Ogletree, who is also black and teaches constitutional law and social ethics at Harvard Law School. Like Thomas, she points out, Ogletree "has scaled walls that at times seemed insurmountable. But unlike Thomas, Ogletree took the time to retain the rope, fashion of it a ladder, throw it over the wall and, via mentoring and extensive community service, encourage other [blacks] to follow."

Clarence Thomas, whose beliefs place him squarely in lockstep with the radical right, clearly doesn't identify as black, or even as one who has risen from the underclass of our society. For example, nothing made Thomas angrier than word getting out that he himself had benefitted from affirmative action when he was admitted to Yale Law School. Apparently, he thought he didn't need it, and a logical corollary, to him, was that if he could do it, so could every other black person. Hence, his public skewering of his own sister, who was at the time of his nomination still on welfare. The radical right adopted Thomas as their own, led in their holy war by Senator John Danforth, a conservative Republican from Missouri.

It is scary to think about how Thomas and his group gathered together to pray, in Danforth's private Senate bathroom, as the hearings were about to commence. It is equally weird to imagine Thomas, as reported, writhing in a fetal position on the floor of his bedroom the night before the vote. Or his chanting something about the Lord and Jesus as he was being evaluated by the senators. The man said he didn't believe in natural law anymore, that it had been an intellectual exercise of his youth, but he certainly hasn't behaved as a rational man might. Nor did he behave as a

moral man would. He said he'd never discussed abortion or *Roe.*
Because he was at Yale Law School when that decision was
handed down, no one believed him.

Anita Hill went back to Oklahoma right after the hearings with
the issue of sexual harassment, although illegal under Title VII,
still very much unresolved. The rest of us mobilized to get
women elected to the Senate and onto the Judiciary Committee.
Hill's coming forward and exposing Thomas for what he was ushered in 1992 as the Year of the Woman. With it, came the election in California of two U.S. Senators, Dianne Feinstein and
Barbara Boxer. The fact that they were both elected was especially sweet to me because of a huge argument I'd had with many
members of the Hollywood Women's Political Committee
(HWPC), then one of the country's most powerful PACs, who
feared that endorsing Feinstein would lessen Boxer's chances of
victory. I felt that it was not only politically and morally impru-
dent to stand behind only one woman on the grounds that two
can't win, but also that two women running at the same time for
the U.S. Senate from one state was a truly historic moment that
wouldn't be lost on the nation—or the press. Finally, the HWPC
endorsement was secured, and I'm convinced it was the major
reason that both Feinstein and Boxer were elected. Other organizations from around the country were waiting to see what the
HWPC would do, and when it endorsed Boxer and Feinstein,
these groups also threw their support to both candidates.

Shortly after the Democratic primary, Alexis graduated from
high school, on the horns of a dilemma about where to go to college. Much to my delight, she eventually settled on Berkeley.
Marc, too, was pleased, despite his continuing qualms about losing his daughter to California. By the time Alexis was a college
sophomore, she had become a member of a sorority, and soon, as
its program chair, she invited me to Berkeley to give a talk on
women's rights.

Originally, I was appalled at the idea of her joining a sorority.
Then I realized how different—at least at Berkeley—sororities
now are from what they were when I was in college. I realized

A big march and rally against the right was staged in San Francisco while Alexis was an undergraduate at Berkeley. She and I marched together, then rested under a banner that means a lot to both of us.

The perfect shirt for the event; I wore it proudly.

that the young women in Tri Delta were actually feminists. I narrowed the subject of my remarks to date rape, acquaintance rape and sexual harassment. When we reached the question-and-answer period, one of them timidly raised her hand and asked whether she should have bitten off a guy's penis when he forced her to go down on him. I was tempted to say yes but refrained. I told her instead that what he did was a crime and that she could press charges. During our back-and-forth, I heard a strange sound, which I soon realized was her sorority sisters' clicking their fingers in support of the young woman who'd admitted aloud the abuse she'd suffered. The day after my talk and the question-and-answer session, which lasted almost four hours, Alexis proudly told me that her friends had been so impressed they wanted me to move in with them as a kind of den mother.

The issue of sexual harassment kept heating up, and I had an enlightening conversation with Ruth Bader Ginsburg about the subject just before she took her seat on the Supreme Court in October 1993. It was at the fortieth anniversary celebration of the graduation of the first class of women admitted to Harvard Law School, and as Ruth and I were talking together after the lunch honoring her, I asked her to clarify something I'd read in the *New York Times.* An important case, *Harris v. Forklift Systems, Inc.,*[52] had been accepted by the Supreme Court and was about to be argued, and I wasn't sure what the article meant when it referred to the issue before the Court in *Harris* as being whether the "reasonable woman" standard would be applied or whether the issue devolved on the reaction of the victim—and plaintiff— Theresa Harris.[53]

Ruth explained in her patient way that the "reasonable woman" standard would probably be interpreted to mean "the reasonable person" (in other words, man) standard. If the Court were to rule that the proper standard was the "reasonable woman" standard, Theresa Harris might lose her case. Instead of suffering severe mental anguish as a "reasonable" woman might—a reaction that a majority of the Court could well say would be a woman's natural response—Harris had finally left her job without suffering severe psychological harm.

We parted ways, and less than two weeks later, Ruth, now officially a Justice of the Supreme Court, distinguished herself during the oral argument in that case. She took apart the attorney for the owner of the trucking company who had subjected the company's female manager (Harris) to his crude comments and lewd behavior. The issue before the Court was whether plaintiff Harris was required to have proven serious emotional suffering to win the case, or whether the fact that she was subjected to the owner's behavior, which caused her to quit her job, was sufficient for her to recover damages.

In shorter order than usual, the Court handed down its opinion. In *Harris,* it reaffirmed an earlier case, *Meritor Savings Bank v. Vinson,*[54] in which the Court had held that "Title VII [of the Civil Rights Act of 1964] is violated when the workplace is permeated with discriminatory behavior that is sufficiently severe or pervasive to create a discriminatorily hostile or abusive working environment."[55]

Writing for a unanimous* Court, Justice O'Connor took "a middle path between making actionable any conduct that is merely offensive and requiring the conduct to cause a tangible psychological injury."[57] She wrote that there must be "an objectively hostile or abusive work environment that a reasonable person would find hostile or abusive." Most important for guidance on future cases, the Court stated that "Title VII comes into play before the harassing conduct leads to a nervous breakdown. A discriminatorily abusive work environment, even one that does not seriously affect employees' psychological well-being, can and often will detract from employees' job performance, discourage

---

* The fact that Justice Thomas, accused of sexual harassment during his confirmation hearings, didn't recuse himself from this case is not surprising. Recusing himself might be tantamount to admitting that he had some personal interest in the subject. And during the *Harris* arguments, according to news accounts, he was silent and spent most of the oral argument staring at the ceiling or fiddling with his nails. And in three days on the bench the same week, he did not ask a single question.

employees from remaining on the job, or keep them from advancing in their careers."[58]

Ruth joined in the majority opinion in *Harris* but wrote an even stronger concurring opinion of her own, in which she clairified any remaining ambiguities:

> [The] inquiry should center, dominantly, on whether the discriminatory conduct has reasonably interfered with the plaintiff's work performance. To show such interference, "the plaintiff need not prove that his or her tangible productivity has declined as a result of the harassment." It suffices to prove that a reasonable person subjected to the discriminatory conduct would find, as the plaintiff did, that the harassment so altered working conditions as to "make it more difficult to do the job."[59,60]

Thus, even though Ruth referred to a "reasonable person" in her concurrence, she qualified that phrase by adding that it's enough that the harassment in question makes it more difficult to do the job. This endorses the notion that anyone subjected to the kind of harassment that Harris was would find it more difficult to do the job, because the *conduct* would be found unreasonable by a reasonable person. Ruth, therefore, looked to the conduct of the offender rather than to the response of the victim, who may or may not be a "reasonable woman."

Today, sexual harassment law has evolved to the point that judges consider two different kinds of claims: *quid pro quo* and hostile work environment. The former, according to federal district judge Susan Webber Wright, presiding over *Jones v. Clinton,*[61] required the plaintiff to show that her refusal to submit to unwelcome sexual advances or requests for sexual favors resulted in a tangible job detriment.[62] But less than three months after Judge Wright made her ruling, on June 26, 1998, the Supreme Court contradicted her in one of two definitive sexual harassment case decisions.[63] In a 7-to-2 majority opinion (Clarence Thomas, of course, and Antonin Scalia dissenting), the

Court held that an employee, Kimberly Ellerth, who was sub-jected to, but resisted, a supervisor's advances, need not have suf-fered a tangible job detriment, like dismissal or loss of promotion, to be able to pursue a lawsuit against her company, Burlington Industries. The Court went on to note, however, that such a suit cannot succeed if the company has an antiharassment policy with an effective complaint procedure in place and the employee has unreasonably failed to use it.[64]

Some of Paula Jones's supporters urged her to appeal her own case because of this subsequent Supreme Court decision. One reason Judge Wright had dismissed Jones's suit against the presi-dent was that in her view Ms. Jones had failed to show any tangi-ble detriment in her job. But Judge Wright seems to have covered herself; she was aware of the *Burlington* case and said that it was not relevant, because Ms. Ellerth had been threatened while Ms. Jones had not. A clear threat was to Judge Wright a prerequisite for a claim of harassment.

Finally, sexual harassment law is becoming clearer, and early in March 1998, Justice Scalia, writing for a unanimous Court, ruled that same-sex harassment is also prohibited under Title VII. And at the very end of the 1998 term, the Court clarified many of the unresolved issues within the rubric of sexual harass-ment law. Although Ruth didn't write the majority opinions, she of course joined them, and I know she exerted significant influ-ence on her colleagues.

But that wasn't the end of the subject, although it may have put employment issues to rest for a while. In May 1999, the Court ruled, with Sandra Day O'Connor writing for the majority, that school districts can be liable for damages under federal law for failing to stop a student from subjecting another to severe and pervasive sexual harassment. A year earlier the Court had ruled that teachers would be liable for harassing students, so this was a logical next step. The case involved a fifth-grade Georgia girl who was subjected to months of taunting and unwanted touching of her breasts and genital area by a male classmate. (The boy was eventually charged and convicted in juvenile court of sexual battery against her.) Despite repeated complaints, school officials had refused to take action. When the case reached the Supreme Court, it declared that Title IX, barring sex discrimination in schools that accept federal money, covers student-on-student harassment.

In her opinion, Justice O'Connor emphasized that "damages are not available for simple acts of teasing and name-calling among schoolchildren," but rather for behavior "so severe, pervasive and objectively offensive that it denies its victims the equal access to education" guaranteed under Title IX of the Education Amendments of 1972. She went on to state that school officials must have known of the harassment and, acting with "deliberate indifference," failed to take reasonable steps to stop it.[65]

This brings me to the story of my last encounter with Ruth. In October 1993, I had visited Cambridge for Harvard Law School's "Celebration 40," forty years since the first class of women graduated from Harvard Law School. I hadn't seen Ruth, who was being honored, in a long time. After the luncheon and her eloquent acceptance speech, I was sitting outside with my old friend Kimba Wood when Ruth came over. After we discussed the "reasonable woman" issue, as it related to sexual harassment cases, she mentioned that Justice O'Connor wanted her to join an 8:00 a.m. aerobics class that "Sandra Day" was trying to organize for all the women employees of the Court, including herself. Knowing that, like me, Ruth is not fond of early-morning activities, a fact that she confirmed was as true in 1993 as it had been twenty-five years earlier,* I suggested that she start an alternate afternoon class in the Court's gym. The reason, I said, was that she had to stay in shape because I (and many, many others) would like to see her live long enough to become the next, and

---

* In the October *New York Times Magazine* article, I read that a former clerk of hers (David Post) commented on Ruth's hours, saying that she works most efficiently alone, and at home, often staying up until two or three in the morning for long periods of concentrated writing and thinking. "She likes to sleep late, work at home and come in when she's ready to do whatever faces her there. When the Court isn't sitting, she can come into the office between noon and 6 in the evening."[66]

the first woman, Chief Justice. She merely smiled, somewhat shyly, in response.

I didn't have an opportunity to communicate with Ruth after that weekend in Cambridge until the winter of 1997, when I decided to send her a holiday card, featuring her and Justice O'Connor as The Supremes. In response, I received a note from Ruth—very impressive envelope, her return address simply "Justice Ruth Bader Ginsburg"—thanking me for the card I'd sent, in which I'd told her that Alexis was at Berkeley's Boalt Hall, her law school education entrusted to the dean and Ruth's old friend and collaborator, Herma Hill Kay.

In addition to her intellect, Ruth is a person whose temperament, for the present Court in particular, is perfect. She is someone to whom even those in political or philosophical disagreement listen. She is calm, soft-spoken, but clearly in control. Whenever she speaks, it is obvious that she has carefully thought through what she is saying. It is therefore not surprising to me at all that Justice Scalia thinks highly of her. As for Justice O'Connor, I believe that already we are seeing Ruth's influence. Before Ruth, Justice O'Connor probably had the right instincts in many areas of the law about which I have written here, but now she has a colleague who is there to support those instincts. Ruth probably would have joined in almost every opinion written by former Justices Brennan and Marshall, but their personalities may have seemed more "radical" to their colleagues. Her manner is more that of a scholar with a well-reasoned thought process at work. I believe she will accumulate a tremendous amount of persuasive power on the Court.

For a long time I thought I was alone in speculating on Ruth's becoming the next Chief Justice. But I wasn't. The point was emphatically made in the above-mentioned *New York Times Magazine* article.[67] Jeffrey Rosen, the author, in a comprehensive review of Ruth and her role on the Court, observed that "Justice Ginsburg has continued to style herself as a cautious codifier of public opinion rather than a crusader for social change."[68] He

added that "more than any of her colleagues, Ginsburg often conceals or subli-
mates her personal views of the merits of a
case by focusing on legal process."[69] This

*Marc, Alexis and I at her
graduation from
Berkeley—Phi Beta
Kappa in economics—
May 1997*

fact has, in the opinion of that writer, no doubt helped her sustain her longtime friendship with Antonin Scalia, dating back to
their days together on the U.S. Court of Appeals for the D.C.
Circuit. So in that article the author's conclusion was: "Because
of the respect Justice Ginsburg has earned from liberals, who
appreciate her feminist advocacy, and from conservatives who
recognize her otherwise restrained sensibility, she is increasingly
mentioned as a plausible candidate to succeed William Rehnquist as Chief Justice."[70] And the author of that *New York Times
Magazine* piece added that even Ruth herself has done little to
discourage speculation about becoming the first female Chief
Justice of the United States. In her speeches, she likes to quote
from a letter by Sarah Grimké, the feminist and antislavery lec-
turer from South Carolina, who visited the Supreme Court in

1853: "In the letter, Grimké says she was invited to sit in the Chief Justice's chair. 'As I took the place,' she wrote, 'I involuntarily exclaimed, "Who knows, but this chair may one day be occupied by a woman." The brethren laughed heartily.' Nevertheless, [Ruth adds] it may be a true prophecy."[71] At this point, the author of the *Times* article noted, "Ginsburg pauses and looks at the audience. 'Today,' she says with a little smile, 'no one would laugh at that prophecy.' "[72]

Chapter 11

A VACUUM OF VISION?

Have we feminists lost the vision we once had? Or if we still have one, what is it? Of course, there is the NOW Legal Defense and Education Fund, and plenty of individual women—like Roxanne Conlin, an attorney friend of mine in Des Moines, Iowa—who have been bringing sex discrimination lawsuits, often successfully, for many years. There are global women's strikes for equal pay, and informative events like the Feminist Expo put on by the Feminist Majority, which also lobbied hard to ensure that American women would have access to a morning-after pill, RU486. There are lawsuits and actions by pro-choice groups to ensure that the rights we won in *Roe v. Wade* are not eroded; that has been a rough and rocky road, with failures that have included the loss of lives because of horrible actions by anti-choice fanatics. But my question is, Do we as feminists share an overall vision for the future?

When I have tried to raise this subject with Gloria, prodding her for clarity about what she thinks the goals of the Women's Movement should be, she generally responds that "goals" sounds utopian and therefore unreachable. Of course, Gloria wants things to change. She annually hands out the Gloria Steinem Reproductive Freedom Awards to those who have helped to gain the freedom to choose whether to have an abortion or a baby. She fights for the rights of poor and minority women, to raise them from the downward spiral in which they all too often find themselves. Except for stating at one point that she wanted to see an end to nationalism, she rarely discusses theoretical issues. But I feel strongly that we feminists should try to envision the society in which we'd like to live and then let our goals be known to one another.

In November 1997, Gloria was a speaker at a special inaugural dinner of the Third Wave, a group of young feminists between the ages of fifteen and thirty who want to help other young women. Gloria cares about them. The next day, she was the keynote speaker for the Twenty-fifth Anniversary Celebration of the Sisterhood Bookstore. Not long after she left Los Angeles, Joanne and I stayed at Gloria's apartment in New York to celebrate the thirtieth anniversary of the Women's Liberation Movement, sponsored by the Veteran Feminists of America, which was honoring all of us. It was a poignant reminder not only of how many of us had struggled in our own way to make a feminist revolution but also of how time has passed and how much more still has to be done. Some of it was sad. Bella, who has since died, was too sick to attend. Flo Kennedy, in her wheelchair, sat at the table with Joanne, Gloria and me, as well as several other old friends. She could barely speak, having recently come out of a coma that she'd been in for a number of months. Kate Millett was there, drinking and chain-smoking, just like the old days. There had been, of course, painful times in the past when we watched our sisters act oddly or not in their own best interests: Ti-Grace Atkinson, barefoot in the snow, defending the Mafia; Kate being institutionalized and/or drinking herself into oblivion; Anselma Dell Olio running off with a rich Italian count (and now, I hear, overseeing five mansions in various parts of Europe in her role as his wife); Dory Cavanaugh dying because she was too vain to let her doctor perform the then necessary mastectomy.

Robin Morgan had her own take on that Thirtieth Anniversary Celebration. She wanted to be as far away as possible. She had problems with who had been invited—and who hadn't. And she didn't like the militaristic sound of the group's name, with the word "veteran" in it.

I've wondered whether the old feminist friends from the early

Kate Millett (left) and Gloria Steinem (right) compare notes at the Thirtieth Anniversary Celebration of the Women's Liberation Movement in New York City. Joanne and I flew in to join old feminist friends there.

1970s feel that what they hoped for a quarter century ago has come to pass, whether we're on the way, whether they're disappointed. Most important, I wonder what they now envision as a feminist future. But somehow at that Thirtieth Anniversary Celebration, there was never a right moment to raise any of these questions.

Flo Kennedy, who had recently been hospitalized, with Gloria, who cheered her with memories of their days together on the lecture circuit

In December 1998, I received an encouraging mailing from the Redstockings Women's Liberation Archives Distribution Project, an all-volunteer grassroots effort. It teaches women's liberation history "for activist use." What pleased me most was to read their mission statement: "We have to alert our sisters to the vital radical storehouse in the feminist tradition and get our movement going in a direction which will actually win some of the things we need."[1]

Even though they probably weren't thinking about women in law school—hardly a radical group by the old Redstockings standards—at that moment I was. After a talk I gave in April 1999 at Yale Law School, I was given a copy of the *Yale Journal of Law and Feminism* that had been published the previous year.[2] I read it eagerly. For an article entitled "Just Trying to Be Human in This Place," the author had interviewed twenty women from the Yale Law School class of 1997 (twenty-eight years after I graduated from Harvard Law School). Her findings were alarming:

• One student reflected: "Here I am sitting in class, and I'm silent. . . . I spent a lot of time thinking I don't have anything to contribute."[3]

• The author backed this up by declaring that several "empirical studies have shown that female students engage in classroom discussions less frequently than male students."[4]

• Another student: "I feel like men are so much more comfortable in the classroom [and] with the professors calling on them. . . . I think the men feel entitled . . . and just spout off, whereas the women want to be prepared and say something they think is intelligent."[5]

• On this, the author observed that although women's feelings about volunteering in class ran from terrified to bored to eager, the majority were not participating, mostly because of some kind of discomfort with the classroom environment. Many also identified feelings of intellectual inadequacy. Their own silence became evidence that "they are not as smart as their more vocal male peers."[6]

• Another woman, in commenting on small group participation: "It would have been a good thing for a professor to encourage me and force me, almost, to speak. Otherwise, I would just sit there quiet, as I did in all my classes. . . . I didn't feel like I had anything impressive to say that was worth fighting with the professor for talk time."[7]

I wish I could have shared my own experiences at Harvard with those Yale Law women before they began their legal training in 1994. I also wish I shared the Redstockings' optimism that simply by studying our history as feminists we could find the way to accomplish our goals today. The problem is that while in the early seventies our demands were clear, shouted loudly, and usually reinforced by action taken, now, I feel, the Women's Movement has neither a clear focus nor a plan for really addressing and acting on many issues that affect women's lives. I'm not sure what our collective dreams are—where we want to be twenty years into the third millennium—or whether we can agree on what we need. It's as though all we have time to do is put out brushfires, such as stop the right wing's assault on choice or curb sexual harassment and sex discrimination in the workplace.

Although the case law discussed earlier might indicate otherwise, being a feminist does not mean merely wanting equal rights with men. Feminists want to revolutionize society and reshape its basic values, while still addressing issues that arise in women's everyday lives.

In the late 1960s and early 1970s, feminists like me were dubbed "liberal," because we wanted to change the system, not overthrow it.[8] Many of our goals, including the ERA and abortion rights, could be accomplished by amendments to the U.S. Constitution, by Supreme Court rulings or by lobbying legislatures, including Congress, to pass laws. Radical feminists didn't believe that change could happen within the system, whereas we "liberal" feminists didn't see how it would come from outside. During the ERA hearings, a small group of disruptive women, calling themselves "feminists" and refusing to use their own names, stood with their *backs* to the Senate panel and chanted, "Down with imperialism." They cared not at all about the ERA; they hated the system.

Because women have had so little power, I knew equality was a necessary (although by no means a sufficient) goal, and I thus took issue with many self-dubbed radical feminists. They didn't seem to understand that the power to influence society cannot be achieved while the playing field is uneven. To me, once women are imbued with equal rights, we as a gender will have a real chance to achieve equal power and therefore control over our lives.

Even today the issue of equality creates debate. Two camps developed—"equalist" and "difference" feminists—after the publication of Carol Gilligan's book, *In a Different Voice,* in 1982. It may not have been Gilligan's intention at all that her work would be used this way, but five years later clashing briefs, reflecting two different viewpoints, were submitted to the Supreme Court before arguments were heard in the Calfed case.* One set of briefs argued that because women and men should be treated equally under the law, pregnancy, with its necessary leave of absence, should be viewed like any other disability. The other set insisted that because pregnancy is a state unique to women, different and more favorable rules should apply. Well-known linguist and best-selling author Deborah Tannen, who is also a feminist, dislikes polarizing issues and groups of people, as she clearly states in her book *The Argument Culture.*

> In one camp are those who focus on the ways that women are different from men. . . . Some emphasize that women's ways are equally valid. . . . Others believe that women are superior. Both these views—called "difference feminism"—contrast with those in the other camp, who claim that women are no different from men by nature, so any noticeable differences result from how society treats women. Those who take this view are called "social constructionists."[9]

---

* See discussion in preceding chapter.

It sounds as though social constructionists are very much the same as equalist feminists, and many equalist feminists are lawyers who are asking that women be accorded the same treatment under the law as men. In any event, the polarity that arose from the *Calfed* case was, it seems to me, inevitable. Both *In a Different Voice* and the briefs in that case contributed substantially to women's studies, as well as feminist jurisprudence. According to Gilligan, men and women do not, in general, share the same moral values. Men's morality is based more on a sense of rights, women's more on a sense of responsibility. Male development is mainly a matter of increasing separation from others to achieve autonomy and independence, whereas women's development involves a continuing and unresolved struggle to balance their responsibilities to others with their commitment to themselves.[10]

Gilligan demurs when it comes to the reasons for these differences:

> No claims are made about the origins of the differences described. . . . Clearly [they] arise in a social context where factors of social status and power combine with reproductive biology to shape the experience of males and females and the relations between the sexes.[11]

Gilligan has enunciated, probably more clearly than most other feminist academics, the different feelings that she believes women and men have:

> Sensitivity to the needs of others and the assumption of responsibility for taking care lead women to attend to voices other than their own and to include in their judgment other points of view.[12]

She goes on:

> Women not only define themselves in a context of human relationship but also judge themselves in terms

of their ability to care. Women's place in man's life cycle
has been that of nurturer, caretaker and helpmate.[13]

Meanwhile, Gilligan ascribes to men the goal of:

favoring the separateness of the individual self over
connection to others, and leaning more toward an
autonomous life of work than toward the interdepen-
dence of love and care.[14]

Without expressing a value judgment about whether women's
ways are better or worse than men's, Gilligan, unfortunately—
maybe even unintentionally—reinforces differences that even
today might still exist between the sexes simply by describing
those differences as fact. That very description could turn into a
prescription for keeping women in their "roles" as nurturers.
(Doesn't it make sense to assume that those whose morality has
been described as one of responsibility take care of the children?)
Worse, it creates an argument for not treating women as men's
equals. If women's values put more emphasis on relationships
than on power, and if this is as good as or better than whatever
men value, then a plausible argument could be made that not
only should we stay as we are, but also anything that keeps us
from maintaining our nurturers' values is undesirable. This could
lead to the situation in which men continue to wield power while
we women deal with relationships in our families and among ourselves, as well as those between women and men. While Gilligan
may believe that well-balanced adults of both sexes should incorporate both sets of values, she doesn't suggest how we should go
from having different moralities to having a blend of the two.

Although we've discussed Gilligan only indirectly, Gloria seems
to be precisely the kind of woman Gilligan describes, not with
respect to men but when it comes to groups of other women.
Issues pertinent primarily to young or poor women, women of
color and women from other countries—usually Third World
countries—resonate most strongly for her. Choice is an important

issue to Gloria, but again, what concerns her most is how it affects young, usually poor or minority women. While she puts a lot of energy into helping young women become feminists, she does not focus as much on how little power women who are more her peers, women in the professions, business or government, have.

Catharine MacKinnon does not seem to accept that the different voice of women that Gilligan found is woman's true voice. She points out that women have been "forced into this situation of inequality," so it therefore "makes a lot of sense that we should want to negotiate, since we lose conflicts."[15] MacKinnon, like other feminists Tannen describes as social constructionists, argues that our working definition of woman was born in the wake of women's oppression by men, and that what was created through oppression will only perpetuate oppression.[16]

So-called difference feminists believe that men's way of doing things is the norm, and therefore that we must impose a female norm in order for women to survive successfully in the competitive job market and in life in general. But defining what is a male as distinguished from a female norm is not only a difficult exercise, it's often a dangerous one.

Even the *Calfed* case reinforces the problems with Carol Gilligan's observations that women's morality leads them to care more about relationships, especially with their infants, while men deal with the real, competitive world and the morality—or lack thereof—that it fosters. Gilligan is not trying to change society so that women cease playing the role of primary nurturer; she's saying that because we *are* society's nurturers, we have different values and different ways of seeing the world. So, in essence, even if Gilligan, being a good social scientist, is merely describing what she found in her studies, she apparently did not take into consideration the effects her observations would have in the real world. And Gilligan is not just another feminist academic. She is a titled professor of gender studies at Harvard, so she has tremendous influence in that field.

My fear is that as long as women, but not men, are assigned the role of primary caretaker, we will be destined to fill it. Why aren't men considered equal candidates for nurturing? I know many who are nurturers by what seems like instinct. When I was growing up my father was, in fact, much more nurturing than my mother, who was always pushing me to go for the brass ring (whatever it was at any given moment). I remember vividly my father's repeating to me that he just wanted me to be happy. It was he who would hold my hand when I was scared at night and he who would patiently take me to visit my favorite Bushman the Gorilla every Sunday in the Lincoln Park Zoo. When I was little, my father, a lawyer, made my bed every morning—even though my mother didn't work outside the home. My father was content just to be with me; my mother took me to piano and ballet lessons (both of which I hated). My mother cared that I got all A's; my father didn't.

Continuing to wonder about feminist theory as it had evolved since the early 1970s, I pursued the subject while in New York, during the spring of 1994 and again in the winter of 1997. There I had a long talk with Robin Morgan, the mother of a son who's a few years older than Alexis. Robin has always intrigued me with her views on the rearing of sons to ensure that they be feminists. Her basic thesis is that yes, men and women, boys and girls, are different, not only biologically but culturally. And I don't disagree. Alexis, the daughter of two feminists, conformed even before she'd been exposed to school or the world to fairly typical female behavior. Although she wouldn't play with dolls (except, much later, the Cabbage Patch variety), she would spend hours with her Lego blocks building structures that would accommodate her "people," who would proceed to have conversations with one another from different rooms in her "buildings." These little wood people were, to her, like humans. She had no interest in more inanimate objects like cranes. (I actually bought her a crane, thinking it would help her to function in a world where hitherto only men operated cranes, but she totally ignored it, possibly because she'd never seen one before in her life, but probably because it was so very inanimate.) And then there was Alexis's fifth birthday party, at which the boys, upon entering our apartment, immediately joined in a game of throwing themselves stomach first onto our hardwood foyer floor to see how far they could slide. The girls, meanwhile, were huddled in the living room talking. I could relate to the girls' pastime a lot more than I could to the boys'—but so would any reasonable adult male.

Robin's theory is that since men have an overload of testosterone, it makes no sense to put them in charge of anything that might remotely spell danger—like the button to the bomb. Both of us, of course, subscribe to the theory that differences in the ways we raise boys and girls play a large part in how they are socialized as adults. In order to pave the way for a more feminist, nonviolent society, we both agree, we must encourage girls to be assertive and involved in matters outside themselves and their intimate relationships, while we foster boys' nurturing instincts. To prescribe how to raise boy children in the future, it helps to look at the way most women were raised: not to repress our emotions, not to be tough and strong at all costs. We have no interest in waging wars; we didn't play with war toys as we were growing up. We talked to ourselves and to others. We didn't punch one another; we put our arms around the friends we really cared about. And when we disagreed, our fights may have ended in tears; they didn't end with bloody noses.

Any discussion of male and female behavior leads to the question of how differences—whether innate or cultural—between the sexes should be treated. Feminist law professor Chris Littleton and former speaker pro tem of the California State Assembly Sheila Kuehl have chastised me for helping to "invent" the concept of joint custody. Many women have come to agree with them that this is nothing more than an additional weapon in the arsenal men already have at their disposal, to gain leverage so they are required to pay insufficient child support to the mothers of their children, or even none at all. But while some vicious men in the throes of divorce do sue for sole custody as a way to divert the courts from the issue of support, many fathers really want and deserve joint custody of their children.

It would have been inconceivable to either Marc or me that

one of us, but not the other, would have sole custody of Alexis. A key premise of our marriage was that we both were, and would continue to be, involved in her life.

Gloria seems to (and in our case did) support the concept of joint custody, stating firmly that differences between men and women, except those specifically related to reproduction, are cultural. As I reviewed the transcripts of the 1970 ERA hearings, I was amazed at how much of what she said in her testimony is exactly what she would repeat today, thirty years later:

> What we do know is that the differences between two races or the two sexes is much smaller than the differences to be found within each group. . . . Women are not more moral than men. We are only uncorrupted by power. . . . Perhaps women elected leaders . . . will not be so likely to dominate black people or yellow people or men; anybody who looks different from us. After all, we don't have our masculinity to prove.[17]

Another point about women elected leaders has been made by Kim Campbell, the former prime minister of Canada. She is also the head of the Council of Women World Leaders, which consists of every woman alive who has ever run a country. There are twenty-three of them. Her view is that women—even those in the most powerful positions—tend to lead in what University of California business professor Judy Rosener calls an interactive style of leadership, which includes asking questions. Men, on the other hand, seem to follow a command-and-control leadership style.[18] Campbell's theory appears to jibe with that of anthropologists Daniel Maltz and Ruth Borker, who add that women also give more "listening" responses—little words like "mhm," "uh-huh" and "yeah"—providing a running feedback loop.[19]

I met Kim Campbell in late 1999, and when I asked her whether she thought women would be more effective if they had a leadership style more like that of men—wondering if that had something to do with why we haven't had a woman president in the United States—she gave me a logical response consistent with Gloria's sentiment: We should all incorporate both styles of leadership. Regardless of the origins of what are thought of traditionally as male and female values, I believe that most thinking people would want to incorporate both into their lives. I want to win at tennis, but I also care about relationships, especially those with my life partner, my daughter and my close friends. I've come to realize that I can be both logical and intuitive.

By the 1980s, within the world of women's studies a problem—having nothing to do with equality or difference—was emerging. All sorts of books were being published, and I was getting more and more confused. For years, I had been visiting the Sisterhood Bookstore in Los Angeles, one of the oldest and most feminist shops of its kind in the country.* It had an entire bookcase devoted to women's studies. Because I had studied political theory—feminist theory, in particular—my interest in the subject drew me to that bookcase.

At first I was pleased at the sight of nothing but books on feminist theory. But then I realized that something unsettling had happened. Facing me were books on "postmodernist feminism," "poststructuralist feminism," "post-Freudian feminism," "post-Marxist feminism" . . . And as I leafed through them, I could tell the task was futile. Though I'm not a women's-studies scholar, I felt I should have been able to understand these books, but by now women who are interested in women's studies, which today has almost universally transformed into "gender" studies, have gone on to advanced degrees that require them to speak in a jargon understandable only to themselves.

They write to qualify for tenure both in women's (or "gender") studies, as well as in fields like philosophy and economics. Their writing has nothing to do with eliminating sexism in the real world or with tackling practical problems—like how to improve

---

* Unfortunately, in the summer of 1999 it closed its doors, shut out by a Borders across the street with its own Women's Studies section and books at discounted prices.

life for battered women or for women banging their heads on glass ceilings, let alone for women in Africa still suffering under the brutal custom of "female circumcision" or the women under Taliban rule. Does anyone except these academics truly believe that deconstructing postmodernism is more important than solving the real problems that women face in all corners of the globe?

I decided to poll my feminist friends. Not surprisingly, the reactions were divided: Gloria Steinem, Robin Morgan and Kate Millett, pragmatists all, found recent developments in women's studies troubling, while Professors Kate Stimpson and Nancy Baker lined up with two UCLA academics, Chris Littleton and Sandra Harding. The academics seemed to be enjoying the intellectual challenge of a new "field" of study. In her foreword to the recent book *Coming of Age in Academe* by Jane Roland Martin, Professor Emerita of Philosophy at the University of Massachusetts, Gloria expresses her own concerns: "I share Martin's worry that the academy . . . is gradually co-opting women and new areas of scholarship. . . . I would go a step further and add that . . . the academy is tougher to change than business. There, popularity with consumers creates a bottom line. . . . [Martin also] is making an intellectual plea: words are meant to communicate, not cover up. Theory that isn't understandable will be left on the page."[20]

As far as I'm concerned, feminist theory is only valuable if it sheds insight on how to better women's lives. This is not the goal of most academics. What has become known as postmodernism, although interesting to women's-studies scholars, doesn't do that job, nor does deconstructionism or lots of the other isms that cropped up during the 1980s.

To sociologist Kathleen Barry,* many feminist academics

> drifted away from political action as their research began to move away from a feminism rooted in women's real lives, and they no longer wanted to be called feminists because it might jeopardize their careers. . . .

---

* Barry was an associate professor at Penn State University and author of *Female Sexual Slavery* (New York: New York University Press).

> Inevitably theory became divorced from politics; research narrowed itself to "objective science," which distanced itself from women's experience. The defeminism of women's studies was under way.[21]

But I have friends who are feminist academics, scholars whom I admire, so I couldn't let the matter rest with what has happened in the field of women's studies in general. I talked with Sarah Lawrence philosophy professor Nancy Baker again, and what she said intrigued me:

> Hundreds of feminist academics over the past two or three decades have been very, very courageous in bringing the subject of women into everything, and in changing the frameworks used for everything. They have lost their jobs, not gotten tenure. . . . They have their own history, their own heroes, their own failures and their own work to be done. They need to be honored and seen as sisters.[22]

How glad I was that I had asked Nancy for her views, but how much I wish that the tribulations of these professors had been made known more widely. I would have liked to have helped.

Much to my delight, other feminist academics have their feet firmly planted in the real world. I read in the *New York Times Magazine* around Thanksgiving of 1999 that a feminist philosopher and professor at the University of Chicago, Martha Nussbaum, believes that feminist academics should be encouraging women to engage on their own behalf in the real world.[23] Nussbaum had castigated well-known radical feminist philosopher Judith Butler "for proffering a 'self-involved' feminism that encouraged women to disengage from real-world problems—like inferior wages or sexual harassment—and retreat to abstract theory."[24]

It's interesting that this comes from a feminist philosopher, not a social scientist. It's even more interesting that one of the most sweeping calls for real-world change came from the other feminist philosopher I respect so much, Nancy Baker: "Every single social institution and conceptual framework has to be radically transformed, washed clean, before we're finished."[25] While Baker feels that this is the work of academics, social scientists, political theorists, psychologists and so forth, I would say that it should be first and foremost a united effort of all different kinds of feminists. We in the Women's Movement collectively need to articulate what we want transformed and what the end results should look like. That would constitute the vision I want us to have.

Eventually I found a book, maybe representing another step forward by a feminist theorist, that coherently addressed the issue of power—an important subject, since women have so much less of it than men. In the introduction to her book *Money, Sex and Power* (with the baffling subtitle *Toward a Feminist Historical Materialism*),[26] Nancy C. M. Hartsock complains that "over the . . . years [from 1968 to 1983] . . . the subject of power has not received sustained feminist attention." She proceeds to speculate that "perhaps this is . . . a result of the effort feminists devoted to avoiding the exercise of power." Hartsock observes that in the early 1970s we believed in a "kind of personal, structureless politics; a widespread opposition to leadership; an insistence on working collectively; and an emphasis on process, often to the exclusion of getting things done."[27]

This was certainly true when, during our early efforts to achieve various feminist goals, from rallying for ratification of the ERA to creating viable child-care centers in our neighborhoods, some feminists worried about what could happen if any one of us really took charge—and whether there were any appropriate ways for her to wield power.* They worried a lot about abuse by self-designated or even elected leaders, when in fact leadership is exactly what we needed then and what the Women's Movement needs today. To Hartsock: "The political practice of much of the contemporary feminist movement has indicated the tacit accep-

* Back in the 1970s, one remarkably good article was written warning about this problem within the Women's Movement: Jo Freeman, "The Tyranny of Structurelessness." [28]

tance of the view that the exercise of power *is* the exercise of domination."[29]

Hartsock raises the question of whether power should be understood as energy or ability: "If we look more closely at the exercise of power over others, can it really be connected with masculinity? If so, is there a way of exercising power that could be characterized as feminine or female?"

I like Hartsock's approach—defining power as energy or ability—although I don't see how we can avoid some form of dominance to maintain an orderly and just society. (For example, people who disobey laws must be punished by others who, acting within our system of justice, exercise dominance over them.)

The best and most straightforward way for women to exercise power is through our political system. Women must run for office with feminist platforms. If we believe that Clinton's $305.4 billion proposed military budget for 2001 or even the space program should be abandoned, because of its exorbitant cost, in favor of programs that will foster human welfare, we should say so—loudly. We must call attention to ourselves as feminists, not try to blend into the background—or worse, start alternative societies that no man dares enter. And we should want our values to dominate. Rich, powerful, usually sexist and racist, men are no longer, if they ever were, the proper caretakers of society.

Feminism, to me, is about helping ourselves, women, first. It's not about us women using our power to save others before we save ourselves. Why is it that most women will fight to save anyone with less power than they have—which is very little? Why is it that many feminists today spend time worrying about the plight of women in other countries, from very different cultures and traditions, but they do not also worry that the United States, the most powerful nation in the world, is still totally dominated by men? Do our nurturing skills, on which Carol Gilligan focuses, play a role? Feminists must support women who'd like to be CEOs of large corporations, foundations or universities, young women like the Yale Law students who still feel the sting of discrimination. Feminists should work to *assure* that at least 50 percent of the

The 1992 Pro-Choice March on Washington. The "uniform" was all-white to recall the suffragists in their rallies for women's right to vote. With me (right to left) are Meredith Baxter, her son, his fiancée and her mother and stepfather.

The march culminated in a rally that even the police agreed had attracted hundreds of thousands of pro-choice activists, including many proclaiming their support for U.S. Senate candidate Barbara Boxer.

House and Senate—together with state legislatures*—is female. Feminism must be about achieving a position from which we really will have the power to help everyone, including women at all levels of society. We will never have the feminist revolution we all dreamed about in the late 1960s and the 1970s unless we collectively demand power—assume meaningful decision-making positions and stand up for what we believe once we are in those positions.

Women are gradually gaining ground in jobs traditionally held by men: as of the middle of 1999, two Supreme Court Justices, six members of the U.S. Senate, three top members of Clinton's Cabinet and one commander of a space shuttle mission.

Women in academia—not just feminist academics—are still shabbily treated, and while they may be university professors, they do not command the same prestige that male professors do. There are not enough women presidents of major universities. A front-page *New York Times* story led off with the announcement that "in an extraordinary admission, top officials at the Massachusetts Institute of Technology, the most prestigious science and engineering university in the country, have issued a report acknowledging that female professors here suffer from pervasive, if unintentional, discrimination."[31] Based on a five-year study initiated by female faculty members in the School of Science, the report documented discrimination in areas including hiring, awards, promotions and inclusion on important committees to decide on allocation of valuable resources such as research money and laboratory space. In 1994, while there were more undergraduate women than men in biology, at the highest level—faculty—there were only one-sixth as many women as men. In math, more than one-third of the undergraduates were women, but there was one female professor among forty-seven males. So by the time women became senior faculty members, they felt

---

* As of February 1999, Washington State boasted the highest percentage of women (40.1 percent) in any state legislature in the nation's history. At the other end of the spectrum was Alabama, with 7.9 percent women, while the national average that year was 22.3 percent.[30]

themselves (and indeed were) increasingly marginalized and overlooked by male-dominated networks. The report also noted that in the School of Science there had never been a female department head or associate head.[32]

Back at my alma mater, as of April 1999, women were 12 percent of Harvard's tenured faculty.[33] And at research universities across the country, women constituted only 28.3 percent of the teachers. Meanwhile, nationwide, according to a report from the American Association of University Professors, men who were full professors earned 9.2 percent more than their female peers in 1975, but 12.5 percent more in 1998. Pay disparities among associate and assistant professors also grew.[34] I'd like to know why the situation is getting worse in a profession that is supposed to include the most enlightened!

Possibly, the court victory in Connecticut won in February 1999 by a former Trinity College professor will scare some of these institutions. That professor was awarded $12.7 million, the jury agreeing that she had been denied tenure because of her sex.[35]

So we go on: How many female doctors are chiefs of staff of the hospitals with which they are affiliated? How many women are the managing partners of major law firms anywhere in the country? How long will it be before the United States has a woman president? As for the military, women still aren't even eligible for most combat positions. It will be a long, long time before there are women in the Navy SEALs, the Delta Force, the Green Berets and the other special forces, especially if they're prevented from doing more than sitting behind computer consoles.

Finally, though, a strange and wonderful thing happened. On July 23, 1999, a female Air Force colonel, Eileen Collins, became the first woman to command an American spaceflight as the space shuttle *Columbia* blasted off just after midnight. Mission Control's statement from the Kennedy Space Center: "We have a liftoff, reaching new heights for women and astronomy." NASA took thirty-eight years to put a woman in charge of a spaceflight. (The Soviet Union launched a woman into orbit aboard a one-person spacecraft in 1963, although she was not allowed to take the controls, as the male cosmonauts were.)

Women have made progress in sports. In the big tennis tournaments women winners now earn about what men do. But most women's tennis tournaments continue to be based on the ridiculous assumption that women have the endurance only for a maximum two-out-of-three-set match, while men in all the major tournaments play by the three-out-of-five rule—this, while it is common knowledge that although women may not have the muscle mass of men, we have far more endurance when it comes to almost any physical activity.

Of course, the Women's World Cup Soccer Championship in July 1999 put women's sports on newspapers' front pages worldwide. And those women hardly looked as if they needed physical protection. I was delighted, as the Americans beat the Chinese in the final game, to have been a cog in the wheel of passage of Title IX. As Pat Schroeder, former Congresswoman and now president and CEO of the Association of American Publishers, put it: "Now Title IX is the toast of the land. It's been in effect long enough to nurture and train these fantastic athletes. Their performances will propel women forward in leadership roles during the next century, because they have shattered the stereotypes of what women can and cannot do."[36]

I'd had the same feeling as I watched the opening game of the Women's National Basketball Association—Los Angeles against New York—and saw up close the size and might of Lisa Leslie, Rebecca Lobo and their teammates.

When it comes to women in business, there are female corporate executives, but they usually bump into the glass ceiling of vice president. In 1978, there were two women heading Fortune 1000 companies; in 1985, 2 percent of the Fortune 1000's senior-level executives were women. A 1990 salary and compensation survey of 799 major companies showed that of the highest-paid officers and directors, less than one-half of one percent were women. By 1992 the number of Fortune 1000's senior-level executives hadn't changed much since 1985—it reached 3 percent. In 1994, there were still two women heading Fortune 1000 companies; in 1996, the number had climbed to four. Finally, in July 1999, a woman was named to head a blue-chip company with revenue of $47 billion in 1998. Carleton Fiorina was named chief executive of Hewlett-Packard Company, the number-two computer company in the country. Unfortunately, Ms. Fiorina doesn't sound much like a feminist: "I hope that we are at a point that everyone has figured out that there is not a glass ceiling. . . . My gender is interesting but really not the subject of the story here."[37] Ms. Fiorina seems to be complimenting herself with this statement. She is saying that only the best (like herself) make it—the other women who tried just weren't as good as she was. I wish that the few women who have really reached the highest level wouldn't assume that because they have achieved their own personal goals it's so much easier for other women. Later, in 1999, a woman became CEO of Avon—high time for a company that aims virtually all of its products at women.

The disparities do not exist only among those at the top: In the United States, the possession of a bachelor's degree adds $28,000 to a man's salary but only $9,000 to a woman's. A degree from a high-prestige school contributes $11,500 to a man's income but *subtracts* $2,400 from a woman's.[38] Although the *New York Times Magazine* article in which I learned this information did not speculate as to the reason for the last statistic, I suspect that men from those high-prestige schools end up in business (which is more lucrative than anything else), while their female counterparts take the more traditional routes of going into the professions, including academia, or government service.

Even women who have made it to the very top of their professions have problems that men don't. Justice Ruth Bader Ginsburg described how she was reminded that women, including herself and her female colleague, have not yet really arrived:

> Just last Term . . . our Acting Solicitor General three times called me Justice O'Connor, and the same slip was made by a distinguished advocate, Harvard Law

School Professor Laurence Tribe. The National Association of Women Judges, anticipating that such confusion might occur, presented Justice O'Connor and me with T-shirts the month after my appointment. Hers read: "I'm Sandra, not Ruth"; mine, "I'm Ruth, not Sandra."[39]

Ultimately, we come back to the question of how comfortable women are reaching for power. Achieving long-range goals means that we must articulate values that correspond with them. Nevertheless, without power, articulating both values and goals may seem a futile exercise. The only solution is to resolve to set our goals so that once we do have power (which may be gained in part by setting those goals), we'll know what to do with it.

Perhaps one problem is that we haven't spelled out what women could do differently to make the workplace or the product made in that workplace better. A woman is rarely tapped to run something, and when she does she doesn't want to jeopardize her newfound power. She may fear that if she follows her instincts and does things differently from the way a man in the same position would, she might be accused of doing substandard work.

I believe that the biggest difference between men and women in relation to power is a sense of entitlement. By entitlement, I mean the self-confidence to know and to act on the knowledge that one is due more credit, more pay, more space for what one has achieved. Women have as much right to a good education, as much right to be elevated to top positions in our places of work, as much right to be president of the United States. We have the right to control our bodies, and to be free from harassment and assault by men, whether they are in equal or superior positions, at home or at work or in our communities. We have the right to respect if we've earned it—just as men do.

One of the reasons so many of us women have failed to live up to our own potential is that we don't like to complain too much or ask too much for ourselves. I worry that we will never revolutionize much more than we have if we don't get our share of power. It's fine to talk of feminist utopias, in which all women, white or of color, rich or poor, educated or not, have equal access to pride, enrichment, nobility. But the question remains of how we are to create such a state if we don't seize the power to create a viable alternative to what exists now.

And if we are to run things our way, what is that way? Once a vision is articulated, it will be easier for women to play the game by our (newly found) rules, because, so far, if a woman has been anointed to a top post, she has probably played the game by men's rules, uncomfortable though it may have been to do so.

We feminists must start to articulate what we want, as well as make known our specific criticisms of the male-dominated society in which we live. When events happen, if we disagree with the policy taken, we must say so and take action to make our disagreement felt. For example, before Operation Desert Storm, in the early 1990s, I wrote and published a statement saying that feminists opposed the impending war because it would cost billions of dollars that would better be spent on health care, on Medicaid, on fighting breast cancer and on numerous other benefits important to Americans.

Twenty-four-hour, universally available child care was one of the three most important issues to us in the 1970s, up there with the ERA and abortion rights. Today, in the United States, we have nothing resembling this kind of care. A few corporations have instituted private policies but most have not.* This means, of course, that even though many fathers share some child-care responsibilities (after they get home from work), the vast majority of American mothers must relinquish their jobs or make what are usually inadequate arrangements for their children. Most families can't afford to hire private nannies. Even if they can, movies

---

* On a recent visit to Paramount Studios, I visited a small child-care center on the lot for employees' children. When I remarked to a woman who was nine months pregnant about how easy it would be for her, since the center was right outside her building, she responded glumly that there was a year-long waiting list.

like *Stepmom*, the big Christmas 1998 release starring Julia Roberts and Susan Sarandon, reinforced the notion that it's the mothers (and even stepmothers) who should give up their jobs and stay home with the kids (who in that movie got out of school at 4:30 p.m.!)—not the fathers. Susan Sarandon's character surrendered a respectable position as an editor at Random House; Julia Roberts's, a career as a rising star in the world of photojournalism. Ed Harris, playing the father, and successive husband to the two women, takes no time out of his busy lawyer work life to deal with his children. None of the characters in the movie once suggested child care of any kind. It's as though it were a dead issue. I, however, remember the days when Walter Mondale ran for president on a platform that included child care as one of his top priorities. Where are today's feminist actions on this issue?

In the film industry the contrast between the power of men and that of women is striking. As of this writing, there are only three women executives with real power in Hollywood studios. Actresses earn less than male costars as a matter of course. One verified story from a few years back is that a big female star was offered a certain fee for her services; her male costar said that he wouldn't do the part offered to him unless he earned more than whatever she was being paid, and the studio agreed. Not only do studios pay male stars more to get them in their movies, they do it because most of the executives are men, who still think it only right that a man earn more than a woman.

Sadly, the few women who have "made it," so far, seem to be running their operations in the same cutthroat way men do. They pay established talent huge fees and rarely let in fresh blood. When they do, it's because that special individual is someone's best friend or relative. And they make deals with the same producers over and over again.

I know that if I were a movie studio executive and fed up (as I am now) with the gratuitous violence in popular, commercial movies, I would exercise my power and refuse to give producers like Joel Silver a deal. (He has been publicly quoted as saying that the only way he wants women in his movies is either prone or dead.) Meanwhile, female studio executives today continue to renew contracts with men like Silver, instead of exercising their authority to make deals with producers whose films would have more women-friendly content.

Fighting racism along with sexism has always been a maxim of feminist politics.* Sometimes, however, there are problems that arise when one is declared more evil than the other. In June 1994, O. J. Simpson brutally killed his former wife, Nicole Brown, and her friend Ron Goldman. After the double murder trial began, Judge Lance Ito decided to allow some testimony about the abuse of Nicole by her husband. The defense, led by Johnnie Cochran, claimed that proof of domestic "discord," the word he preferred because it put the onus as much on the wife as the husband, bore no relevance to whether or not Simpson committed the murders of which he'd been accused.

Although Cochran obtained an acquittal for an obviously guilty client, to get there he went the unconscionable jury-nullification route. He made the trial into a referendum on race and on whether blacks suffer from police abuse. Of course they do. But the trial was about whether O. J. Simpson had murdered two people. The mostly black jury acquitted Simpson in less than three hours after a more than nine-month-long trial. When I and most of the people I know heard the verdict, we were stunned. As for the connection between the abuse of Nicole and her murder, one of the black female members of the jury, right after the verdict was announced, stated, "Domestic abuse doesn't matter." She didn't seem to realize that domestic abuse can and does lead to murder.

Not surprisingly, in reaction to the Simpson trial, Gloria proved—emotionally, at least—to have carved her own path.

---

* The inverse, unfortunately, is not true. For example, the NAACP did not object to rampant sexism when it recently protested discrimination against blacks by the broadcast networks.

When I called her moments after the verdict, knowing that her opinion would be sought out by the press from all over the world, and determined that we feminists put up a strong front, I was dismayed by her focus. "This shows," she said sadly over the long-distance wires, "just how alienated blacks are from the system."

I felt strongly that as feminists our attention should be on how an admitted wife batterer bought his way to freedom, in the face of what had appeared to be certain conviction. It mattered that Johnnie Cochran behaved in a racist manner, exploiting, if not creating, animosity by blacks against whites.[40] Meanwhile, Gloria's reaction got translated down to masses of feminists who traditionally wait for her cue.

In the July issue of *Ms.* magazine there appeared an article entitled "How NOW,"[41] and Patricia Ireland, president of National NOW, was quoted as saying that NOW "must offer a clear understanding of what it means to be a feminist organization concerned with ending discrimination based on *race, class, and other issues of oppression* [emphasis mine] that come from a patriarchal structure."[42] The next quote in that article was from Gloria: "To be feminist, we have to take on the entire caste system."

So by the July after the verdict, some feminists actually seemed more concerned about issues of caste systems and race than about issues that specifically affected women, such as domestic violence. Certainly a paralysis had been created, so that feminists who would normally have taken to the streets in angry demonstrations against the verdict stayed home, quiet.

The Simpson civil trial came and went—doling out some justice at last. Of course, Simpson was found liable for the deaths of his former wife and Ron Goldman. Whether this verdict was a result of the jury's being, this time, primarily white (the trial was held in Santa Monica instead of downtown Los Angeles, where many of the criminal trial jurors had been black) or whether the plaintiffs' lawyers just did a better job than the district attorney's office is hard to say. In any case, the Simpson trials caused domestic violence to become a red flag—at least for a while. On talk shows and in newspaper columns, the subject came out of the closet, with women admitting to having been beaten by their husbands and finally seeking shelter away from them. The Feminist Majority Foundation even started emphasizing domestic violence within police families at its third annual National Center for Women and Policing conference in April 1998.[43]

Not too long after the Simpson trials, a national crisis began, caused by President Clinton and his womanizing. Paula Jones had begun a lawsuit, in which she accused Clinton of sexual harassment. Not knowing for sure what the facts were and waiting for the trial court to resolve the matter, most feminists did not publicly come to her defense. Nor had other women who would come forward against Clinton later done so yet. But then came Monica Lewinsky, and soon all the world knew for sure that Clinton had lied under oath about his behavior with Paula Jones. (In fact, in April 1999 a federal judge found him in contempt of court for that lie and by that summer she ordered him to pay approximately $90,000 to Jones's lawyers.) A few feminists rose to the occasion and criticized Clinton for behavior that clearly would violate Title VII were he a private-sector employer. Others refused to get caught up in the debate about whether what he'd done was sexual harassment, preferring to focus on the outrageous nature of his conduct and what it said about his ability to command the respect necessary for the leader of the most powerful nation in the world.

The first inkling of a real schism within the Women's Movement over this issue came when Gloria wrote an op-ed piece for the *New York Times* in which she characterized Clinton's dropping his pants, exposing himself, and asking for a blow job as a "clumsy sexual pass." That was okay, she said, because he took no for an answer, although Gloria did add that Clinton "may be a candidate for sex addiction therapy."[44] Unfortunately, Gloria also criticized Clinton's detractors, among them other feminists, for disqualifying Clinton's "energy and talent, [which] the country needs."[45] (As far as I was concerned, he was the one who had disqualified his energy and talent, especially the energy and "talent" he was using to discredit the many women he used for his own sexual pleasure.)

Gloria's piece would be interpreted as *the* position of the Women's Movement with regard to Clinton. So I drafted a piece for the *New York Times* op-ed page to counter what Gloria had said. In my opinion, Clinton's dropping his pants (when he was governor of Arkansas) and asking Paula Jones, an Arkansas state employee, for a blow job constituted sexual harassment. He had the power to ensure her being fired if he so chose—or to reward her if he liked the performance he was trying to get out of her. I added that what Gloria had written did not represent the views of all feminists.

Before I sent it off to the *Times,* I had already decided, out of courtesy, that I would fax to Gloria what I'd written. Her response back was: "Remember, I'm not a leader, and have never been elected to anything. I'm a writer and organizer who says what I think."[46]

While I'd tried to write as though I were just expressing the views of another feminist, it sounded like a rebuttal to the *Times* editors, and they say they never publish op-eds that are rebuttals to other op-eds. My little piece never saw the light of day.*

As to the matter of Monica Lewinsky, *Time* magazine in its June 1998 cover story, entitled "Is Feminism Dead?," made my point:

> The doyen of second-wave feminism startled many . . . when she penned an op-ed piece for the *New York Times* arguing that the allegations of a sexual dalliance between the President and a 21-year-old intern were nothing to get worked up about. If the stories were true (and she believed they were), then Clinton was guilty of nothing more than frat boyishness, Steinem wrote.[47]

Gloria had also said in her *New York Times* article that "femi-

---

* A. M. Rosenthal, on the other hand, because of his position as an editor of the *New York Times,* wrote an editorial *and* an op-ed piece criticizing Gloria's position.

nists will . . . have been right to resist pressure by the right wing and the media to call for [Clinton's] resignation or impeachment." I told Gloria that I resented her implication that we might cave in to the right, even if the outcome we wanted might have been the same as theirs. In fact, I actually feared that feminists might feel pressured by Gloria to play partisan politics and blindly support a Democratic president—good as he may be on a few issues, especially choice. On this the *Time* magazine writer observed that

> Conservatives have an easy explanation for these forgiving attitudes toward the President's private treatment of women. They say Clinton-loving feminists . . . have chosen to overlook the faults of a man who has been their best provider. Ideals be damned for the President who vetoed the ban on partial-birth abortions.[48]

Soon after Gloria's and my disagreement aired, Bella Abzug died, and in our mourning for our dearly loved friend, we ended that debate. Meanwhile, I found other allies, Kitty MacKinnon and the *Times*'s Abe Rosenthal. Patrick Caddell, Jimmy Carter's trusted lieutenant (pollster and overall adviser when he was president), assured me that he thought Gloria was wrong, as a feminist, about Clinton and that she would, no doubt, influence other women. Liberal, intellectual men, disgusted by Clinton's behavior vis-à-vis first Paula Jones and now Monica Lewinsky (in addition to a few isolated feminists), were becoming my new best friends.

The next time I saw Gloria was in her apartment in New York, where I asked her to realize, please, that she was perceived as a leader who spoke for the Women's Movement and therefore she should crank that in when she next went public with her views about Clinton. Gloria said that she feared a "sex police" if we spoke out against Clinton's behavior. Certainly, I don't want that kind of atmosphere to prevail—one that encourages snooping into the private lives of public figures. But I do see the distinction between Clinton's actions, which caused him to be impeached for obstruction of justice and perjury, on the one hand, and an at-large unit of the federal government sending spies to hide in people's closets or even offices, on the other.

After the Starr Report and the president's videotaped deposition on August 17, 1998, before the grand jury in the Whitewater-turned-Zippergate hearings, many in the feminist community seemed to lose their critical faculties when it came to Clinton. One friend said that she hated all laws because they usually work against women, and that therefore she didn't care about Clinton's alleged perjury or obstruction of justice. When Joanne and I attended a meeting of a new group headed by the executive director of the Ms. Foundation and calling itself the White House Project, the purpose of which is to get a woman into the White House sometime soon, I raised my hand in support of the project and noted that now was a perfect time to push for a woman president because surely Clinton's "boys will be boys" behavior wouldn't happen if a woman were in the White House. My remarks were met with derision by a theoretically feminist group in Los Angeles whose main spokespeople were spooked by the theory that after Clinton was removed from office, Congress would "get Gore" too, leaving our land in the hands of Newt Gingrich. I had become persona non grata at a Los Angeles feminist event, attended by, among others, Peg Yorkin, founder of the Feminist Majority, who was to become one of the biggest contributors to Clinton's legal defense fund.

On the same day as the White House Project meeting, September 24, 1998, a few women, calling themselves feminist leaders and including in their number Betty Friedan; Patricia Ireland, president of NOW; and Eleanor Smeal, president of the Feminist Majority, held a press conference to state that women supported Clinton because he'd been so good on all our issues.* They echoed the increasingly popular refrain to bolster their point: "Who's on third?" And they urged women to demand that the

---

* In my opinion, any Democratic president would have supported choice and would have made as many appointments of women to Cabinet-level and Supreme Court positions.

Republican-controlled Congress drop efforts to impeach Clinton or to hound him from office.

In fact, had those feminists called for Clinton to resign, Gore would be president going into the November 2000 election and we would have much less reason to panic that George W. Bush— representing everything that feminists abhor, including a litmus anti-choice test for Supreme Court nominees—might become our leader. Gore, by virtue of already being in office, would have had a chance to prove that he could be a decent president. He's certainly not my ideal candidate for the job, but he'd be the incumbent, with all the benefits that bestows, not a vice president trying to distance himself from the weakened and, some might say, disgraced President Clinton. The feminists who backed Clinton were, to me, extremely short-sighted in their thinking that morally, or in any other way, he deserved their support.

Sometime during this period, I read an essay entitled "The Diverted Left," by Howard Zinn, the author of A People's History of the United States and a well-known progressive.[49] Referring to "those on the Left" who were outraged by the impeachment-removal proceedings, he observed, "Their concern, they say, is not Clinton, but the danger posed by Right Wing Comstockites who will move on from Clinton to the rest of us, that the right of sexual privacy will be imperiled, that the prurient puritans will poison the freedoms won by the cultural revolution of recent decades." Zinn suggested that this was an "overheated reaction to a last-ditch attempt of a [right-wing] minority—loud and powerful, but still a minority—to impose on the people of the country a set of sexual restrictions they have already rejected." In other words, the public, except for the small minority of the "righteous right," has already accepted the principles of sexual freedom, making that issue beside the point. Zinn was convinced that progressives, in general, deserted a battlefield dominated by Clinton and the Republicans, who joined, through all the years of his presidency, "to act against the poor, to make the corporate rich richer, to maintain an enormous military apparatus, and to use it against helpless people."*

Shortly after the so-called feminist leaders came to Clinton's defense (either forgetting or not caring enough about these issues), the Hollywood community did, too. Predictably, they defended his behavior as not being offensive. It was painful to read that Barbra Streisand blamed the press because it no longer "respected the boundaries between public and private behavior," and that she justified Clinton's conduct by observing that many of the greatest presidents seemed to have had affairs.

A recent (male) head of production at Universal Pictures, Sean Daniel, was quite blunt: "Hollywood has seen worse. When it comes to private matters, Hollywood has made its peace with far more scandalous behavior. And there's an understanding here that you can have a messed-up private life and still do good work."[50] It's this kind of attitude that allows the film director referred to earlier in the chapter on Hollywood, a husband and father, to get work even though it is generally known that he sexually abuses little children. I guess that meets the definition of a "messed-up private life." In reality, it ought to get that director thrown in jail, as well as shunned by the community in which he works.

The very word "immoral" seemed to send shivers up the spines of erstwhile feminists and their Hollywood colleagues, since they then fell back on the argument that if we called Clinton immoral, the rest of the world would tag all of us with the same label. It's as though criticizing him was coming down on one of their own for behavior they felt was commonplace.

By December 1998, a political sea change was occurring. Liberals of all varieties—from Hollywood stars to the New York intelligentsia, from the ACLU to Jesse Jackson's Rainbow Coalition to Larry Flynt (who demanded that he be considered a liberal)—

* This article was made available to me by Cliff Pearson of the Dallas Peace Center in Dallas, Texas.

were lining up behind Clinton. But far, far worse, so were feminists—from Gloria to NOW to the Feminist Majority to Robin Morgan. Robin really surprised me when we received an e-mail instructing us and everyone else on her mailing list to get behind Clinton and do it in the way she outlined. Joanne and I wrote Robin back, saying that we wouldn't support Clinton, because of his callous behavior toward women—coupled with his lies. We received a curious note back from Robin saying that while she realized we live in lala land, we ought to get real and understand that the fuss was not about protecting Clinton but about stopping Trent Lott and his ilk.

On the issue of "sex," which to me, again, the whole thing is only slightly about, it was terribly sad to see former radical feminists, not to mention liberals, defend Clinton, instead of taking the position that what he did may well reinforce the adulterous behavior of many married men. It may signal young men that it is okay to approach women for sex without regard to emotional involvement, and it may encourage young women to behave "inappropriately" (Clinton's word) with men in order to get ahead. These are lessons that we feminists have tried to unteach for over thirty years. Larry Flynt's political alignment with "liberals" is no surprise. He thinks sex—no matter what kind and how dangerous—is good and to be defended wholesale.

What strange bedfellows have come out of this whole mess! I, the liberal feminist who supported the ERA in the face of early opposition to it by feminists like Robin Morgan,* became the radical, refusing to be a member of the Democratic Party's Ladies' Auxiliary (joining gays, lesbians and other groups to whom Clinton made promises he didn't keep). Now Larry Flynt was on the same side as feminist "leaders," who had lost a crucial opportunity to tell the world that President Clinton did not deserve the

---

* Robin's position had been that the ERA might wipe out protective legislation that women in labor unions had fought so hard for. But when CLUW (Coalition of Labor Union Women), the UAW and others became pro-ERA, so did Robin and other feminists who had earlier and misguidedly, in my opinion, opposed it.

support of feminists. Even though he had been on the right side of issues involving choice, even though he'd made some very good appointments, that just was not enough.

Regarding sexual harassment (which was not technically an issue in Clinton's doings with Monica Lewinsky), it took Republican Senator Kay Bailey Hutchinson to make the broader point that it would be a "very bad standard to set, if a superior could have an affair with an underling." Maybe she, like me, was concerned with the effect Clinton's actions with Monica had on the other interns. Clearly he was playing favorites with Monica. Did they wonder whether if *they* came on to him, they'd get all sorts of job offers from important people, not to mention the potential of millions from writing a book about the affair itself? Weren't the more moral of them being put at a disadvantage? Perhaps a new tort should be created that could be brought by other employees who are damaged by the boss's singling out one for special favors.

To be sure, there were a few rational voices during the impeachment debacle, which went to the real issues, cheering me enormously. As journalist Lindsy Van Gelder summed it up:

> My objections to Clinton's recent conduct are objections I would have to anyone, but I've been troubled by Clinton for a long time; Lani Guinier, Joycelyn Elders, the welfare bill . . . don't ask/don't tell . . . the attack on the Sudanese pharmaceutical plant . . . most of which liberals seem oblivious to as they check their stock quotes. So what I'm wondering is, where were all the email petitions and phone banks and faxes from all these noble anti-Puritan, rightwing-fearing, pro-sex liberals when Clinton was signing DOMA?[51]

The Defense of Marriage Act (DOMA) especially, and for obvious personal reasons, had been sticking in my craw. That's the legislation, discussed in an earlier chapter, that Clinton approved allowing states to refuse to recognize same-sex marriages performed in other states—in my opinion, a clear violation of the Full Faith and Credit Clause of the Constitution, just as "don't ask, don't tell" strikes me as a blatant violation of the First Amendment freedom-of-speech guarantee.*

I have always opposed that policy of Clinton's, established early in his presidency. I take the position that gays and lesbians must be able to serve openly in the armed forces. In fact, aside from the constitutional issue, there has been a personal toll, as related in a *New York Times Magazine* profile, "The Shadow Life of a Gay Marine," which explored the difficulties of living a clandestine homosexual life within the "don't ask, don't tell" structure.[52] And figures released by the Defense Department on January 22, 1999, showed that the Army, Navy, Air Force and Marine Corps discharged 1,145 gay men and lesbians in the 1998 fiscal year, a 13 percent increase from the year before and nearly double the number in 1993, the last year before the "don't ask, don't tell" policy took effect.[53] In late 1999, both candidates for the Democratic presidential nomination, Al Gore and Bill Bradley, as well as Hillary Rodham Clinton (running for the U.S. Senate from New York), announced their opposition to the "don't ask, don't tell" policy. And the *New York Times,* one week into the year 2000, ran an editorial saying that allowing "gays to serve openly in the military . . . is the only fair and rational course now that five years of experience has shown the compromise policy of 'don't ask, don't tell' to be a failure that should be abolished."[54] One too many young men in the military had been murdered by homophobic comrades-in-arms. Many "liberals" supported "don't ask, don't tell," because they thought it signaled some progress. They were wrong.

Some of the same liberals, including many leading feminists, supported Clinton's shenanigans with Monica. But others of us think the president of the United States should set a moral exam-

---

* David Mixner, a gay leader and Democratic party bigwig who roused support for Clinton during his campaign, apparently didn't mind Clinton's broken promises to gays and lesbians, his positions on DOMA and "don't ask, don't tell." He was in the forefront of supporters of Clinton during the impeachment hearings.

ple for the citizens of the nation. Not by what he does or doesn't do in bed—or wherever—but by how he handles a crisis of confidence that arises because of a situation of his own making. The president needs credibility to run the country effectively; by the time he was impeached, in my opinion, Clinton had lost his completely. He may even be disbarred in Arkansas.

I was relieved, at the very beginning of 2000, to read that the presidents of NOW and Planned Parenthood of America, as well as Gloria and other feminists, were no longer in lockstep with Clinton. They accused the administration of a position that was "extremely detrimental to women" in negotiations over a new United Nations treaty on sex trafficking. They were referring to the administration's support for wording in the treaty that would define "forced prostitution"—but not other types of prostitution—as a form of "sexual exploitation."[55] I agree. Is prostitution really something to which women freely consent? To me, the issue bears a strong relationship to that of "voluntary" sterilization when a woman is too poor to be able to choose to voluntarily consent. In both situations, if a woman is addicted to drugs or desperately needs money for something else it can hardly be said that she's able to exercise her choice freely.

One issue that should have been and should continue to be at the top of the list of feminist priorities for years is fighting breast cancer. It affects one in eight women and kills more people than AIDS does. But AIDS is a more popular cause, probably because it hits mostly men, even though many are gay. It also attracts more attention from women, most of whom are drawn like moths to a flame in their role as caregivers rather than receivers of care. I've been wearing a little pink ceramic breast-cancer ribbon button for years. And in the early 1990s, when I attended the Emmy Awards, I refused the request (almost a demand) at the door that I wear a red AIDS ribbon, because, I said, until they start passing pink ribbons around too, I was boycotting the red ones.

I realize that AIDS is not just a gay disease, but because so many gay men in the visible entertainment and fashion industries have died of it, it's chic in Hollywood to speak out about finding a cure for AIDS. Elizabeth Taylor made it her number-one cause, despite her own very real health problems. Even macho Bruce Springsteen wrote and performed the wonderful song "Streets of Philadelphia." I'm just grateful that Candice Bergen's character Murphy Brown got breast cancer so her show's millions of viewers had a glimpse of what that disease can be like. But *Murphy Brown* went off the air in 1998, and no version of AIDS' ACT UP has yet arisen to express serious outrage at this ongoing epidemic and to demand that significant government funds be allocated to prevent, better treat and cure it.

Then the matter became personal. On June 3, 1999, I myself was diagnosed with breast cancer. I had noticed a flattening of the nipple of my right breast for about a week, during which time I kept thinking that it would go back to normal, that it was probably my period—or something. But it didn't go away, so I had a mammogram and sonogram. The radiologist—a very nice woman—tried to feel the lump behind my nipple but had trouble. So, armed with a report that my mammogram was abnormal, I was sent off to find a breast surgeon. Trembling, I called my two favorite gynecologists from my cell phone in the parking lot. Each had a different suggestion. I met first with a male surgeon that night. He seemed to be pushing the idea—if the lump was malignant—of a full mastectomy, because he thought the "cosmetic results" might be more pleasing than keeping my own breast minus a nipple.

The next day, I saw a female surgeon. Pat Wolfson is someone you would never guess is a doctor, let alone a surgeon. With long blond hair and a sense of humor, she could be an ad executive or a soccer mom, but she seemed awfully smart. She looked, prodded and sent me to St. John's Hospital for a fine-needle biopsy. Off we schlepped. Upon our arrival, Joanne and I were sent into a small room that looked as if it was more suited for storage than medical care. A nurse and an administrator were there, and soon we were joined by a young doctor in his thirties. He advised me that it was best for him to do the biopsy without using a local pain killer, like Novocain or lidocaine, because they might dilute the results. So before I could catch my breath, let alone exhale as he exhorted me to do, he stuck a long, thin needle right into the center of my nipple. The pain was extraordinary. He repeated the procedure about five times. Through my haze of pain, I realized that Joanne had sunk to the floor, which she later told me was because she couldn't stand to see me in so much pain. She also couldn't believe I wasn't screaming. In fact, the nurse was holding my hand and I made a point of not squeezing hers too tightly, knowing from my Lamaze classes twenty-five years earlier that my job was to keep my body relaxed and try to forget my breast—an attempt at a kind of out-of-body experience.

A few minutes after the painful ordeal, the young doctor returned, ashen-faced, and announced that the tumor contained malignant cells. He left immediately, shutting the door behind him, at which point Joanne and I both burst into tears, hugging each other for dear life. Almost immediately, the phone in the hall outside our little room rang, and it was Dr. Wolfson. Sounding reassuring, sympathetic and professional, she started to tell me what we'd do next, including scheduling my surgery for the next week. But after a few minutes, she asked if she could speak to Joanne. That's when I realized that she knew I wasn't taking in the information she was giving. And then a sweet white-haired woman came out from behind a desk and offered me an ice pack and comfort. Joanne, an ex-Catholic, later informed me that the woman was a nun.*

When we got home, I called Gloria. She'd had breast cancer twelve years earlier and is doing fine. She reassured me that radiation treatments left her feeling no worse than having a bad cold. She didn't have chemo, because no nodes were involved. I'd find out my status in that regard after the surgery. Meanwhile, my

---

* While we took for granted that Joanne would be by my side throughout the whole ordeal, many lesbian couples aren't so fortunate. Some even feel the need to form support groups that are separate from those attended by straight women who are uneasy in the presence of lesbians (*New York Times,* November 23, 1999).

brain stayed blurred. Names of friends, let alone doctors, began to escape me, and worse, I couldn't remember any phone numbers, a talent I'd had since I was a child.

I managed to call Alexis. I'd already told her that my mammogram was abnormal, but now I had to tell her the really bad news. She seemed to take it calmly, concerned only that I was in the best professional hands. Early the next morning, though, when Marc called to express his sympathy and concern, I realized that Alexis, usually early to bed, had called him at 3 a.m. During our next chat, she said she wanted to come down right away, take a few days off from her law firm job in San Francisco. I reassured her that I was okay, but she insisted, and when she arrived two days before my surgery, I was, of course, delighted to have her with me. We went to the Huntington Gardens in Pasadena; for once she wanted to do whatever I wanted. The tables had turned.

On the day of the surgery, Alexis, Joanne and I trooped off to the hospital. I was scheduled to stay overnight but was dismayed to learn that all they had was a semiprivate room. As they led us to it, I gave Alexis a look. She knew what I wanted and disappeared. About fifteen minutes later, the head nurse came in and said they'd just found a private room but it didn't have a view. I grinned at Alexis proudly as I told the nurse that was just fine.

After the surgery, I learned that I had a not very aggressive-looking 1.5-centimeter tumor, as well as one positive node. The next day, the doctor called, greeting me with the words "two positive nodes!" I told her that sounded bad and she responded, "Well, two out of seventeen (the total she'd taken) is a whole lot better than two out of four."

Meanwhile, Alexis and Joanne had their own tales to tell, and both agreed that they had needed each other throughout the ordeal. It warmed my heart when Joanne raved about how great and mature Alexis had been during the whole thing. She also told me that she'd received a message from our friend Lily Tomlin, who'd called at about 6:00 a.m. to remind Joanne to let her know as soon as I was out of surgery. Lily called again while I was still in surgery. Then when Joanne called Vicky while I was in the recovery room, she reached Vicky's answering machine and left a message about the cancer having spread to at least one node. Vicky later told Joanne that as she listened to the message she burst into tears, partly because she felt so helpless being so far away. When I heard about the reactions of all the people Joanne had spoken to, I was very moved.

About 5:00 p.m. the day after my surgery, I was released to start healing from surgery and to get ready for the next big thing: chemotherapy. Marc called as soon as we walked into the house, wanting to know how I felt after the surgery.

Medically, the question at this point was which medical oncologist I would choose. As I was dealing with that, flowers began to arrive from all over. I had called practically none of my friends because I hadn't had my wits about me, but word seemed to have spread. The house looked beautiful, if a bit like a funeral parlor. But I tended those flowers carefully. Arranging them was, in fact, one of the few things that took my mind off my troubles.

All the female doctors I respected told me that the one oncologist they really trusted was Marilou Terpenning. Her offices are in Santa Monica, she teaches at UCLA, and she just might be on her way to becoming chief of staff of St. John's Hospital. Armed with a tape recorder, as we'd been admonished to do, Joanne and I went to our meeting with her. The medical jargon was almost impossible to fathom, but she seemed confident that the proper course of treatment for me was Adriamycin and Cytoxan (AC)— administered intravenously every three weeks, six times in a row, over an eighteen-week period. Although I liked Dr. Terpenning and could tell she was smart, I wanted to get a few more opinions. All the books I'd read—and there were many—had said to get three opinions.

The next doctor I saw was at Cedars Sinai, a big breast cancer center within a very established hospital. He thought I needed only four cycles of the same treatment and then, without a single question from me about the subject, volunteered that vaginal skin could be taken and made into an areola and nipple. I was so turned off by his assumption that I'd want to have myself mutilated to make my breast look better that I decided against him on the spot, although I later questioned Dr. Terpenning about his view that I only needed four treatments. I knew enough to realize that I'd have to trust someone else, such as her, because I just couldn't make sense of the differing opinions. Thinking I had decided definitely on Dr. Terpenning, I spent a relatively peaceful weekend in anticipation of starting chemo the following Thursday.

But on Monday morning, I got a call from UCLA. A big-deal oncologist there, Dr. Peter J. Rosen, who had been too busy when I'd tried to make an appointment—my third opinion—had just had a cancellation. How would I like to come in that afternoon? Exhausted at the thought but wanting to be thorough, Joanne and I mustered our strength and arrived at UCLA armed again with our tape recorder. Dr. Rosen's visit to me was preceded by that of a young female doctor, who shook my hand far too vigorously given my recent surgery. Dr. Rosen was a nice avuncular doctor. He seemed sure that the right treatment for me was not what Dr. Terpenning had suggested—and he knew and respected her, he said. He wanted me to enter a UCLA clinical trial to test a drug called Neupogen, a drug to help replenish white cells destroyed by the chemotherapy, which was necessary no matter what but which they were testing for a one-shot, instead of seven-shot, protocol. The chemo he'd be using was a combination of Adriamycin and Taxotere (AT)—six cycles. He was convinced that Taxotere—stronger than Cytoxan—was necessary and said that he'd use it on his own wife. (Of course, his wife didn't have breast cancer, and who knew if she'd need that or something less, I later realized.) By this time I was hopelessly confused—again, after I'd been so sure of Dr. Terpenning's suggested way to go. I asked Dr. Rosen to call Dr. Terpenning and see if they could come to some sort of agreement.

The next morning I got a call from Dr. Terpenning. This was

now the second time I'd challenged her approach, but she took it in stride. She did say, however, that if I wanted to go the AT route, she'd already scheduled me to start the following Monday at UCLA. She just totally disagreed with that approach, and although she had the drugs and could easily administer them, she wouldn't in my case. I didn't need a drug as strong as Taxotere, which has significant side effects. As she continued to explain, I started crying. I just couldn't handle the confusion. Dr. Terpenning then very kindly observed that I'm the kind of person who needs to understand things intellectually, that she's the same way and that if she ever needed a lawyer she'd call on me. But for now, I should just realize that no amount of her explaining could bring me up to her speed. Translated, that meant trust her. And I did; I had to.

At some point in our conversations, I told her about the Cedars' doctor's suggestion that he cut part of my vaginal skin and shape it into a nipple and areola. She sighed and exclaimed, "Are they still doing that?" Afterward, we agreed that although the male doctors in the field aren't exactly sexist, they are very paternalistic and seem to feel they know what women want: perfect-looking breasts. Dr. Terpenning also revealed that she'd been part of the Boston Women's Health Collective back in the early 1970s and that she's a feminist. I'd already decided that she was the best doctor. This information just reinforced my feelings that feminist professionals usually are the very best.

On June 24, 1999, I started my first round of chemotherapy. I didn't want to be given a sedative, preferring instead to have as clear a head as possible and ask questions about what would be happening when. I got an earful from the nurse who had to sit there administering the Adriamycin by hand. (It's so strong that if it gets on your skin, you get a third-degree burn.)

The chemo wasn't fun. As my hair started to fall out, Lily took me wig shopping, in anticipation of the total baldness that would be upon me soon. And unlike before the chemo started, when I was busily running hither and yon with Joanne trying to find the very best doctors, I now had enough time to feel depressed and, totally irrationally, as though I were the only one in the world with breast cancer.

When Marc called to check on how the chemo was going, I told him that when this was all over, I was going to become actively involved in helping figure out how to prevent this awful disease. It's not like me simply to put it behind me, assuming I'm lucky enough to be able to do just that.

Meanwhile, Joanne signed up for the three-day, 55-mile Avon breast cancer walk from Santa Barbara to Malibu, scheduled for the end of October. Not only was I glad for the cause that she would do the walk, I was also delighted that she'd be doing something for herself, an excuse to stop being my nurse, if only for one weekend plus some weekend training out of 18½ weeks.

By the fourth cycle of chemo, I was experiencing horrible chemically induced hot flashes, so bad that Dr. Terpenning put me on medication for them. Herbs are fine for normal menopausal symptoms, she advised us, but I needed more now.

The fifth cycle was by far the worst. I felt sicker than I had and got really worried that the sixth (and last) cycle would be unbearable. When I told the nurse, she said that was never the case. The fifth is always the worst. The last, whether it's because you know that's what it is and feel the end is in sight, or whether it's because your body has gone through the worst already, is better. In fact, by the time that one was administered, I noticed that fuzz was growing back on my head. Then I worried that it would fall out because of more chemo. It didn't. In fact, soon very soft hair, lighter in color than what I'd had before, began to grow.

But my focus was really now on the radiation, which was to begin two weeks after the last chemo. I had been tattooed earlier—a painful process, because I had to lie in one uncomfortable position in a very cold room for over an hour, without moving a muscle, while they did the physics to find the vectors to get the beams into exactly the right places. Then, with small black dots, they tattooed the areas to be assaulted just under my skin.

My first male doctor in this ordeal, the radiation oncologist, proved to be funny, kind and smart. After a few weeks, when he saw that part of my skin was getting way too red, he told the technicians to let that area take a break. I worried that I wouldn't get enough radiation if he shortchanged that part, but he reassured me. Finally, I was finished, after going to radiation every day (except weekends) for thirty-three days. I hadn't anticipated, even though I'd been warned, that the fatigue from the radiation, which I felt mostly in the small of my back, would be so bad. So just as I did during chemo, every late afternoon I'd have to lie down, impatient because I had piled-up work to get to. It's awfully hard for me to put the care of my body first, especially for a six-month stretch, but I had to learn.

As the treatments were ending, I found myself fascinated by the new hair that was growing on my head and returning to the rest of my body. I actually could go out without wondering if I needed a hat, let alone a wig.

After all I went through, my prognosis is good. My oncologist, who "hates recurrences," will see me every three months for a few years. Then the visits will taper off and this whole episode will be behind me. Nonetheless, almost every day I hear about someone else who has either had or has been diagnosed with breast cancer.

While I'm delighted that Avon and Revlon (with its big annual ball) are putting money into breast cancer research, that still isn't enough. The Women's Movement has to deal with this disease the way ACT UP dealt with AIDS. We have to make it so the government, hospitals, researchers and doctors take us as seriously, and get to work *now*. We have to ensure that the chances of getting breast cancer, the chances of recurrence and the chances of dying from breast cancer decrease dramatically. We have to demand answers to the many still open questions and let no one off the hook. We have been passive patients, victims of this awful disease, for far too long. I do not write these words because I got breast cancer, but I do regret that it took my own getting sick for me to see the different standards of care applied not just around the country, but within a single city like Los Angeles. The ignorance that I—an educated woman—found enshrouding me was scary. Every decision I had to make felt like a tremendous leap of faith, not one made by an informed consumer. I want all this to change for other women. I intend to see that the Women's Movement has as one of its primary goals eradicating this disease by prevention as well as cure. Breast cancer is a feminist issue!

My feeling is that the Women's Movement hasn't made the issue of breast cancer a priority because it is not a "movement" acting on a vision that we have clearly defined. Rather, it consists of isolated individuals and groups who speak out if something horrendous happens, or who react to hot political issues of the day. The energy of the early 1970s is missing, replaced by a certain satisfaction that we have already made a difference—to some degree. Why have we slowed down so much, when so many problems need to be addressed? Men are in charge virtually everywhere we look. There are a few token women hither and yon, but it sure still looks like a man's world, and I, as well as other women, am still not one of the boys.

If we can't get it together to see that breast cancer is a feminist issue, that we've been shortchanged by public health officials, researchers, doctors and insurance companies, we hardly are the Women's Movement we once were. Breast cancer is an issue about which we should have been screaming for decades. If it afflicted one in twenty women in 1950 and it now affects one in eight, something's been wrong for a long time. The fact that most breast cancer research money is going to "awareness" (urging women to get mammograms) and "cures," instead of to prevention, speaks volumes about the power of big chemical and other companies that put out into the environment toxins that are probably causing breast and other cancers. Something has been spread in the air, water or food that wasn't there (very much, at least) in 1950. Feminists in the United States should be challenging industries that could be at fault to prove they're not. Feminists should be shifting the burden in that direction, not sitting by hoping that (usually male) scientists and doctors will have the same priorities that we do. But what we think of as the Women's

Movement isn't doing that.* Instead, more energy seems to be focused on working to preserve rights like choice or joining UN groups to help underprivileged women in underdeveloped countries. We badly need women who will speak out for us today, here and now, about all the battles, such as the fight against breast cancer and ovarian cancer, that we still have to wage and win. We need leaders and spokeswomen who are not ashamed to call themselves feminists and who will speak out for *all* women, not only the most underprivileged.

The Women's Movement still exists, but it could be more powerful by bringing an independent, fresh approach to issues that really matter to women. It should provide a vision of how we women are going to take our rightful place as leaders in society, leaders who will be guided by feminist values.

Perhaps, as the Redstockings stated, it is important to remember our history in moments like those recently past, when there seem to be such muddled priorities, such a vacuum of vision and absence of action, permeating the current Women's Movement. The Women's Movement in the United States is not only that about which I have been writing—the "Second Wave" of feminism through which I have lived and in which I have participated. It is a 150-plus-year legacy in this country, if we date it from the 1848 Seneca Falls Convention, in which women, led by Elizabeth Cady Stanton, first demanded the right to vote. Throughout that history, there were difficult times, such as the years right after the Civil War, when the movement split into two factions over whether to support the Fifteenth Amendment to the Constitution. That amendment would enfranchise black men but no women, black or white. Later, on a different occasion, another split occurred over a resolution passed at the

* To be fair, recently NOW, the Ms. Foundation, the Women of Color Resource Center, the Coalition of Labor Union Women and other groups have joined the Breast Cancer Fund's environmental initiative, calling for further research into environmental links to breast cancer and for curbs on environmental toxins. The issue is how much these feminist groups are really *doing* besides lending their names.

National American Women's Suffrage Association. There, Susan B. Anthony vehemently protested the censuring of her friend, movement founder Elizabeth Cady Stanton, for having criticized organized religion (which men dominated, of course) by writing what she called "The Women's Bible." During those times, our foremothers felt alone, abandoned by their sisters and former colleagues, as I have during certain crises discussed in this book. But they went on. They didn't give up the fight. Then, the vision that was lost eventually was regained, just as I feel ours will be— sooner, I hope, rather than later—as the vast majority of us endeavor to make the world a better place for women.

As Martin Luther King once said, "The arc of the universe is long and it is bending toward justice." Many of us will continue to travel that path toward justice, freedom, equality and power for women—encouraged, supported and joined now by our feminist children.

Notes

INTRODUCTION

1. Judith Hole and Ellen Levine, *Rebirth of Feminism* (Quadrangle Books, 1971), p. 350, citing Margaret Lawrence, "Statistics Submitted by National Association of Women Lawyers," *Green Hearings,* pp. 1120–28.
2. Ibid.
3. Honorable Ruth Bader Ginsburg, "Remarks on Women's Progress in the Legal Profession in the United States," *Tulsa Law Journal,* vol. 33, no. 1 (Fall 1997), pp. 13–15.
4. B. N. Current, A. DeConde, and H. L. Dantes, *United States History* (Scott, Foresman, 1977), p. 639.
5. Ibid., p. 641.
6. 335 U.S. 464 (1948).
7. Ginsburg, "Women's Progress," p. 15.
8. Ibid., p. 14.
9. Ibid., citing *Peter W. Huber, Sandra Day O'Connor: Supreme Court Justice* 33 (1990).
10. Current et al., *U.S. History,* p. 642.
11. Ginsburg, "Women's Progress," p. 18, citing *City of Los Angeles Dept. of Water & Power v. Manhart,* 435 U.S. 702 (1978).
12. Ibid.
13. Dorothy Clancy, "Harvard Law School Survey, Women in Law: The Dependable Ones," *Harvard Law Bulletin,* June 1970.

CHAPTER 1

1. Simone de Beauvoir, *The Second Sex* (Bantam, 1961); originally published in France, 2 vols., as *Le Deuxième Sexe: I. Les Faits et Les Mythes: II. L'Expérience Vécue* (Paris: Librairie Gallimard, 1949).
2. Judith Hole and Ellen Levine, *Rebirth of Feminism,* (New York: Quadrangle Books, 1971), p. 342.
3. Ibid., p. 350.

4. *Bradwell v. Illinois,* 83 U.S. 130 (1873).
5. Gerda Lerner, *The Grimké Sisters from South Carolina: Pioneers for Woman's Rights and Abolition* (New York: Schocken, 1971), back cover.
6. Harry N. Abrams, 1994, p. 122.
7. Susan J. Douglas, *Where the Girls Are: Growing Up Female in the Mass Media* (Harmondsworth: Penguin Books, 1995) p. 169.
8. New York: Holt, 1997, p. 27.
9. Addison-Wesley, 1997.

CHAPTER 2

1. Sheila Rowbotham, *A Century of Women* (New York: Viking, 1997), p. 464.
2. Toni Carabillo, Judith Meuli, and June Bundy Csida, *Feminist Chronicles 1953–1993* (Women's Graphics, 1993), p. 80.

CHAPTER 3

1. 2 ACLU Women's Rights Project Report 5, note 19, at 5 (1980).
2. 404 U.S. 71 (1971).
3. *Goesaert v. Cleary* 335 U.S. 464 (1948).
4. "Legal Battle of the Sexes," *Newsweek,* April 30, 1979, p. 69.
5. 411 U.S. 677 (1973) would be the cite once the decision was rendered by the Court.
6. 83 U.S. 130 (1873).
7. 335 U.S. 464 (1948).
8. Brief of the ACLU, *amicus curiae,* p. 39.
9. 335 U.S. at 467.

CHAPTER 4

1. Honorable Ruth Bader Ginsburg, "Remarks on Women's Progress in the Legal Profession in the United States," *Tulsa Law Journal,* vol. 33, no. 1 (Fall 1997), p. 19.
2. Ibid., p. 20, citing Nancy D. Polikoff, *Why Are Mothers Losing?: A Brief Analysis of Criteria Used in Child Custody Determinations,* 7 WOMEN'S RTS. L. REP. 235, 239 (1982).

CHAPTER 5

1. *The Male Machine* (New York: McGraw Hill, 1974), p. 94.
2. New York: Alfred A. Knopf, 1999, p. 247.
3. Ibid.
4. *Going Too Far* (New York: Vintage, 1978).
5. Ibid., p. 180.
6. Ibid.
7. "Legal Battle of the Sexes," *Newsweek,* April 30, 1979, p. 68.

CHAPTER 6

1. The Guerrilla Girls, *Confessions of the Guerrilla Girls* (New York: Harper-Perennial, 1995), p. 13.
2. Fact Sheet on the Earnings gap, Employment Standards Administration, Women's Bureau, Department of Labor Commission.

CHAPTER 7

1. *New York Times,* December 13, 1998, Arts and Leisure Section, p. 17.
2. *New York Times,* January 31, 1999, Arts and Leisure Section, p. 13.
3. "Shooting for a Role in a Male Film Genre," *Los Angeles Times,* September 25, 1997.
4. Joanne Parrent, "Creative Control: Women & Power in Film and Television," ms., 1998.
5. Ibid.

CHAPTER 8

1. *Los Angeles Times,* September 25, 1997.
2. Ibid.
3. *New York Times,* January 31, 1999, p. AR30.
4. Ibid.
5. Ibid.
6. Ibid.
7. Ibid.
8. Ibid.
9. Ibid.
10. *New York Times,* February 21, 1999.
11. *New York* Times, January 31, 1999.
12. Ibid.
13. Ibid.
14. Ibid.

CHAPTER 9

1. 413 U.S. 15 (1973).
2. Ibid., p. 24.
3. Ibid., p. 32.
4. *Harris v. Forklift Systems, Inc.* 114 S. Ct. 367 (1993).
5. See, for example, *Boos v. Barry,* 485 US 312 (1987).
6. Conversation with Professor Catharine MacKinnon in Los Angeles on February 11, 1997.
7. *NYU Review of Law and Social Change,* Vol. 8, no. 2, 1978–79, Panel Discussion: "Regulation of Pornography," Opening Statement of Brenda Feigen Fasteau, p. 283.

8. Ibid., p. 294.
9. Ibid., p. at 285.
10. *American Booksellers Assn. V. Hudnut* 771 F. 2d 323 (7th Cir. 1985), summarily aff'd, 106 S. Ct. 1172 (1986).
11. Ibid.
12. Catharine A. MacKinnon, *Only Words* (Cambridge: Harvard University Press, 1993).
13. Ibid., p. 17.
14. Germaine Greer, *The Whole Woman* (New York: Alfred A. Knopf, 1999), p. 191.
15. Drucilla Cornell, *The Imaginary Domain: Abortion, Pornography and Sexual Harassment* (New York: Routledge, 1995), p. 106.
16. Ibid.
17. Ibid., p. 107.
18. Nadine Strossen, *Defending Pornography: Free Speech, Sex and the Fight for Women's Rights* (New York: Scribner, 1995).
19. Ibid.
20. *New York Times,* April 4, 1999, p. AR 11.
21. Marjorie Smith, "Private Action Against Pornography: An Exercise of First Amendment Rights," *NYU Review of Law and Social Change,* vol. 3, no. 2 (1978–79), p. 248.
22. *Daily Variety,* February 20, 1997, p. 32.
23. *New York Times,* February 26, 1997.
24. Tonya Flynt's statement at press conference with Gloria Steinem, Women against Pornography, NOW, etc. in Manhattan, January, 1997.
25. *Hustled: My Journey from Faith to Fear* (Westminster: John Knox Press, 1998).
26. Russell Publications, 1993.
27. Houston, Texas, 1985.
28. Texas Attorney General's Pornography Commission Survey (Houston, 1985), p. 140.
29. Ibid.
30. Neil Malamuth and Edward Donnerstein, eds., *Pornography and Sexual Aggression* (New York: Academic Press, 1984).
31. Ibid., p. 127
32. Diana Russell, *Against Pornography* (Russell Publications, 1993).
33. Malamuth and Donnerstein, *Pornography and Sexual Agression,* p. 127
34. *Los Angeles Times,* February 12, 1995, Letters to the Times, "Violence and Pornography."

CHAPTER 10

1. 416 U.S. 351 (1974).
2. Ruth Bader Ginsburg and Brenda Feigen, *Report of Columbia Law School's*

Equal Rights Advocacy Project (U.S. Commission on Civil Rights, Washington, D.C., 1974).

3. *Edwards v. Healy,* 421 U.S. 772 (1975).
4. *Weinberger v. Wiesenfeld,* 420 U.S. 636 (1975).
5. *Califano v. Goldfarb,* 430 U.S. 199 (1977).
6. *City of Los Angeles, Dept. of Water and Power v. Manhart,* 435 U.S. 702 (1977).
7. *Craig v. Boren,* 429 U.S. 190 (1976).
8. Brief for the American Civil Liberties Union as *Amicus Curiae,* p. 22.
9. *Dothard v. Rawlinson,* 433 U.S. 321 (1977).
10. Section 703(e)
11. *Dothard v. Rawlinson,* p. 332–37.
12. Brief for the American Civil Liberties Union, *Amicus Curiae,* p. 9.
13. Ibid., p. 7.
14. *Los Angeles Times,* August 11, 1993.
15. *Duren v. Missouri* 439 U.S. 357 (1979).
16. Vol. 63, pp. 375, 378.
17. Citing *Mississippi Univ. for Women v. Hogan,* 458 U.S. 718, 724 n.9 (1982), and *Frontiero v. Richardson,* 411 U.S. 677, 691–92 (1973) (Powell, J., concurring).
18. *Craig v. Boren.*
19. For a discussion of how the Court viewed cases of discrimination against men (often brought by Ruth) differently from those dealing with discrimination against women, see generally David Cole, "Strategies of Difference: Litigating for Women's Rights in a Man's World," *Law & Inequality: A Journal of Theory and Practice,* vol. 2, no. 1 February 1984, pp. 33 ff. For a thorough discussion of *Craig v. Boren* from Cole's point of view, see pp. 79–85.
20. *Craig v. Boren,* p. 197.
21. *Walker v. Jones* 733 F. 2d 923 (D.C. Cir.), *cert. denied,* 469 U.S. 1036 (1984).
22. *Mississippi University for Women v. Hogan,* 458 U.S. 718 (1982).
23. *Michael M. v. Superior Court,* 450 U.S. 464 (1981).
24. *Rostker v. Goldberg,* 453 U.S. 57 (1981).
25. *New York Times Magazine,* October 5, 1997, pp. 60, 65.
26. 410 U.S. 113 (1973).
27. *Struck v. Secretary of Defense,* 460 F. 2d 1372, *cert. denied, etc.*
28. Brief for the American Civil Liberties Union in *Struck v. Secretary of Defense.*
29. 410 U.S. 113 (1973).
30. *New York Times Magazine,* October 5, 1997, p. 60.
31. Ibid., p. 65.
32. Delivered as the William T. Joyner Lecture on Constitutional Law.
33. Vol. 63, pp. 375 ff.

34. See, for example, *The New Republic,* "The List," May 10, 1993.
35. Ibid., p. 381.
36. *The New Republic,* vol. 209; no. 5 (August 2, 1993), p. 19.
37. Drucilla Cornell, *The Imaginary Domain: Abortion, Pornography & Sexual Harassment* (New York: Routledge, 1995), p. 53.
38. Ibid., p. 65–66.
39. *Geduldig v. Aiello,* 417 U.S. 484 (1974).
40. *General Elec. Co. v. Gilbert,* 429 U.S. 484 (1976).
41. Ruth Bader Ginsburg and Susan Deller Ross, "Pregnancy and Discrimination," *New York Times,* January 25, 1977.
42. *New York Times,* February 3, 1999, A11.
43. *California Federal Savings and Loan Association, et al. v. Guerra,* 479 U.S. 272 (1987).
44. Wendy Williams, "The Equality Crisis," in Linda Nicholson, ed., *The Second Wave: A Reader in Feminist Theory* (New York: Routledge, 1997), p. 82.
45. Ibid.
46. Ibid.
47. Ibid., pp. 82–83.
48. Boston: Houghton Mifflin, 1994.
49. Jane Mayer and Jill Abramson, *Strange Justice: The Selling of Clarence Thomas* (Boston: Houghton Mifflin, 1994), p. 269.
50. Ibid., p. 268.
51. *Los Angeles Times,* November 11, 1994.
52. 62 U.S.L.W. 4004.
53. *New York Times,* October 1, 1993, p. B9.
54. 477 U.S. 57 (1986).
55. Ibid., pp. 64, 67.
56. *Los Angeles Times,* Oct. 7, 1993, p. A16.
57. 62 U.S.L.W. 4004.
58. Ibid.
59. Citing *Davis v. Monsanto Chemical Co.* 858 F. 2d 345, 349 (CA 6 1988).
60. *Harris v. Forklift Systems, Inc.,* 510 U.S. 17.
61. *Jones v. Clinton,* 990 F. Supp. 657, 671 (E.D. Ark., April 1, 1998).
62. *New York Times,* April 2, 1998, p. 18.
63. *Burlington Industries Inc. v. Ellerth,* 524 U.S. 742 (June 26, 1998).
64. *New York Times,* June 27, 1988, pp. A1, A11.
65. *New York Times,* May 25, 1999, p. A24.
66. *New York Times Magazine,* October 5, 1997, p. 96.
67. Ibid., p. 90.
68. Ibid., p. 65.
69. Ibid., p. 86.
70. Ibid., p. 90.
71. Ibid., pp. 90, 96.

72. *New York Times Magazine,* October 5, 1997, p. 96.

CHAPTER 11

1. "Women for Peace or Women's Liberation?: Signposts from the Feminist Archives," *Vietnam Generation,* Summer/Fall 1989.
2. *Yale Journal of Law and Feminism,* vol. 165 (1998).
3. Ibid., p. 181
4. Ibid., p. 183
5. Ibid., p. 184
6. Ibid., p. 186.
7. Ibid., p. 198
8. This having been said, I read recently in Betty Friedan's memoir, *Life So Far,* (Simon & Schuster, 2000) that "Gloria and Bella brought New York *radicals* like Brenda Feigen Fasteau, a young lawyer, and Flo Kennedy, the flamboyant black lawyer . . . to the [July 1971 NWPC] organizing conference in Washington" (p. 251). I suppose everything is, indeed, relative!
9. Deborah Tannen, *The Argument Culture* (New York: Ballantine, 1999), p. 275.
10. Carol Gilligan, *In a Different Voice* (Cambridge: Harvard University Press, 1982).
11. Ibid., p. 3.
12. Carol Gilligan, "Woman's Place in Man's Life Cycle," in Linda Nicholson, ed., *The Second Wave: A Reader in Feminist Theory* (New York: Routledge, 1997), p. 206.
13. Ibid., p. 207.
14. Ibid.
15. Catharine A. MacKinnon, "Feminism, Marxism, Method, and the State: An Agenda for Theory," *Signs,* vol. 7 (1982), pp. 525, 534.
16. Ibid.
17. "Statement of Gloria Steinem, Writer and Critic," Women and the "Equal Rights" Amendment, Senate Subcommittee Hearings on the Constitutional Amendment, 91st Congress. Edited by Dr. Catharine Stimpson, in conjunction with the Congressional Information Service (New York: R. R. Bowker Company, 1972), pp. 104, 106.
18. Kim Campbell, *Time and Change: The Political Memoirs of Canada's First Woman Prime Minister* (Toronto: Seal Books, 1997), p. 424.
19. Deborah Tannen, *You Just Don't Understand* (New York: Ballantine, 1991), p. 142.
20. Jane Roland Martin, *Coming of Age in Academe* (New York: Routledge, 1999), pp. xi, xii, xiv.
21. "Deconstructing Deconstructionism," *Ms.,* January/February 1991, pp. 83–85.
22. Fax from Nancy Baker to Brenda Feigen, January 20, 2000.

23. *New York Times Magazine,* November 21, 1999, p. 66.
24. Ibid. For more on Nussbaum versus Butler, see Victoria Stanhope, "Bad Writing or Bad Politics? Feminist and Postmodern Relations," *Off Our Backs,* August/September 1999, p. 10.
25. Fax from Nancy Baker to Brenda Feigen, January 20, 2000.
26. Nancy C. M. Hartsock, *Money, Sex and Power: Toward a Feminist Historical Materialism* (Boston: Northeastern University Press, 1983).
27. Ibid., p. 2.
28. *Ms.,* July 1973, p. 76.
29. Hartsock, pp. 1, 2.
30. *New York Times,* February 4, 1999.
31. *New York Times,* March 23, 1999, pp. A1, A16.
32. Ibid., p. A16.
33. *New York Times,* April 29, 1999, Letters to the Editor.
34. Joan Oleck, "Colleges Flunk in Pay Equity," *Business Week,* March 1, 1999, p. 6.
35. Ibid.
36. Patricia Schroeder, "Listen to the Sound of the Glass Ceiling Shattering," *Los Angeles Times,* July 14, 1999, p. B7.
37. *New York Times,* July 20, 1999, p. C1.
38. *New York Times Magazine,* February 21, 1999, p. 50.
39. The Honorable Ruth Bader Ginsburg, "Remarks on Women's Progress in the Legal Profession in the United States," *Tulsa Law Journal,* vol. 33, no. 1 (Fall 1997), p. 15.
40. See *Life After Johnnie Cochran,* by Barbara Cochran Berry and Joanne Parrent (New York: Basic Books, 1995).
41. *Ms.,* July/August 1996, p. 47.
42. Ibid., p. 50.
43. *Feminist Majority Report,* Spring 1998.
44. *New York Times,* March 22, 1998, p. 15.
45. Ibid.
46. Fax from Gloria Steinem to Brenda Feigen, March 30, 1998.
47. *Time,* June 29, 1998, pp. 54, 56.
48. Ibid.
49. *New York Times,* September 26, 1998.
50. *New York Times,* September 29, 1998, A19.
51. E-mail from Lindsy Van Gelder to Brenda Feigen, December 12, 1998.
52. *New York Times Magazine,* June 28, 1998.
53. *New York Times,* January 23, 1999, A13.
54. "The Debate Over Gay Troops," *New York Times,* January 8, 2000.
55. "Feminist Coalition Protests U.S. Stance on Sex Trafficking Treaty," *New York Times,* January 13, 2000.

Index

Page numbers in *italics* refer to illustrations.

fathers, 108; child care and, 50–1, 74,
106–7, 114–15, 123, 247, 250–1,
278–80, 292; joint custody,
114–15, 279–80; nurturing role,
278–80; rights of, 50–1, 106,
114–15, 123
Federal Bureau of Investigation (FBI),
54*n.*, 89, 232, 257
Feigen, Brenda, 4, *18, 19*, 55, 77, 79,
*100, 103, 111, 112, 118, 121, 130,
137, 148, 152, 212*, 253, 260, 267,
286
Feigen, Richard, 12, 17, 27, 38, 39,
58, 94, 99, 121, 129–31, 148,
166–7
Feigen-Fasteau, Alexis, 99–103, *103*,
104–9, *109*, 110–11, *111*, 112,
112, 113, 116, *118*, 119, 120, 123,
124, *137*, 156, *156*, 159, 167, 168,
170–2, 184–5, 192, *261*, 267,
278–80, 308; birth of, 99–101;
education of, 111–13, 122, 128,
213, 259–61, 267; Feigen's lesbianism and, 126–8; feminism and,
213, 259–61; hernia surgery,
104–6
Feinstein, Dianne, 259
feminism, 24, 198; breast cancer and,
313–15; British, 26*n.*; Clinton sex
scandals and, 296–305; "difference" vs. "equalist," 247–51,
273–8; ERA debate, 28–36,
39–41, 76–9, 96; Feigen's discov-
ery of, 25–57; Hollywood and, 198,
200, 209–10, 212–13, 225–35; law
and, 247–51; lesbianism and,
39–41, 59–61, 131–7, 303; liberal,
51, 273–4; 1970s battles, 27–54,
58–71, 72–89, 214, 292; of 1980s,
173, 176; of 1990s, 176, 269–305,
313–16; pornography and, 214–35;
radical, 31–32, 51, 53, 78–9,
273–4, 283; theory, 281–5; vision
for the future, 269–316; *see also*
Women's Movement

Feminist Majority Foundation, 296,
299, 302
film industry, 305; Feigen and,
139–53, 154–94, 195–213, 293;
NAVY SEALS project, 154–94;
politics and, 176, 206–7, 259,
300–301; pornography and,
214–16, 219, 225–35; sexism in,
131–2, 141–53, 165, 172–94,
195–213, 225, 293, 301; women
filmmakers, 158–94, 199–213,
225; *see also* Hollywood
Fiorina, Carleton, 2–90
Firestone, Shulamith, *The Dialectic of
Sex,* 34, 35
First Amendment, 303; pornography
and, 214–35
First Congress to Unite Women
(1969), 26–7, 51, 91
Fleiss, Heidi, 182
Flynt, Larry, 226–35, 301, 302
Flynt, Tonya, 228 and *n.*, 234
Foley, Hoag and Elliott, 14
Ford Foundation, 44, 121
Forman, Milos, 226, 234–5
Fortas, Abe, 22
Fourteenth Amendment, 29, 30, 50,
73, 244–7
Frankenheimer, John, 201
Freund, Paul, 9–11, 73
Friedan, Betty, 25, 27, 39–41, 66, 299;
The Feminine Mystique, 25; NOW
and, 29, 39–40; views on lesbian-
ism, 39–41, 133
Friedman, Leon, 67–8
Frontiero, Sharon, 79–88
Frontiero v. Richardson, 79–89, 241;
sex discrimination after, 236–8

Galbraith, John Kenneth, 43–4
Gannon, Happy, 99, 102–3, 107, 109,
109
Garland, Lillian, 248–9

A Note About the Author

Brenda Feigen was born in Chicago. She earned degrees at Vassar College in 1966 and at the Harvard Law School in 1969. She was admitted to the bar in Massachusetts and New York. She practiced as an attorney in New York and worked as a motion picture and literary agent, in addition to her work in the Women's Movement, which included serving as legislative vice president of NOW (with responsibility for work on the ERA and abortion rights), cofounding *Ms.* magazine with Gloria Steinem and directing with Ruth Bader Ginsburg the Women's Rights Project of the ACLU. In 1987, her focus shifted to Hollywood, where she produced *NAVY SEALS,* a 1990 Orion Pictures release, and worked with Jane Fonda on a feature for MGM, and on films for CBS, ABC and Warner Bros. While maintaining her New York–based law practice, in California she serves as a literary manager, and as copresident of and general counsel to Reel Life Women, a production company. For several months, starting in January 2000, she served as manager of "Entertainment Goes Global," a joint project of the Annenberg School for Communication's Norman Lear Center and the Pacific Council on International Policy. She is on the board of California Lawyers for the Arts and has been a contributor to the *Harvard Law Bulletin, Harvard Women's Law Journal, Ms., Vogue, The Village Voice* and various entertainment newsletters.

A Note on the Type

This book was set in Fairfield, the first typeface from the hand of the distinguished American artist and engraver Rudolph Ruzicka (1883–1978). Ruzicka was born in Bohemia and came to the United States in 1894. He set up his own shop, devoted to wood engraving and printing, in New York in 1913 after a varied career working as a wood engraver, in photoengraving and banknote printing plants, and as an art director and freelance artist. He designed and illustrated many books, and was the creator of a considerable list of individual prints—wood engravings, line engravings on copper and aquatints.

Composed by North Market Street Graphics,
Lancaster, Pennsylvania
Printed and bound by Quebecor Printing,
Fairfield, Pennsylvania
Designed by Anthea Lingeman